MY BELIEF

Books by Hermann Hesse

PETER CAMENZIND

BENEATH THE WHEEL

GERTRUDE

ROSSHALDE

KNULP

DEMIAN

STRANGE NEWS FROM ANOTHER STAR

KLINGSOR'S LAST SUMMER

WANDERING

SIDDHARTHA

STEPPENWOLF

NARCISSUS AND GOLDMUND

THE JOURNEY TO THE EAST

THE GLASS BEAD GAME

IF THE WAR GOES ON . . .

POEMS

AUTOBIOGRAPHICAL WRITINGS

STORIES OF FIVE DECADES

MY BELIEF

REFLECTIONS

My Belief

ESSAYS ON LIFE AND ART

HERMANN HESSE

Edited, and with an introduction, by
THEODORE ZIOLKOWSKI

Translated by
DENVER LINDLEY

With two essays translated by
Ralph Manheim

Farrar, Straus and Giroux
NEW YORK

Contents

All the essays in this book were translated by Denver Lindley, except for "From a Diary" and "Anti-Semitism," which were translated by Ralph Manheim

The year of composition follows each title; in most cases, first publication in German also occurred that year

PART TWO
I · EUROPEAN AND AMERICAN LITERATURE

II · INTELLECTUAL HISTORY

III · ORIENTAL LITERATURE

Introduction

IN MAY 1922, T. S. Eliot visited Hermann Hesse in Montagnola, the isolated Swiss village above Lugano where Hesse had recently settled and where he was to live until his death in 1962. But it was not the author of the recently sensational novel *Demian* (1919) to whom Eliot was paying his respects. Nor was it the fashionable writer of popular prewar fictions from whom he hoped to elicit contributions to his journal *Criterion*. Rather, as Eliot had explained in an earlier letter of introduction, a slender volume of essays entitled *Blick ins Chaos* (1920; *In Sight of Chaos*) had aroused his admiration. "In your book *Blick ins Chaos* I detect a concern with serious problems that has not yet penetrated to England, and I should like to spread its reputation." It is a fact of literary history that Eliot attempted to do precisely this by citing *Blick ins Chaos* in his Notes to *The Waste Land*. Yet this publicity effort obviously failed, for fifty years later Hesse's essays constitute an aspect of his writing that is virtually unknown in the English-speaking world, even among his most fervent devotees, and that is still too little appreciated even in Germany.

Hesse's essays can be grouped roughly, for purposes of initial discrimination, into three categories. First of all, we find a large group of writings dealing with literary matters. These range from general reflections on "Language" or "About Good and Bad Critics" to reconsiderations of his own work: the gloomy "Poet's Preface to His Selected Works," the account of a typical "Night's Work," the 1941 postscript to his novel *Steppenwolf,* or the recollection of the circumstances surrounding the composition of the novella *Klingsor's Last Summer.* In addition, there are reviews of books both German and foreign, appreciative essays on favorite writers, and introductions to various anthologies as well as to editions of works from world literature. A second major category includes essays of a more personal nature. These are sometimes frankly confessional like the "Letter to a Philistine." And at times they amount to such statements of personal credo as "My Belief" or "A Bit of Theology." Finally, there remains a substantial group of essays that address themselves to frankly political issues or, more generally, to questions of cultural criticism.

Yet there are really no clear lines separating these three loose categories, which adumbrate the principal areas of Hesse's essayistic interest rather than specify the subject matter of individual pieces. In general, it may be observed that Hesse's earliest essays revolve around more narrowly literary topics. During his middle years, from about 1917 to 1933, the essays frequently take on a more philosophical tone. And the late essays tend increasingly to become classically concrete; instead of beginning with a literary or cultural situation, the author moves from a specific "Description of a Landscape" to general reflections on life and art. Yet all these preoccupations are anticipated in the early notes "At Year's End" (1904), which start with the young author's personal situation, then move on to express his disenchantment with contemporary "culture," and conclude with the literary appreciation of a medieval chronicle. For Hesse, the realms of Life and Art are so closely intertwined that any reflection which begins in one area leads almost inevitably into the other.

This tendency is conspicuous in the volume that attracted Eliot's attention. Its two central pieces, which constitute a significant statement on European civilization at the end of World War I, begin ostensibly as studies of Dostoevsky's novels *The Brothers Karamazov* and *The Idiot*. (The third essay of the volume, a topical and dated piece on German poetry, is not included in this selected edition.) The first essay, which bears the subtitle "The Decline of Europe," argues that the spirit of Europe is being undermined by what Hesse calls the "Asiatic" ideal of the Karamazovs: "a turning away from every fixed morality and ethic in favor of a universal understanding, a universal validation." Reluctant to make absolute distinctions between good and evil, right and wrong, "Russian man" worships a God who is at the same time Satan. As this new spirit gradually invades the West, the decline of traditional Greco-Roman, Judaeo-Christian Europe becomes imminent. The "decline of Europe," however, will be no violent upheaval, but an inner revolution: "the reinterpretation of worn-out symbols, the transvaluation of spiritual values." These rather Spenglerian ideas—developed independently, by the way, before Hesse read Spengler's *The Decline of the West*—are elaborated in the second essay, "Thoughts on *The Idiot* by Dostoevsky." Myshkin, the hero of the novel, is misunderstood and feared by his friends, because his manner of seeing reality differs so radically from theirs. Whereas they are European men, clinging to the values of an outmoded system, he accepts all of life as it thrusts itself upon him. Notably during certain visionary moments (his epileptic seizures) he has stood at the magical boundary where all opposites are canceled out. As long as we remain within the framework of traditional reality, we see life in terms of clashing opposites. But if we can step outside the system, only for a moment, it becomes evident that these apparent opposites actually constitute complementary parts of a greater whole. "Magical thinking" is Hesse's somewhat romantic term for the act of mental projection that permits us to escape the sphere of seeming polarities: it is a spiritual revaluation of life, proceeding from an uncompromising examination of the chaos in our own souls. The very antithesis of anarchy, "magical thinking" implies the acknowledgment of a meaningful totality beyond chaos, for chaos is "chaotic" only from the standpoint of conventional concepts of order.

Readers acquainted with Hesse's novels will quickly realize that these two essays supply the theoretical background for the novel *Demian,* which was written only a short time earlier. And it should be immediately evident why Eliot was attracted to these essays, which he cited as a footnote to his vision of "those hooded hordes swarming / Over endless plains" in Part V of *The Waste Land*. When we consider the essays of *Blick ins Chaos* in the light of Hesse's own work, however, at least two principal points need to be discussed.

First, the two Dostoevsky essays were composed in 1919, at a critical point in Hesse's own development. However extensively Hesse's early writings may be seen to foreshadow his later works, it can safely be said that up to about 1916 he was concerned primarily with his own life and work, choosing by preference to ignore political developments in the world outside. But the events of World War I shattered this happy idyl and impelled Hesse to speak out in a series of pacifistic essays (collected in the volume *If the War Goes On* . . .) that contrasted sharply with the general euphoria with which most European intellectuals greeted the war. (A notable exception to the nationalistic and militaristic fervor of the times was Romain Rolland, to whom Hesse later dedicated *If the War Goes On* . . .) The experience of suddenly being branded a traitor because of his pacifism produced a spiritual crisis from which, in 1916–17, Hesse sought relief through psychoanalysis. The illuminating essay on "Artists and Psychoanalysis" (1918) helps us to understand the role of psychoanalysis in Hesse's life and works. He soon realized that many of the insights of Freud, Jung, Stekel, and others had been anticipated in the works of the great writers of the past—that psychoanalysis represented, in other words, a systematization of existing knowledge rather than a radically new approach. At the same time, psychoanalysis forced him to acknowledge precisely those problems of consciousness that Western society had effectively repressed for generations. In response, Hesse shifted the focus of his works, both fictional and essayistic, from the private to the public. In the novel *Demian* as well as in the essays on Dostoevsky, he used a literary occasion as an opportunity to investigate the general upheaval of values in European man. What was previously accepted as the disgruntlement of the alienated intellectual in the midst of a contemptible "culture" is now unmasked as a much broader crisis of values: European man is being displaced by Russian man, while conventional assumptions regarding morality are turned topsy-turvy by magical thinking.

Second, the essays on Dostoevsky alert us to the basically dialectical nature of Hesse's thought. In the revealing statement entitled "My Belief" (1931), Hesse maintains that the idea of the underlying unity of all being is the only dogma in his faith. But the experience of unity is a synthesis that can be achieved only through the reconciliation of conflicting opposites. This dialectical process shows up over and over again in Hesse's novels. In *Demian* it underlies the "Two Worlds" with which Emil Sinclair is confronted in the first chapter and which he seeks to reconcile through the aid of his friend Demian. In *Siddhartha* (1922) the hero makes his way from the realm of the spirit to the realm of the senses before he finally achieves the liberating synthesis on the river that flows between the two realms. Harry Haller is obsessed with the dual aspects of his personality, is torn between the poles of bourgeois and Steppenwolf, until he realizes that any simple duality of thesis and antithesis is an oversimplification that can be resolved only through the acceptance of a higher and more complex unity. And in *Narcissus and Goldmund* (1930) the thesis and antithesis of spirit and nature are embodied in the lives of the two central figures, who achieve a symbolic unity to the extent that they complement each other's existence.

Now this dialectical process, which underlies all of Hesse's major novels, provides both the substance and the form of his most important essays. In the pieces on Dostoevsky the thesis and antithesis of European man and Russian man are resolved in the synthesis of magical thinking, which refuses to accept conventional divisions into polarities and opposites. Hesse's playful delight in the dialectical process shows up also in the "Variations on a Theme by Wilhelm Schäfer" (1919), which opens with the assertion that any real truth must be capable of inversion. (Here Hesse is close to one of the basic assumptions of modern science and philosophy. Niels Bohr, for instance, was fond of saying that the opposite of a merely *correct* statement is a false statement; but the opposite of a *truth* can often be an equally profound truth.) Similarly, the extract "From My Diary" (1918) consists of a dialectical dispute between two voices—the voices of consciousness and of vision—concerning the necessity of suffering.

Hesse is of course fully aware of the dangers inherent in the dialectical process. In his "Bit of Theology" (1932) he warns that nothing is more detrimental to philosophy than a strict and literal belief in typologies of any sort. Yet as a hermeneutic model he again presents us with the polarity of two fundamental human types, which he calls the man of reason and the pious man, characterizing them in considerable detail. But even here we see the possibility—indeed, the necessity—of synthesis. For Hesse combines his dialectical theory of types with another idea outlined in the first part of the essay: the triadic rhythm of humanization. According to this pattern, which Hesse perceives in all mythic and religious systems, the course of humanization begins with innocence (paradise, childhood, a pre-stage without any sense of responsibility). From there it leads into guilt, into the knowledge of good and evil, into the behests of culture, morality, religion, and human ideals. But the realization that these ideals are unattainable in reality plunges the individual into despair. This despair leads either to a downfall or to "faith"—a third level that corresponds in its acceptance of all being to the magical thinking of the Dostoevsky essays. It is on this third level, Hesse argues in his concluding paragraph, that the man of reason and the pious man achieve the synthesis that cancels out their opposition and that permits them to enter a state of true humanity. It is worth pointing out that in the pattern of his thought, if not in its content, Hesse remains within a familiar tradition of German philosophical speculation: Schiller, Hegel, and Marx—to cite only three examples—produced systems of thought that involve a binary opposition operating and being transformed within a ternary historical sequence.

Most of Hesse's writings during the twenties and thirties tend to focus on the dramatic moment of dialectical struggle, when the antithesis has just asserted itself in opposition to the thesis. In the novels the heroes are forced to question and, ultimately, to reject their initial values when they develop a new consciousness. And in the essays, notably those on politics and culture, Hesse is concerned primarily with expressing his opposition to the currently accepted values. He opposes his pacifism to the prevailing militarism, his cosmopolitanism to nationalism, his tolerance to anti-Semitism, his conception of a world culture to a narrow "European" civilization, and his belief in a broadly ecumenical religion to any insular sectarianism. In the late essays, in contrast, we share the reflections of a man who has retreated from the strife of dialectics into the third stage, synthesis. In these pieces on "Happiness," on "Old Age," or on "The Peach Tree," Hesse writes from the standpoint of one who has achieved resolution and whose sense of the unity of all being enables him to deal with such matters with greater detachment, as when the tension of civilization and primitivism is synthesized in "Description of a Landscape."

It would be tempting to apply Hesse's theory of the triadic rhythm of human development to his own life and work. We could then set up a tidy scheme according to which Hesse emerged from the solitude that is praised in so many of his early essays ("At Year's End," "Old Music," "The Refuge") to confront the political reality of the twenties and thirties, only to retire again in old age into the solitude and harmony implicit in all the late essays. But any such scheme, as plausible as it seems at first glance, would be a grand oversimplification contributing to the legend of Hesse rather than to a true understanding of him.

It is easy to forget—especially for the more enthusiastic members of the current Hesse cult—that Hesse was never an otherworldly guru, but a professional writer who produced, in the course of an active literary career of some sixty years, a quantity of work so vast that it has yet to be thoroughly catalogued. As a young writer with a wife and three children to support, he could hardly afford the pose of the hermit. Even though he preferred to live away from the bustle of cities—from 1904 to 1912 in the village of Gaienhofen on the German shore of Lake Constance and from 1912 to 1919 in a suburb of Berne—he was constantly involved in many activities that took him away from his own writing and prevented any solipsistic obsession with his own consciousness. Between 1910 and 1955, for instance, he edited over fifty volumes of works from various periods of world literature. In the year 1913 alone he produced six volumes, ranging from a collection of Oriental tales to an anthology of German Romantic poetry. In 1918–19, as general editor of a series of books for German prisoners of war, he brought out twenty-two volumes: these included both contemporary and medieval texts, but they focused principally on the period in which, as he constantly reminds us, Hesse felt spiritually most at home—German literature from 1750 to 1850—and in which he acquired a knowledgeability matching, and indeed often exceeding, that of many professional scholars. And during the twenties this editorial activity continued unabated. The year 1925 saw the appearance of five volumes, including those on Hölderlin and Novalis whose introductions are reprinted here.

Although this activity was certainly dictated in part by financial considerations, it was by no means simply hackwork. Thomas Mann, for one, recognized the valuable contribution that Hesse made to German culture by providing reliable and convenient editions of important writers whose merit was not yet commonly acknowledged. For instance, Hesse contributed significantly to the rehabilitation of the Romantic novelist Jean Paul (see the essay "About Jean Paul"), whose works had been ignored for almost a century. But more than that: Hesse believed passionately in the living reality of a cultural tradition that he consistently opposed to the phony "reality" (often indicated by quote marks) of everyday life. (His observations on "A Virtuoso's Concert" are representative in this connection.) His editorial endeavors must be seen as a serious aspect of his effort to keep that cultural tradition intact in the face of two world wars and the general disintegration of values that he witnessed during the twenties and thirties and that he analyzed in many of his essays (e.g., "Our Age's Yearning for a Philosophy of Life").

The impressive extent of Hesse's professional literary activity is just barely suggested by the books he edited. As co-editor of the journal *März* from 1907 to 1912, he contributed well over a hundred reviews, many of them discussing several different titles. (In 1910 he wrote to a friend that he had read, for purposes of review, over three hundred books that year; but it was his lifelong principle, as he once remarked to Jung, to review only those books about which he could say something favorable.) *März* was a liberal journal of opposition to the policies of Kaiser Wilhelm; yet in this period before his political awakening, Hesse rarely took advantage of the opportunity to express himself on political or even cultural issues. His contributions are almost wholly literary. The same applies to his pieces for the journal *Vivos Voco,* which he co-edited from 1919 to 1921. This journal was founded for the purpose of stimulating the cultural renewal of a Europe that had been shattered by the war. But despite the fact that Hesse was writing, during this very period, many of his most important political essays and his sharpest cultural criticism, he restricted himself in *Vivos Voco* to the task of literary reassessment in order to provide a basis for a renewed intellectual and cultural life. It has been estimated, in fact, that Hesse wrote well over a thousand reviews in the twenties and thirties—for a variety of newspapers and journals in various countries. His role as one of the major German literary critics is gradually beginning to be appreciated as the extent of his activity and influence comes to light.

We can get a full appreciation of the range of Hesse's activities during the productive years between *Demian* (1919) and *The Journey to the East* (1932) only if we keep in mind the fact that he produced, in addition to the mentioned reviews and editions, three major novels—*Siddhartha, Steppenwolf,* and *Narcissus and Goldmund*—several volumes of poetry and stories, many of his finest essays, and several long autobiographical accounts (the latter collected in the volume *Autobiographical Writings*). He became a passionate gardener—a fact that accounts for the increasing importance of landscape and nature in his later essays. And he painted hundreds of water colors, many of them as illustrations for holograph editions of poems and fairy tales that he produced to supplement the often uncertain income from his books. In other words, the view of Hesse as a sage lost in the contemplation of his psyche is distorted. Even later, when increasingly poor eyesight caused him to give up reviewing and limited his writing largely to essays, he wrote hundreds of letters to friends and readers all over the world.

A word remains to be said about Hesse's activities during the thirties. His principal essays on politics and culture appeared in the years immediately before and after the end of World War I. When it became apparent to him—much sooner, by the way, than it did to the somewhat younger generation of committed writers of the thirties, like Brecht—that literature can have little direct impact upon politics and society in general, Hesse turned away from those efforts and directed himself principally to the development of the individual. As he observed in the Foreword to the 1946 edition of his political essays, *If the War Goes On . . . :* "When I call my articles 'political,' it is always in quotes, for there is nothing political about them but the atmosphere in which they came into being. In all other respects they are the opposite of political, because in each one of these essays I strive to guide the reader not into the world theater with its political problems but into his innermost being, before the judgment seat of his very personal conscience."

It was during these years, characteristically, that he wrote his most significant autobiographical pieces, most notably "A Guest at the Spa" and "Journey to Nuremberg." And such general analyses of culture as the essays on Dostoevsky gradually give way to the more individual concerns of "A Bit of Theology."

Disenchanted very early with the political developments in Weimar Germany, Hesse became a Swiss citizen in 1923. As a result, when the Nazis came to power in 1933, his position was quite different from that of most German writers. First of all, since he was already living abroad, he was not forced to emigrate. Second, since his experiences during World War I had destroyed his faith in petitions and political pronouncements, he felt a deep skepticism regarding the value of public comment on developments in Germany, noting that excessive and ill-considered attacks could even be harmful to opponents of the regime who were unable to escape. (At the same time, Hesse unostentatiously devoted a considerable part of his income to helping victims of Nazi repression flee Germany and gain a foothold in emigration.) His notes "From a Diary" (1933) give an indication of his reasons for refusing to join in the general public condemnation of the Nazis.

Unlike most of the émigrés, Hesse was tolerated by the cultural watchdogs of National Socialism until about 1938, and his works were not officially proscribed until 1943. This meant that he was one of the few non-party members permitted to publish in German journals. From 1933 to 1936 he reviewed extensively for the leading literary journal, *Neue Rundschau,* and took it upon himself to introduce to the German public many writers, principally foreign, whose works were not available in Germany and whose names would otherwise have remained unknown (e.g., Faulkner). In this same spirit of cultural mediation, he reviewed German books for *Bonniers Litterära Magasin* (1935–36), where he sorted out current publications for the Swedish audience, rejecting the official products of Nazi propaganda and singling out for praise such writers as Kafka, Musil, and Broch, whose reputations were virtually lost in the general anti-German hysteria that was growing in Europe. Although a few contemporaries like Thomas Mann were able to appreciate Hesse's often valiant efforts during these years, he was generally assailed from both right and left. For his reviews in Sweden he was viciously attacked as a Bolshevik and an enemy of the people by Nazi spokesmen, and this led to the condemnation of his works in Germany. At the same time, many émigrés, so embittered by their fate that they were unable to make rational distinctions, slandered Hesse as a tool of the National Socialists.

As a result of this abuse and soon reduced to a limited audience that rarely extended beyond Switzerland, Hesse in effect gave up the activities of editing, reviewing, and essay writing that had occupied him for so many years. It was only after the war and after the award of the Nobel Prize (1946) that he again addressed himself from time to time to a more general public. But in these late essays—virtually the only form that he practiced during the last twenty years of his life—we find few concessions to worldly concerns. At peace with himself, Hesse wrote only for those readers who wished to join him in his realm of the spirit. These quiet contemplations often begin as an idyl of childhood or as a reverie in the garden. But they invariably lead to such compelling issues as the quest for personal identity, moral responsibility, and the search for unity in a world that has become fragmented. It is not so much the substance of these essays as their tone that distinguishes them from the earlier works. Here we no longer find the sometimes self-indulgent pathos of the youthful rebel against conventional values, but the smiling irony that enchanted Thomas Mann and André Gide. These late reflections do not represent the flagging of Hesse's sense of commitment or the capitulation of a former rebel to the powers of the world, but rather what might be called the classicism of revolt. Here he speaks with the serenity of Joseph Knecht, who in one of the last essays relates stories of the Zen masters to his disciple Carlo Ferromonte. It is characteristic of the classical objectivity of his old age that Hesse, in the interests of detachment, translated these highly personal thoughts into the fiction of an epistle between figures from his last novel, *The Glass Bead Game*.

From all that has been said, it should be evident, first, that any valid assessment of Hesse's achievement as a writer must take into account his substantial activities as essayist, reviewer, and anthologist; and, second, that an acquaintance with his essays can contribute significantly to our understanding of his fiction. But to date only a few of his essays have been available in English. The two reflections on Dostoevsky's novels were translated by Eliot's friend Sydney Schiff (pseudonym, Stephen Hudson) and published in a limited edition in Zurich in 1923 under the title *In Sight of Chaos;* only two or three other essays have appeared in American periodicals.

My Belief, therefore, fills a conspicuous gap by presenting within a single volume most of Hesse's important essays and a representative selection of his reviews and introductions. Virtually all the significant essays are collected here, with the exception of two groups: the political pieces that have been published separately in *If the War Goes On . . .* and the specifically autobiographical reminiscences that make up *Autobiographical Writings*. Otherwise, this volume embraces examples from the three principal areas of Hesse's essayistic endeavor—literary criticism, personal credo, and cultural criticism. And it includes essays from every period of his life, from the early notes "At Year's End" (1904) down to the letter "Joseph Knecht to Carlo Ferromonte" (1961).

It is obviously impossible to reprint in this volume more than a highly select number of Hesse's hundreds of book reviews. Bibliographers are still attempting to compile a complete list of the pieces that appeared over a period of more than fifty years in a wide variety of newspapers and journals. I have tried to suggest the range of Hesse's interests by making a selection of reviews from three general areas: his remarks on European and American literature, from medieval times to the present; his interest in Western intellectual history, extending from Jung and Freud to Marx and Spengler; and, notably in the second half of his life, his increasing fascination with Oriental culture and literature.

Surely no one who has read *My Belief* can return to Hesse's novels with the usual preconceptions. Although by choice Hesse remained in the social isolation of the small Swiss village where Eliot sought him out, he was intellectually engaged not only with world culture of the past but also with the most compelling issues of modern civilization. In these writings we come face to face with those beliefs concerning life and art that underlie Hesse's major fictions and that have recently seized the imagination of yet another generation of readers.

THEODORE ZIOLKOWSKI

PART ONE
ESSAYS, 1904–1961

At Year's End

1904

T HE MAIL was heavy again today. Ten journals, each
addressed to the truly cultivated and edited from an
exclusively artistic viewpoint, send New Year's greetings,
and twenty publishing houses announce that they are vigorously extending their celebrated lists. All of them speak in
the same lofty, deadly serious language and present rosters
of "top names"; all are fully aware of the new currents of
our times, and all would be happy to make a little more
profit. As happens every few years, a young novelist is extolled whose work deserves to be put alongside *Green Henry*,
and so is a new lyric poet who is a true original and beyond
question will soon be considered in the same class with
Liliencron and Mörike; there is a picture of him in the
catalogue.

All this, of course, is not new and basically perhaps not
especially vicious; I have found entertainment a hundred
times in just this sort of cultural country fair. On this particular day, however, it does not make me want to laugh or
even to scold. A brief hour ago I was out on the hills looking at the clouds; each one drifted past, or strode or swam
or danced by like a miracle, like a word or a song or a jest
or a solace from the lips of God, and pressed on eagerly into
the distance, cradled in the cool pale blue, and it was more
beautiful and sang more enchantingly than any songs printed
in books. Now I had come back to the flea market and com-
mercial fair of the poets and artists and publishers as though
into a crowded room where the air was terrifyingly oppressive, and all at once it seemed to me that I was wading hopelessly through deep dead sand, I was suddenly as tired as
though from a fruitless hectic day, and I rested my head

in my hands and felt a malevolent melancholy assail me like a fever from that jumble of "culture" lying in front of me. In self-defense I pushed the rubbish aside, took the lamp in my hand, and went up to my room where my many old books stand in tight-packed rows and outside the windows sparrows and gulls fly. An old book is always comforting; it speaks out of the distance, and you can hearken or not; if suddenly great words flash out, you accept them not as you would in a book of today, not as coming from such and such a well-known author, but rather as something immediate like a sunbeam or a gull's cry.

And I read. I read in the *Heisterbach Chronicle,* in the pleasant easy good-humored Latin of the monk Caesarius, a little anecdote of the monastery.

The Abbot Gebhard used to lecture every morning to the monks about God, His essence and His attributes. It must be that he did this not only as a scholar and dogmatist but also with truly reverent feeling, for otherwise he would have been stricter and more severe with his pupils. As it was, these pupils believed they had long since learned enough about the essence and attributes of God, they hardly paid any attention but played the fool, daydreamed, and frequently went to sleep—as is indicated by a special chapter entitled "De Temptatione Dormiendi," in which Caesarius represents falling asleep as a besetting temptation. The Abbot went right on talking; perhaps he hardly looked at his pupils. But one morning in the course of his lecture his glance fell on the rows of auditors and he saw his monks dreaming, staring, smiling, winking, woolgathering—or asleep. He chose not to upbraid them but rather made use of a small ruse, a completely innocent small ruse, for this man would not have been capable of any other sort. What he did was to pause, change the tone of his discourse as though introducing something new, and then he said: "The following incident occurred at the famous court of the great King Artus . . ." Whereupon all the sleepers awoke and the winkers and dreamers suddenly looked alert, the whole audience leaned forward in attention, avidly interested in an anecdote about King Artus. But the Abbot gazed around at them and saw what was in their eyes, and then he said in good-natured reproof, "Alas, if I start to tell you a story about the court of King Artus you open your ears and are full of attention. But if I wish to talk to you about God you fall asleep!"

I put the old book back in its place and went to the window. In the blue mist below, the smooth lake lay in twilight, the windowpanes of the villages beyond flashed in the sunlight, and on the Thurgau mountains long pale narrow snowfields lay between the trees. Those mountains, separated from me by the lake, rose in such silent solemn beauty into the veiled sky and stood in such quiet holy repose in the approaching winter night that it seemed to me if I were over there, I could be a holy man and understand all the secrets of the earth. Over there the pale snow lay in a different fashion than on my roof, over there the beech forest and the black pine trees were indescribably beautiful and reserved in a way I never saw in my neighborhood; perhaps God Himself walked over there along the slopes, and whoever met Him there could touch Him and speak to Him and look closely into His eyes.

Yes, over there! Now here, in my beautiful quiet village, on my hill, in my woods, I do not dare to think of God, I do not touch His hand, do not hear His step—I see Him over there, across the lake, behind the light mist. And just suppose I were now in one of our cities, in Munich, Zurich, Stuttgart, or Dresden? Is there any place in any of them where I would not be ashamed and terrified if God encountered me? Is not every house and every stone full of lustful longing—for a story about King Artus? Only a few days ago an artist friend of mine asked me in what city it would be pleasant and agreeable to live. We took counsel and considered the names of many cities; we selected and rejected, but we could not find a city in which we would have liked to live permanently or even for a long period. Instead we live, one here, one there, in villages, in the mountains in country cottages, one in the Tyrol and another on the coast, one on a heath and another on Lake Constance, and we do not venture to get together in the same place nor can we find a city we would like to call home. Must it be this way?

I have often asked myself: Has it always been this way? But that is useless. Whoever has taken an honest look at what we call world history must know that every former time and race and culture is shut away from us by a hundred seals and will remain forever mysterious.

I stood and thought about the Abbot of Heisterbach, about God, and about King Artus. My eyes ran along the rows of books; many of the books, at other times my favorites, were lifeless and had nothing to say to me, but here and there an old brown volume with leather back looked out at me alertly and challengingly. There they stand arranged and waiting, and God is in each of them, but He does not speak at all hours, and often when I want to avoid Him and begin some merry story, I am like one of the Abbot's pupils and instead of the delightful tale I was eager for, I see a sad affectionate glance and hear a voice saying, "But when I talk about God you fall asleep!"

On Little Joys

1905

GREAT MASSES of people these days live out their lives in a dull and loveless stupor. Sensitive persons find our inartistic manner of existence oppressive and painful, and they withdraw from sight. In art and poetry, after the brief heyday of realism, dissatisfaction has arisen everywhere, the clearest symptom of it being nostalgia for the Renaissance and Romanticism.

"What you lack is faith!" cries the Church, and "What you lack is art," says Avenarius. They may be right. I believe what we lack is joy. The ardor that a heightened awareness imparts to life, the conception of life as a happy thing, as a festival—that is, after all, what dazzles and attracts us in the Renaissance. But the high value put upon every minute of time, the idea of hurry-hurry as the most important objective of living, is unquestionably the most dangerous enemy of joy. With a wistful smile we read the idyls, the sentimental journeys, of past epochs. What didn't our grandfathers have time for? Once when I was reading Friedrich Schlegel's elegy on idleness I could not help but think: How you would have sighed if you had had to work as hard as we do!

That this aggressive haste has influenced us detrimentally from our earliest schooldays is sad but inescapable. Unhappily, moreover, the increasing speed of modern life has long since done away with what meager leisure we had then. Our ways of enjoying ourselves are hardly less irritating and nerve-racking than the pressure of our work. "As much as possible, as fast as possible" is the motto. And so there is more and more entertainment and less and less joy. Whoever has witnessed a great celebration in a town or city or has visited the entertainment spots in a modern metropolis will retain in his memory a painful and displeasing impression of those feverish, distorted faces with their greedy eyes. This morbid pursuit of enjoyment, spurred on by constant dissatisfaction and yet perpetually satiated, is to be found in the theaters too, and the opera houses, in the concert halls and art galleries. To visit a modern art exhibition is hardly ever a pleasure.

The rich man is not spared these evils either. He might be but he cannot be. You have to conform, remain *au courant*, stay on top.

No more than anyone else do I have an infallible prescription against these abuses. I would simply like to recall an old and, alas, quite unfashionable private formula: Moderate enjoyment is double enjoyment. And: Do not overlook the little joys!

Well then—moderation. In certain circles it requires courage to miss a première. In wider circles it takes courage not to have read a new publication several weeks after its appearance. In the widest circles of all, one is an object of ridicule if one has not read the daily paper. But I know people who feel no regret at exercising this courage.

Let not the man who subscribes to a weekly theater series feel that he is losing something if he makes use of it only every other week. I guarantee: he will gain.

Let anyone who is accustomed to looking at a great many pictures in an exhibition try just once, if he is still capable of it, spending an hour or more in front of a single masterpiece and content himself with that for the day. He will be the gainer by it.

Let the omnivorous reader try the same sort of thing. Sometimes he will be annoyed at not being able to join in conversation about some publication; occasionally he will cause smiles. But soon he will know better and do the smiling himself. And let any man who cannot bring himself to use any other kind of restraint try to make a habit of going to bed at ten o'clock at least once a week. He will be amazed at how richly this small sacrifice of time and pleasure will be rewarded. The ability to cherish the "little joy" is intimately connected with the habit of moderation. For this ability, originally natural to every man, presupposes certain things which in modern daily life have largely become obscured or lost, mainly a measure of cheerfulness, of love, and of poesy. These little joys, bestowed especially upon the poor, are so inconspicuous and scattered so liberally throughout our daily lives that the dull minds of countless workers hardly notice them. They are not outstanding, they are not advertised, they cost no money! (Strangely enough, it is precisely the poor who do not know that the loveliest joys are always those that cost no money.)

Among the joys mentioned above are those granted us by our daily contact with nature. Our eyes, above all those misused, overstrained eyes of modern man, can be, if only we are willing, an inexhaustible source of pleasure. When I walk to work in the morning I see many other workers who also have just crawled sleepily out of bed, hurrying in both directions, shivering along the streets. Most of them walk fast and keep their eyes on the pavement, or at most on the clothes and faces of the passers-by. Heads up, dear friends! Just try it once—a tree, or at least a considerable section of sky, is to be seen anywhere. It does not even have to be blue sky; in some way or other the light of the sun always makes itself felt. Accustom yourself every morning to look for a moment at the sky and suddenly you will be aware of the air around you, the scent of morning freshness that is bestowed on you between sleep and labor. You will find every day that the gable of every house has its own particular look, its own special lighting. Pay it some heed and you will have for the rest of the day a remnant of satisfaction and a touch of coexistence with nature. Gradually and without effort the eye trains itself to transmit many small delights, to contemplate nature and the city streets, to appreciate the inexhaustible fun of daily life. From there on to the fully trained artistic eye is the smaller half of the journey; the principal thing is the beginning, the opening of the eyes.

A stretch of sky, a garden wall overhung by green branches, a strong horse, a handsome dog, a group of children, a beautiful face—why should we be willing to be robbed of all this? Whoever has acquired the knack can in the space of a block see precious things without losing a minute's time. Moreover, this kind of seeing is not tiring; on the contrary, it strengthens and refreshes, and not the eye alone. All things have their vivid aspects, even the uninteresting or ugly; one must only want to see.

And with seeing come cheerfulness and love and poesy. The man who for the first time picks a small flower so that he can have it near him while he works has taken a step toward joy in life.

There was a girls' school opposite the house in which I worked for quite a long time. A class of ten-year-olds had their playground on my side of the building. I had a great deal of work to do in those days, and at times I suffered from the noise of the children playing, but the amount of joy and lust for life that a single glance at that playground gave me is greater than I can express. Those bright clothes, those lively, merry eyes, those supple, sinewy movements heightened my delight in living. A riding school or a chicken run would perhaps have served the same purpose. Anyone who has once observed the play of light on an evenly colored surface, the wall of a house for instance, knows how easily contented, what a source of pleasure, the eye is.

Let these examples suffice. Readers will certainly have thought of many other small joys, perhaps the especially delightful one of smelling a flower or a piece of fruit, of listening to one's own or others' voices, of hearkening to the prattle of children. And a tune being hummed or whistled in the distance, and a thousand other tiny things from which one can weave a bright necklace of little pleasures for one's life.

My advice to the person suffering from lack of time and from apathy is this: Seek out each day as many as possible of the small joys, and thriftily save up the larger, more demanding pleasures for holidays and appropriate hours. It is the small joys first of all that are granted us for recreation, for daily relief and disburdenment, not the great ones.

Letter to a Young Poet
1910

THANK YOU for your charming letter and for your poems
and stories. The letter expresses a confidence that I
must, alas, disappoint. Even if I were not suffering from eye-
strain and burdened by a much too heavy correspondence I
would have to disappoint you, for what you ask of me is
something I do not have to give.

You present me with your poetic efforts and request me to
read them and then tell you what I think of your talent.
You ask for severe judgment and candid appraisal, flattery
will be of no use to you. Simply put, your question is: Am
I a poet? Am I talented enough to be entitled to publish
poems and, if possible, to make writing my calling?

I would like nothing better than to be able to give a
simple answer to this simple question, but that is not possible. I consider it altogether out of the question to draw from
sample poems by a beginner whom one does not know
personally and intimately any conclusions about his lasting
qualifications to be a poet. Whether you have talent can, of
course, be made out, but talent is no rarity, the world is
teeming with talent, and a young man of your age and education would have to be actually lacking in normal endowment if he were not able to write acceptable poems and
essays. Further, I will no doubt be able to see from your
work whether you have read Nietzsche or Baudelaire, if
this or that present-day poet has influenced you; I will also
be able to see whether you have already formed a taste for
art and nature, which nevertheless has not the slightest
thing to do with poetic endowment. At best (and this would
speak well for your verses) I will be able to discover traces
of your experiences and attempt to form a picture of your

character. More is not possible, and whoever promises on the basis of your early efforts to appraise your literary talent or your hopes for a poetic career is a highly superficial character, if not a swindler.

Consider this: it is not hard after reading *Faust* to pronounce Goethe a significant poet. It would be quite possible, however, from Goethe's early works, and also from some of his later ones, to put together a slim volume of poems from which no one could draw any conclusion except that the young author had read his Gellert and other models attentively and that he had a knack for rhyming. And so, even with the greatest poets, the manuscripts of their first attempts are by no means always really original and convincing. In Schiller's youthful poems one can find quite astonishing blunders, and in those of C. F. Meyer often complete absence of talent.

No, the judgment of young talent is not as simple as you think. If I do not know you intimately, I cannot tell at what stage of your development you are. Your poems may show immaturities at which you yourself will smile in six months' time. It could be that favorable circumstances have brought to bloom in you just at this moment a certain talent that is incapable of further development. It may be that the poems you sent me are the best you will ever write in your whole life, but it is equally possible that they are the worst. Some talents reach their heights in a writer's early twenties and then quickly wilt; others first become evident in the thirties or often later.

And so the question of whether perhaps in five or ten years you will be a poet does not depend at all on the verses that you write today.

But the matter has another side to which we should devote a moment's attention.

Why do you want to be a poet? If it is from ambition for fame, then you have chosen a poor field: the German of today doesn't care very much about poets and gets along quite well without them. It is the same with making money: if you were to become the most famous poet in Germany (not counting the theater), you would, in comparison with a director or an assistant manager of a stocking or needle factory, be little better than a beggar.

But perhaps you have hit upon the ideal of being a poet because you see a poet as an original, a perceptive and a pious man, pure in heart, with delicate sensibilities and an exalted emotional life, a man who is capable of awe, who yearns for an inspired, in some way ennobled existence. Perhaps you see the poet as the opposite pole to the money-man, to the man of power. Perhaps you strive for a poet's career not on account of the verses or fame but because you feel that the poet only seems to enjoy a certain freedom and isolation but actually is responsible in the highest degree, and must dedicate himself totally if his poetic vocation is not to be a masquerade.

If this is so, then you are following the right road with your verses. But in that case too it is of no consequence whether in time you become a poet or not. For these high qualities, tasks, and goals which you ascribe to the poet, that loyalty to himself, that awe in the face of nature, that acceptance of unusual self-sacrifice, that responsibility which is never satisfied with itself and gladly pays the price of sleepless nights for a successful sentence, a well-turned phrase—all these virtues (if we may call them so) are the hallmarks not only of the true poet. They are the hallmarks of the true human being per se, of the unenslaved, unmechanized man, of the reverent and responsible human being, no matter what his profession.

Now if you have this ideal of a human being, if you are not inspired by a desire for notoriety and fame, money and power, but rather desire a life centered in itself and unshakable by worldly influences, then, to be sure, you are not yet a poet, but you are the poet's brother, you belong to the same species. And then too there is profound meaning in the fact that you write poetry.

For writing poetry, especially when one is young, does not have just one social function, that of bringing pretty works of art into the world and through them delighting or exhorting; rather, writing poetry can have, completely independent of the worth and possible success of the poems produced, an irreplaceable value for the poet himself. In earlier ages writing poetry was as a matter of course considered part of the development of a young man's personality. To follow the way of the poet, not simply to practice the use of language but to learn to know oneself more profoundly and more accurately, to advance one's individual development farther and higher than the average of mankind succeeds in doing, through setting down unique and wholly personal psychic experiences, to see better one's own powers and dangers, to define them better—that is what writing poetry means for the young poet, long before the question may be raised as to whether his poems perhaps have some value for the world at large.

The word "personality" today no longer implies an unqualified ideal as it did, for instance, in Goethe's time. From both the bourgeois and the proletarian side the unique personality is rejected as an end in itself—there is no attempt to rear outstanding individuals but rather normal, healthy, hard-working, average people. The factories thrive on this. But in a very short time, in Germany for instance, it has become obvious that vital functions of the body politic suffer damage and deathly crisis when there is a lack of that energy, responsibility, and inner purity which can be produced only by the high-minded individual. The horrifying deterioration of political activity, of party action and of parliamentarianism, shows this lack clearly, and those very parties that made it impossible for a man even slightly above the average to remain in their midst now belatedly cry out for a "strong man."

Pay no attention if you have to put up with some teasing from your friends because of your poetry. Perhaps it will help you to mature and to attain a somewhat higher stage of humanity than is possible for the masses. Perhaps after a while you will find quite by yourself that for you poetry is dispensable—not in order to make a base peace with mediocre ideals but to gain for yourself in other fields that nobler, more worthy, more inspired kind of life to which you feel yourself called.

Old Music

1913

O UTSIDE THE WINDOWS of my lonely country house the
gray rain was falling persistently, hopelessly. I had
little desire to put on my boots again and make the long
muddy journey into the city. But I was alone and my eyes
ached from long hours of work. Along all four walls of
my study stood golden rows of books staring at me with
their intolerably solemn questions and challenges, the children were long since in bed and asleep, and the little fire
on my hearth had died. So I decided to go, searched out my
concert ticket, pulled on my boots, chained up the dog,
and in my raincoat set off through the mud and damp.

The cool air smelled bitter, the lane wound its way in
capricious curves around the neighboring properties between tall crooked oak trees. A light shone from a gatekeep-
er's lodge. A dog began to bark, grew furious, barked louder
and louder until its voice broke and it suddenly fell silent.
The sound of a piano reached me from a country house
behind black shrubbery. There is nothing more beautiful and
moving than to walk alone like this in the fields at night and
hear music from a lonely house; it brings intimations of
everything good and lovable, of home and lamplight, of
evening solemnity in quiet rooms, of women's hands and
ancient family traditions.

Soon came the first streetlight, silent pale outpost of the
city, and then another, and close at hand the shimmering
gables of the suburbs, and then suddenly around a corner
the glare of the arc light at the streetcar station, people in
long coats waiting, conductors chatting in dripping wet
caps, the buttons of their wet uniforms shimmering palely.
A streetcar clatters up, bright and warm with broad glass

windows, blue lightning playing under it. I get in, we move away, from my bright glass cage I look out at the nighttime streets, broad and deserted; here and there at a corner a woman under an umbrella waits for the car, and now come brighter and livelier streets, and suddenly beyond the high bridge the whole city lies glowing in the evening brilliance of shopwindows and streetlamps, and far down under the bridge is the valley of the river with the dark mirror of its waters and the white foam of spillways.

I get out and walk through the arcades of a narrow side street toward the cathedral. The streetlights are reflected pale and cool in the wet pavement of the small cathedral square; the chestnut trees on the terrace wave in the wind. Above the portal bathed in reddish light the Gothic tower disappears into the wet night, narrowing upward to immense height. I linger for a little in the rain, finally throw away my cigar and walk under the high pointed arch. There people in damp clothes are crowded together, behind his bright window sits the cashier, a man asks for my ticket, I move into the cathedral, hat in hand, and at once from the huge dimly lighted vault a hallowed atmosphere streams toward me, laden with anticipation. Weak lights shed their timid beams along the columns and clusters of pillars, beams that lose their way among the gray stones and wane warm and tender high up in the arches. A few pews are completely filled; farther on, the nave and choir are almost empty. I steal forward on tiptoe—even my steps echo faintly behind me—through the huge solemn space; in the dark choir are the old heavy wooden benches with carved backs. I pull down a seat; the wooden thump re-echoes from the stony heights.

I settle back contentedly into the wide deep seat and get out a program, but it is too dark to read. I think back but cannot exactly recall what had been announced: an organ piece by some dead French master, an old Italian violin sonata, who knows by whom, perhaps by Veracini or Nardini or Tartini, and then a prelude and fugue by Bach.

A few more black figures steal into the choir, seat them-

selves far apart from one another and burrow themselves
deep into the old seats. Someone drops a book, behind me
I hear two girls whispering. Now silence. Silence. Far off
on the lighted rood loft, between two round lamps and in
front of the cool gleam of the towering organ pipes, a man
is standing; he nods and seats himself, a sigh of expectation
runs through the little congregation. I do not want to look
on. Leaning back, I stare up into the high arches and breathe
the hushed cathedral air. I think: How can people Sunday
after Sunday in the bright light of day sit crowded close
together in this holy place and listen to a sermon which,
however fine and wise it may be, can only sound flat and
disappointing in so lofty a temple.

There—a high strong organ note. Increasing in volume,
it fills the huge space, becomes space itself, envelops us
completely. It waxes, then pauses, other notes come to accompany it, and suddenly all plunge in hurried flight into
the depths, prostrate themselves, do reverence, but still
persist in asserting themselves, controlled by the harmonic
bass. Now they fall silent. A pause sweeps through the hall
like the quiet before a storm. And now once more: mighty
tones rise up in deep and splendid passion, swelling stormily,
crying aloud in resignation their lamentations to God, crying again and more piercingly, louder, and then they fall
silent. And again they arise, again this daring and forgotten master raises his strong voice to God, challenges and
accuses, mightily weeps forth his song in stormy sequences,
and then he rests, enveloping himself and praising God in
a chorale of reverence and dignity, he stretches golden arches
across the lofty twilight, causes columns and clusters of
pillars to resound, and he erects the cathedral of his worship until it stands there alone and unshaken, embracing
us all, even after the last notes have died away.

I am forced to think: How miserable, how paltry, how
bad are the lives we lead! Which one of us would dare to
stand forth like this composer before God and fate, with
such cries of accusation and of gratitude, with such aspir-
ing grandeur from so profoundly reverent a mind? Alas,

one should live differently, one should be different, should spend more time under the sky and among the trees, keep more time for oneself to be closer to the beautiful and great mysteries.

The organ begins again, deep, faint, a quiet chord; and above it a violin melody ascends into the heights in marvelously ordered stages, with little questioning, little complaint, just singing and floating in the fullness of a mysterious bliss, light and lovely like the movements of a beautiful girl. The melody is repeated, it changes, it alters direction, it seeks out related figures and a hundred delicate joyful arabesques, it winds supply along the narrowest paths and emerges free and purified in clear and tranquil emotion. Here there is no grandeur, no outcry or abysmal suffering, no sublime awe, here is nothing but the beauty of a happy, contented soul. It has nothing more to say to us than that the world is beautiful and filled with divine order and harmony and, oh, what rarer message is there, what message do we stand in greater need of than this joyful one!

You can sense without actually seeing that throughout the whole great church there are now smiles on many faces, happy pure smiles. Some may find this simple, ancient music a little naïve and old-fashioned, and yet they too smile and drift along in the clear stream of pure bliss.

During the interval one feels that the little rustlings of the people are happy and cheerful, their whisperings and moving about in their seats. The audience feels happy and released and looks forward to new splendor. And now it comes. With majestic free deportment Master Bach enters his temple, does grateful homage to God, rises from worship and, following the text of a hymn, happily falls to expressing his reverent Sunday mood. But hardly has he made a start and cleared some space for himself than he begins to drive his harmonies deeper, interlace melody with melody, harmony with harmony in animated polyphony; he reinforces and lifts and rounds out his edifice of notes far above the church into a starry space full of nobly perfect systems as though God had gone to sleep and handed over to him

His staff and mantle. He makes the lightning play from towering clouds and throws open serene sunny spaces, he triumphantly guides forth planets and suns, he rests relaxed at high noon and at the proper hour elicits the cool showers of evening. And he ends in splendor and power like the setting sun and, as he falls silent, leaves the world full of glory and of soul.

In silence I walk through the lofty nave and across the little sleeping square, in silence I cross the high bridge over the river and pass the rows of streetlamps on my way out of the city. The rain has stopped, an immense cloud covers the whole country but a few narrow fissures let one glimpse moonlight and a beautiful clear night above. The city disappears and the oak trees along my forest path rustle in the soft cool wind. Slowly I climb up the last hill and enter my sleeping house, the elm tree speaks to me through the windows. Now I am glad to go to rest and for a time give life a trial once more and be its plaything.

Letter to a Philistine

1915

To Herr M. in Z.

YOU WILL BE SURPRISED, Herr M., that I am writing to you, and it will surprise you even more to learn that I do so because of my memory of our last meeting and conversation, for presumably you have long since forgotten them both. Meanwhile, just the reverse has happened to me; that is, at the time I attributed no importance at all to those moments and words. I forgot them, Herr M., I forgot what you said, as it were, while the conversation was still going on, and I left without retaining any perceptible impression of our talk. Later that same day, however, our stupid little exchange suddenly came back to me, already accompanied by a sharp little sting, and thereafter the memory returned more and more frequently and became constantly more urgent and unpleasant. Since then months have passed, yes, almost a whole year, but in each of those months I have been forced to think of you, Herr M., at least two or three times, and I have repeated our conversation and made it the subject of long arguments with you and explanations which you presumably do not deserve and which I shall take care not to share with you.

Let us start at the beginning, since you doubtless have long ago forgotten the whole incident. Well then, perhaps ten or eleven months ago I had arrived around noon in your city, I was carrying a small yellow leather suitcase and a raincoat, and I encountered you on the streetcar on the far side of the tunnel. I was on my way to the outskirts of the city where a friend of mine lives, and you, I suppose, were coming home for lunch from your business (about which

I know nothing at all). You own, as I observed at the time, a fine house with a large garden in that most attractive section.

I greeted you because I remembered you from a number of earlier meetings, at literary lectures, concerts, and similar occasions, and, I believe, you belong as well to some kind of artistic or literary commission. In any case, we had talked to each other several times. You had shown a certain interest in me and I had the impression that you were an agreeable man of the world, well enough educated to have some idea of art but at the same time too much a businessman, too much interested in money, too much interested in nothing, ever to be able to free yourself and breathe the air in which beauty naturally flourishes. You knew beauty well, so it seemed to me, but only as a female slave, a secretly prized and secretly favored slave. From time to time, you felt, so it seemed to me, a yearning for some transfiguration of life, for an echo from that world in which money and business do not exist. This was the reason you sat on art commissions and attended literary evenings, and certainly you would have many a good painting hanging on the walls of your beautiful house.

And so I spoke to you with the innocent friendliness and pleasure one feels on meeting again someone who awakens only agreeable, guileless, undemanding memories. You acknowledged my salutation in the same manner, with a small gratified smile of recognition, and with that small, to me by no means disturbing, trace of condescension which rich or influential people almost always feel toward artists and similar eccentric characters. We could not converse, we were not sitting next to each other, and the noon car was filled to overflowing.

But you got out at the same stop I did and you took the same uphill side street, and so we had an opportunity of shaking hands and chatting together briefly. You genially inquired what had brought me to Z., and I replied that I had come to attend a musical performance to be conducted by a friend of mine, and we talked about this. A third gentleman, whom you had just introduced to me, was walking beside us, and if I remember correctly it was this third person who brought the halting conversation (we were climbing uphill and all of us were hungry) around to the subject that has so often preoccupied me since then. He mentioned a recent book of mine and asked me whether a new one would appear that winter, then half jestingly he added a little comment about the material rewards of literary work, about royalties and printings. Smiling, I tried to dismiss the subject, and this was the single moment out of the whole conversation that I have retained accurately in my memory.

It was then that you suddenly became animated and your voice grew loud and rather unpleasant as you looked at me with a malicious smile and shouted, "Oh, come now, you artists and writers are exactly like everyone else! You think about money and profits and that's all!"

There it was. I made no reply, and as a matter of fact for the moment I was slightly stunned by the oddly aggressive discourtesy of your stupid words; however, I did not pause over it and so did not defend myself in any way. Nevertheless I was disagreeably affected and was glad when you shortly reached your house. I tipped my hat and said good day, but since I was offended I did not shake hands again; and I parted with equal abruptness from the other man and walked on alone the short remainder of my way.

The meeting with my friend and his wife and children, the midday meal, the conversation and music afterward, completely wiped out my encounter with you until that evening. It was then that I suddenly experienced a feeling of discomfort and uneasiness, yes, something like the nasty feeling of being unwashed; I was pursued by the vague shadow of a memory as though I had been insulted on that day, or had witnessed something dishonorable and at the same time had behaved unworthily myself. And suddenly it became clear to me: it was your words, Herr M., your coarse stupid words about me and about artists in general.

Presently I realized that it was not the insult contained

in your comment that had struck me, that had caused me pain, but a feeling of guilt, of bad conscience. I had listened in silence while a person whom I had taken rather seriously and even respected expressed himself coarsely and hatefully about all artists. I had missed an opportunity when a serious word from me might perhaps have touched this man's soul, when this Herr M. might for a moment have been taken aback, and felt inwardly humbled or at least ashamed before a world he recognized as purer than his own.

Since then, as I have said, those words have echoed often in my thoughts. And it has always happened that anger at you as an individual, Herr M., subsided and anger at myself became my principal concern. That I would not greet you again or shake hands with you was a minor matter, settled at once and for good; that did not redeem my failure or justify my negligence. My feeling of discomfort, anger, and shame, when I thought about my unprotesting acceptance of your silly words, was exactly the same as a sensation I had once had two or three years before. I thought I had forgotten that incident but it came back to me again and, together with the later one involving you, began actually to torment me.

That other incident was as follows. In the course of a sea voyage while my ship lay in harbor taking on coal, I went ashore in the company of another traveler. He was well acquainted with that exotic port and was acting as my guide. In two or three hours he succeeded in showing me everything that was to be found there in the way of cheap music halls, low dance palaces, bars, and other evil spots. However, from the time we entered the first of these dens not only did I find them unsympathetic places, but my companion's conversation, winks, and laughs struck me as disagreeable, repulsive, and improper in the highest degree. Nevertheless, I tagged along, sullen and angry, and simply did not summon up courage to free myself, to let the man know my disapproval either explicitly or quietly by leaving him. No, that simply wasn't possible; his fat, merry, naïvely robust character had overpowered my weaker one, I followed him as

though he were my executioner, and while I grew wildly
angry at him and at myself, I listened in silence to his talk.

Yes, there it was. I was not offended because the world
contained ugliness and obscenity; I could overlook them,
even laugh at them. But that I had once unprotestingly
countenanced this aspect of the world, which I despise and
reject, in a way that might make it seem that I was condoning these things and condoning my companion who was
seeking them out and who loved them, that was what had
left its sting behind. And now this little incident with you,
Herr M., had come along as a second little sting.

In no sense do I write you this in order to exonerate myself retrospectively; quite the contrary. I write this for myself, not for you, and I write it in order to admit to a fault.
It was my duty on that occasion not to listen without protest to your unlovely words about artists. Perhaps indeed
they were not even meant that way! Perhaps you, the
affluent moneyman with a secret hunger for art, really simply
wanted to irritate me, to hear my vindication, provoke an
answer from me that would reassure your own doubting
heart about the existence of ideals, the reality of that purer
world. And because I remained silent, that secret confirmation, that secret desire in you to believe, subsided and vanished, and when I walked on silently and in a bad temper,
I completely abandoned your hesitating soul to disbelief
and to that stupid cheap skepticism that is more inimical
and dangerous to art and to the life of the spirit in general
than any vice.

If after almost a year I make this confession to you, it
does not mean in the slightest that I am canceling my private intentions in respect to you. I no longer need speak to
you or give you my hand. Oh, it would be so easy to refute
the silly accusation you made, without sentiment, simply
by facts, figures, and statements. But there is nothing to be
gained by that now. You are not the one I blame, though at
the same time I no longer especially prize you; it is myself
I blame because of the complicity of my silence and also
perhaps because of a slight smile, easy to misinterpret,

which made it seem that I agreed with you, that I shared your view, which I actually reject and abhor with all my soul.

Think of me what you will. Believe, if you wish, that I actually agreed with you on that occasion. Believe, for all I care, that I have always been of that opinion and still hold it today. Consider me one of those who are related to that world of art only by accident and profession . . . It makes no difference to me; I can get along very well without your regard. But, Herr M., you wealthy man with your fine house and garden, just do not believe that one can commit with impunity small murders such as you committed on that occasion by your words! I know you have already begun to feel the punishment, and I know it will grow more and more painful, it will increasingly ruin your life. And until you make some move to restore faith to your soul, until you seriously think once more about the existence of the good, your soul will be sick and will suffer. You will be condemned to see everywhere and always that precisely what is best, precisely what is most beautiful, precisely what is most desirable, money cannot buy! The best, the most beautiful, the most desirable things in the world can be paid for only with one's own soul, just as love can never be bought. And he whose soul is not pure, not capable of goodness or at least of believing in the good, no longer distinguishes the best and noblest clearly and completely and must forever content himself with that diminished, distorted, cloudy picture of the world that his ideas have created for his own suffering and impoverishment.

Language

1917

LANGUAGE IS A DETRIMENT, an earthbound limitation from which the poet suffers more than anyone else. At times he can actually hate it, denounce it, and execrate it—or rather hate himself for being born to work with this miserable instrument. He thinks with envy of the painter whose language—color—is instantly comprehensible to everyone from the North Pole to Africa; or of the musician whose notes also speak in every human tongue and who commands so many new, individual, subtly differentiated languages, from simple melody to the hundred voices of the orchestra, from horn to clarinet, from violin to harp.

For one reason, however, the poet envies the musician constantly and especially profoundly: the musician's language belongs to him alone, it is just for making music! The poet on the other hand must use for his work the same language employed in school and in business, dispatching telegrams and conducting lawsuits. How handicapped he is in having no individual instrument for his art; no dwelling of his own, no private garden, no attic window through which to look at the moon—each and every thing must partake of the commonplace! If he says "heart," meaning thereby the most vibrant of man's qualities, his innermost abilities and weaknesses, the word at the same time signifies a muscle. If he says "power," he must contend for the meaning of his word with the engineer and the electrician; if he speaks of "blessedness," a flavor of theology creeps into the expression of his idea. There is not a single word he can use that does not squint in another direction from the one he intends, that does not in the same breath recall alien, disturbing, contradictory notions, that does not bear within itself restrictions and abridgments; it breaks apart like a voice striking too-narrow walls and rebounding, incomplete and muffled.

And so if a scoundrel is to be defined as someone who gives more than he has, a poet can never be a scoundrel. Indeed, he does not give so much as a tenth, not so much as a hundredth part of what he would like to give; in fact, he is satisfied if he is quite superficially, distantly, and, as it were, accidentally understood by his listener, or at least is not grossly misunderstood on the most important points. He seldom achieves more than this. And wherever the poet is praised or blamed, wherever he is effective or laughed to scorn, wherever he is loved or despised, it is never his real thoughts and dreams that are in question but only that hundredth part of them that can force its way through the narrow channel of speech and into the equally narrow channel of his reader's understanding.

That is why people defend themselves with so much fear, as though from a deadly threat, when an artist or an entire generation of young artists begins to experiment with new expressions and new language and to tug at the bonds that constrain them. For a citizen who has learned it, language (any language that he has painfully acquired, not just that of words) is holy. To the average man everything is sacrosanct that is held in common by society, that he shares with many, if possible with all, that never reminds him of loneliness, of birth and death, of the innermost I. The poet's fellow citizens, like himself, have the ideal of a world language. But the world language of the citizen is not the same one the poet dreams of, a primeval forest of riches, an immense orchestra; rather the citizen's is a simplified telegraphic sign language, the use of which will save people trouble, words, and paper and will not interfere with the earning of money. Alas, writing poetry, composing music, and endeavors of that sort always, as it happens, interfere with the earning of money!

Now, if our fellow citizen has learned a language that he takes to be the language of art, he is content in the belief that he understands art and has mastered it; he then becomes furious if he discovers that this language he acquired so painfully is valid only for a quite small province of the world of art. In our grandfathers' time there were energetic and educated people who had pushed their way ahead in musical appreciation to the point of admitting, beside Mozart and Haydn, Beethoven too. To that extent they "went along." But then with Chopin and Liszt and Wagner, when they were required again and again to learn a new language, to become once more revolutionary and young, flexible and happy in their recognition of something new, then they grew deeply offended; they proclaimed the downfall of art and the degeneracy of the times in which they were condemned to live. What happened to those people is now happening to many thousands more. Art is producing new faces, new languages, babbling sounds and unfamiliar gestures; it is tired of always talking the language of yesterday and the day before, it wants to dance for a change, it wants to kick over the traces, it wants to cock its hat and walk zigzag. And our fellow citizens are furious at this; they feel that they are being mocked and that their values are being attacked at the very root; they hurl curses about in every direction and pull the blanket of their education up over their ears. And the same citizen who rushes off to the law courts at the very slightest slur or affront to his personal dignity now becomes prolific in horrid insults.

This kind of rage and fruitless excitement does not, however, free the citizen, does not unburden and cleanse his soul, does not by any means put an end to his inner unrest and disgust. The artist, on the other hand, who has no less to complain about in the case of this fellow citizen than vice versa, takes the trouble to seek to discover and learn a new language for his anger, his contempt, his bitterness. He feels that insults will not help, and he sees that he who utters them is in the wrong. Since in our time he has no other ideal but himself, and since he wills and desires nothing except to be wholly himself and to do and speak what nature has implanted within him, he converts his enmity toward his fellow citizens into the most personal possible form, the most beautiful, the most eloquent; he does not translate his scorn into venom but rather sifts and kneads it into a new irony, a new caricature, a new insight that transforms what is unpleasant and irritating into what is agreeable and beautiful.

What an infinite number of languages nature has, and what an infinite number men have invented! The few thousand simple grammars that nations have hammered out, from Sanskrit to Volapük, are relatively meager accomplishments. They are meager because they have always contented themselves with what was most essential—and our fellow citizens have always agreed among themselves that what is most essential is earning money, baking bread, and the like. On such fare, language cannot thrive. Never has a human language (I mean a grammatical one) achieved half the animation, wit, elegance, and spirit that a cat reveals in the waving of her tail or a bird of paradise in the silvery plumage of its wedding attire.

And yet man, as soon as he became himself and did not try to imitate the ants or the bees, greatly outdid the bird of paradise, the cat, and all other animals and plants. He thought up languages that permit him to communicate and empathize infinitely better than German, Greek, and Italian do. He conjured up religions, architectures, paintings, philosophies; he created music whose meaningfulness and richness of color far excel any bird of paradise or butterfly. If I think "Italian painting"—what untold riches there are in the words; choirs ringing with reverence and sweetness, instruments of all kinds blissfully singing, a scent of pious coolness in marble churches, monks fervently praying, and beautiful women reigning imperiously in southern lands. Or I think "Chopin": notes descend softly and sadly out of the night; the lonely plaint of homesickness in a foreign land rises to the accompaniment of strings; the most subtle, most personal sufferings are sounded in harmonies and dissonances more profound and infinitely more accurate and delicate than any description of a sufferer in scientific terms, figures, and formulas.

Who seriously believes that *Werther* and *Wilhelm Meister* are written in the same language? That Jean Paul spoke the same language as our schoolteachers? And those are only poets! They had to work with the poverty and brittleness of language; they had to work with an instrument made for something entirely different.

Utter the word "Egypt" and you hear a speech that praises God in mighty, brazen chords, full of intuitions of eternity and deep dread of mortality; kings gaze inexorably out of stony eyes across millions of slaves, and yet beyond all and everything they look simply into the dark eyes of death— sacred animals stare out in earthy solemnity, lotus flowers, delicate in the hands of dancing girls, perfume the air. A world, a starry heaven full of worlds, is contained in this one word "Egypt"; you can do nothing but fantasy about it for a month if you like. But suddenly something else occurs to you. You hear the name "Renoir," and you smile and see the whole world resolved into circular brushstrokes, rosy, bright, happy. And you say "Schopenhauer" and see this same world represented by lines of suffering men who during sleepless nights have turned suffering into a deity and who with solemn faces move down a long, rough street leading to an infinitely quiet, infinitely modest, sad paradise. Or the words "Walt und Vult": the whole world arranges itself in a misty, flexible Jean Paul fashion around a middle-class German home where the soul of humanity, divided between two brothers, moves unruffled through the nightmare of a crotchety will and the intrigues of a mad ant heap of teeming philistines.

The average citizen likes to compare the dreamer to a madman. The average citizen is right in feeling that he would immediately go mad if, like the artist, the man of religion, the philosopher, he allowed himself to become acquainted with the abyss within him. We may call the abyss the soul or the unconscious or whatever; out of it comes every impulse of our lives. The average citizen has set a watchman between himself and his soul, a consciousness, a morality, a security police, and he recognizes nothing that comes directly from that abyss of the soul before it has been given that watchman's stamp of approval. The artist's constant distrust, however, is not directed against the region of the soul but precisely against that border watchman's authority; the artist secretly comes and goes between this side and that, between the conscious and the unconscious, as though at home in both houses.

While he tarries on this side, on the familiar daylight side where the citizen lives, the poverty of all languages presses heavily upon him, and to be a poet seems a thorny life. But once he is over there, in the land of the soul, then, magically, word after word floats toward him from every wind, stars sing out, and mountains smile, and the world is perfect, and it is the language of God in which no word and no letter is lacking, where everything can be said, where everything chimes, where everything is resolved.

The Refuge

1917

FOR MANY YEARS a favorite wish has accompanied me— or rather it has not so much "accompanied" as been rooted in me, nourished itself on me, drawn strength from me in the way certain relatives and friends "accompany" us by letting themselves be favored and led by us and by making our home and our strength their own.

This favorite wish was a pretty one, and not especially immodest if looked at from the outside. Its object was—a refuge. This refuge took very different forms at different times. Sometimes it was a small house on Lake Lucerne with a rowboat at the landing place. Then again it was a woodsman's hut in the Alps with a bunk to sleep in and four hours away from the nearest neighbors. Or it was a cave or a little ruin among the rocks in southern Ticino, close to the airy chestnut forest, placed as high as the highest vineyards, with or without a window and door. Another time the refuge was a steamship ticket good for a small cabin on a ship with no other passengers, for a voyage of three months, no matter whither. And occasionally it was even more modest, only a hole in the ground, a little grave, well or ill dug, with or without flowers above, with or without a coffin.

The meaning and principal point were always exactly the same. Whether a house in the country or a ship's cabin, whether an Alpine hut or a garden in Tuscany, a rocky cave in Ticino or a hole in the ground in a cemetery, the meaning was always—a refuge. As superscription to this wish there always stood the verse of that Swabian pastor, that lovable, ailing eccentric who sat in a tiny village, deserted by the world, with nothing to do, and wrote the line:

Leave, O world, leave me in peace!

Thereby, it seemed, all was to be achieved if somewhere I had a hideaway and a refuge, if I knew of a retreat safe and quiet, with a forest or lake nearby, but in any case no people, no messengers of grief and thieves of thought, no letters, no telegrams, no newspapers, no traveling salesmen of culture. There might be a brook prattling nearby, a waterfall, or the sun falling hot on brown rock, there might be butterflies fluttering or goats grazing, lizards incubating or gulls nesting—no matter, but one thing I was determined to have there, peace, my sleep and my dream. No one would dare enter this refuge unless I summoned him, no one would even know about it, no one there would be acquainted with me or want anything from me, no one would compel me to anything. I would be on no list of addresses, no tax roll.

That was an agreeable wish and dream of mine; it sounded sweet and modest and in its favor there was the precedent of some famous poets. And how well justified it was! For a man who did not seek power, who tried to meet the world's claims on him as well as he could, who was a poet and peaceable citizen—a man like me—was there a more proper, more understandable wish than for a retreat, a spot in the South, a rocky nook in the mountains, a cave, a hiding place, a grave? If perchance a house in the country or a ship's cabin were too pretentious, this certainly could not be said of a bed of straw in a hut or a small nameless grave.

During many hours over many years I elaborated this dream; while walking, working in the garden, before going to sleep, after waking up, on railway trains, and during sleepless nights I turned to it. I constructed it with care, painted and adorned it, made it ever more beautiful through music, more delicate, more noble. I drew it in the shadow of the forest, imagined an accompaniment of goat bells, wove yearning around it, poured love into it. I illuminated my darling tenderly, stroked it with maternal care, wooed and cosseted it. When I pause to think about it, I can say that perhaps I have never devoted so much love to any one thing on earth, or to very few, so much care, so much warmth from my own blood, so much strength and longing.

And how at times that darling dream shone before me, stimulating and comforting, what profound inner echoes it awakened, how rosily it glowed! How enmeshed it was in the most delicate golden threads, how ardently and lovingly painted with colors a thousand times refined!

Now and then in the course of the years it happened that other voices reached me, here and there a warning came my way, an insight that damaged the dream, opened little cracks in its precious painted surface, put one of its strings out of tune, revealed a wilted leaf in its wreath. Instantly I set about mending it, pouring into it new love, deeply deploring the disturbance, giving it new blood to resuscitate it. Soon it was pretty and whole again. And, to be honest, even today it can revive, can glow once more, can win back what it has lost.

But oftener and oftener I entertained perceptions that could not be reconciled with the dream. Some word in conversation with friends, a sentence in a book, a verse from the Bible, a line from Goethe took hold of me powerfully; lonesomeness, loss of friends, sacrifice of pleasures spoke their own rough language to me; pains came to live with me. Simple challenges, simple warnings, each little heeded in itself but all constantly hitting the same raw spot. And all were opposed to my dream. Shakespeare derided it, Kant attacked, Buddha denounced it. Only the pains again and again brought me back to it. Would they not subside and disappear once I had my refuge? Would not sleep and hunger, smiles, an open countenance, full lungs, and a longing for action come back to me there in the cave beside the brook in the heart of nature, far from noise, far from bustle?

But the pains grew more insistent, lasted longer, and turned against my dream: there came hours when I saw that it was worthless. The "refuge" would not cure me, the

pains would not disappear in the forest or in the cabin, I would not become one with the world there nor would I achieve harmony with myself.

All this went on slowly and in many narrow spirals, and a hundred times the wishful dream returned: the brook ran comfortingly over golden-brown pebbles and the lake cradled my deepest, most colorful dreams. But the warnings came more often, and especially the pains, and at times it seemed to me that Job was my brother.

And on one occasion a new realization knocked at my forehead; it was more serious, clearer, more hostile, more threatening. This is what it said: "Your wishful dream has been not simply false, not simply an error, not simply a pretty bit of childishness like a soap bubble. It has been much more than that, much worse, much more dangerous. It has fed upon you. It has drunk your blood, robbed you of life. Have you ever bestowed on your friend, your wife, your child so much as half the love you have given to it, half the care and warmth, half as many days, nights, creative hours? And your weariness and your pains, your aging, your failing—whom have you to thank for them? It—it is to blame for them all, that dream, that bloodsucker, that serpent!"

Even this insight did not triumph immediately, and even today, firmly fixed though it is, it is still open to doubts and defeats. Nevertheless, it has persisted.

And then came a day that knocked the heart out of my dream.

The dream was put to the final test—it was to be fulfilled. There was a refuge available, a little house, high on a mountain above a southern lake, a retreat and hideaway, a resting place and cradle of dreams. It was to be had, it was offered to me.

Behold, here the dream was caught red-handed! Caught in all its pretty falsity. To be specific, it took fright just when it was to be fulfilled. It did not want to be fulfilled, it was cowardly, it searched for objections, it found excuses, it advised against, it drew back shuddering.

Oh, well, there was nothing else it could do. It had been lying for so long, it had been making promises for so long, and promising much too much. Always it had taken and taken, and now for a change when it was its turn to give, there was nothing it had to offer. It drew back cringing like a swindler who has named a false address and now is being taken there where no one will know him, where he will have to be silent, where he will be unmasked.

That was its death blow.

But vampires survive many death blows and revive again, come back and demand to eat again, to feed once more on living blood. This one too is still alive, still has tricks and devices. But now I know it for my enemy.

I have known this since the day I had my final insight.

It came like all insights, in a familiar, oft-encountered guise. It was a saying I came upon by accident in a book, an old saying, a quotation from the Bible, and one with which I had been acquainted for many years and knew by rote. But today it was new, today it was full of significance.

The kingdom of God is within you.

Now I have something again to strive for, something that guides me, to which I sacrifice blood. It is no wish or dream, it is a goal.

This goal is once more—a refuge, but not a cave or a ship. I seek and long for a refuge within myself, a place where only *I* am, whither the world cannot reach and where I alone dwell, safer than mountain or cave, safer and more hidden than coffin or tomb. That is my goal, there nothing shall be able to intrude unless it become completely *I*.

Then let there be storms, let there be pains, let blood flow.

I am still far from that place, I am still on the first stage of the way, but it is now my way, no longer a dream.

O deep refuge! No storm reaches you, no fire burns you, no war destroys you. Little room within, little coffin, little cradle, you are my goal.

Concerning the Soul

1917

THE EYE OF DESIRE dirties and distorts. Only when we desire nothing, only when our gaze becomes pure contemplation, does the soul of things (which is beauty) open itself to us. If I inspect a forest with the intention of buying it, renting it, cutting it down, going hunting in it, or mortgaging it, then I do not see the forest but only its relation to my desires, plans, and concerns, to my purse. Then it consists of wood, it is young or old, healthy or diseased. But if I want nothing from it but to gaze, "thoughtlessly," into its green depths, then it becomes a forest, nature, a growing thing; only then is it beautiful.

So it is with people, and with people's faces too. The man whom I look at with dread or hope, with greed, designs, or demands, is not a man but a cloudy mirror of my own desire. Whether I am aware of it or not, I regard him in the light of questions that limit and falsify: Is he approachable, or arrogant? Does he respect me? Is he a good prospect for a loan? Does he understand anything about art? A thousand such questions are in our minds as we look at most people we have to deal with, and we are considered expert psychologists if we succeed in detecting in their appearance, manner, and behavior whatever it is that will abet or hinder our plans. But this attitude is a shabby one, and in this kind of psychology the peasant, the peddler, the shyster lawyer are superior to most politicians and scholars.

At the moment when desire ceases and contemplation, pure seeing, and self-surrender begin, everything changes. Man ceases to be useful or dangerous, interesting or boring, genial or rude, strong or weak. He becomes nature, he becomes beautiful and remarkable as does everything that is an object of clear contemplation. For indeed contemplation is not scrutiny or criticism, it is nothing but love. It is the highest and most desirable state of our souls: undemanding love.

If we have once achieved this state, be it for minutes, hours, or days (to sustain it permanently would be perfect bliss), then people no longer appear as they used to. They are not mirrors or caricatures of our desire, they become nature once more. Beautiful and ugly, old and young, cordial and offensive, open and taciturn, harsh and mild are no longer opposites, nor are they standards of judgment. All are beautiful, all are remarkable, no one can any longer be despised, hated, misunderstood.

Just as, from the standpoint of quiet contemplation, all nature is nothing but the changing manifestation of eternally creative immortal life, so man's special role and duty is to represent soul. Pointless to argue whether "soul" is something specifically human, whether it does not reside in animals and plants as well! Certainly soul is everywhere, is possible everywhere, is prepared for everywhere, is surmised and longed for everywhere. But just as we think of the animal and not the stone as representative of motion (though stones too move, live, grow, decay, vibrate) so we look for soul principally among men. We look for it in the place where it is most visible, where it suffers and acts. And man seems to us to be that corner of the universe, that particular province whose present duty it is to develop soul—as it was once his duty to walk upright, discard his animal fur, invent tools, make fire.

Thus collective mankind becomes for us a representation of the soul. Just as in mountain and rock I see and love the primal force of gravity, in animals motion and essays at freedom, so in the human being (who represents all these things too) I see first of all that form and promise of life which we call "soul" and which seems to us human beings not just a random beam of vitality among a thousand others but a deliberately selected, highly evolved goal in itself. For no matter whether our thought is materialistic, idealistic, or whatever, or whether we consider the "soul" as something divine or as the oxidizing of matter, we nevertheless all know it and value it highly; for each of us, the inspired eye of man, his art, the formation of his soul constitute the highest, newest, most precious stage and highwater mark of all organic life.

And so our fellow man comes to be for us the noblest, grandest, most precious object of contemplation. Not everyone makes this obvious evaluation at once or without difficulty—this I know from my own experience. In my youth I had closer and more intimate relations with landscapes and works of art than with human beings; indeed, I dreamed for years of a poem in which only air, earth, water, trees, mountains, and animals would appear, no human beings. I saw man so far astray from the path of the soul, so enslaved by desire, so crude and wild in his pursuit of animal, apelike, prehistoric goals, so intent upon rubbish and gimcracks, that temporarily I fell into the serious error of believing that perhaps man had already been discarded as the pathway to the soul and was in process of retrogression, that this fountain must make its way out of nature by some other course.

When one observes the behavior of two average men of today who have just met by chance and really want nothing of each other, one can sense almost palpably how thick and oppressive is the atmosphere surrounding each one, how defensive his protective crust, how he is swathed in a net woven of distractions from the spiritual, of intentions, anxieties, and wishes that are all directed toward the nonessential and that separate him from everyone else. It is as though the soul could not be allowed to speak, as though it had to be walled off by high fences, fences of fear and shame. Only undemanding love can break through this net. And wherever the net is penetrated, soul stares us in the face.

Sit in a railroad car and observe two young gentlemen, who speak to each other because chance has thrown them together for an hour. Their conversation is extremely odd, it is almost tragic. These inoffensive folk seem to be hailing each other from enormous, icy distances of alienation, as though poles apart—naturally I am not thinking of Malayans or Chinese but of modern Europeans—they seem each to live in a fortress of pride, of threatened pride, of suspicion and wariness. What they say, objectively considered, is utter nonsense; it is the calcified hieroglyphics of that soulless world which we are constantly outgrowing but whose icy fragments continue to cling to us. Rare, rare indeed, are the individuals whose souls find expression in daily talk. They are even more than poets, they are almost holy men. No doubt the "simple folk" have a soul, the Malayan and the Negro, and in their salutations and manner of address show more soul than most of the rest of us. But their soul is not the one we strive for and desire, although it is precious to us and closely related. The soul of the primitive, which has not yet encountered any alienation, any of the misery of a profane and mechanized world, is a collective simple, childlike soul, a beautiful and lovable thing, but not our goal. Our two young Europeans in the railroad car have got beyond that. They show little soul or none at all, they seem to be composed exclusively of organized will, or intellect, and plans and schemes. They have left their souls in the world of money, of machines, of suspicion. They must find them again; they will sicken and suffer if they neglect this task. But what they will then have will no longer be the lost soul of childhood but a much finer, more personal, richer, and more responsible soul. Our path does not lead backward to the child, to the primitive, but forward, to personality, to responsibility, to freedom.

With our two young men there is no hint of those goals or any intuition of them. Neither primitives nor saints, they speak the language of every day, a language that fits as little the goals of the soul as does the hide of the gorilla, which we are only now painfully discarding after a hundred tentative tries.

Their prehistoric, crude, stammering speech runs something like this:

"Morning," says one.

"Day," says the other.

"May I?"

"Certainly."

And so what needs to be said has been said. Meaning is completely lacking in the words, they are simply the ritual of primitive man, their point and value being the same as those of the ring that the African wears in his nose.

Extremely odd, however, is the tone in which these ritual-istic words are uttered. They are courteous words, but they sound abrupt, terse, grudging, cool, not to say angry. There is no cause for strife here, quite the contrary, and neither of the two men harbors any offensive thought. But in manner and tone they are cold, formal, stiff, almost as though in-sulted. As he says, "Certainly," the blond man arches his eyebrows in an expression bordering on contempt. He does not feel contemptuous. He is simply using a ritual that through decades of soulless association among men has become a device for self-protection. He thinks he has to hide his inner feelings, his soul; he does not know that the soul thrives only on being shown and being surrendered. He is proud, he is a personality, he is no longer a naïve savage. But his pride is pathetically unsure, it has to fortify itself, has to throw up cold, defensive walls around itself. This pride would be wiped out if one were to win a smile from him. And all this coldness, all this angry, nervous, proud, and at the same time insecure conversational tone between the "educated" is symptomatic of sickness, a necessary and therefore hopeful sickness of the soul, which knows of no other way to protect itself from being overpowered except by such behavior. How timid and weak this soul is, how young and unrecognized it feels itself on earth! How it re-treats, how terrified it is!

Now if one of these two men were to behave as he would like to and as he really feels, he would offer the other his hand or clap him on the shoulder and say something like this: "God, what a fine morning, everything's like gold, and I'm on vacation! How do you like my new tie, beautiful,

isn't it? And by the way, I have some apples in my bag,
will you have one?"

If he actually spoke like this, the other would experience
something uncommonly cheering and touching, something
like a laugh and a sob, for he would realize that now the
soul of the other was speaking, that the subject was neither
apples nor ties but simply the fact that here a breakthrough
had occurred, something had rightfully come to light that
we repress on the strength of a convention—a convention,
alas, still strongly compelling even though we already feel
intimations of its eventual demise!

That's what he would feel, but he would not acknowledge
it. He would take recourse in some mechanical, defensive
action, would toss off some meaningless fragment of speech,
one of our thousand substitutes for communication: "Yes
. . . very nice," or something of the sort; he would glance
away with a jerk of the head indicative of offense and over-
tried patience. He would play with his watch chain, stare
out the window, and by twenty such hieroglyphs show that
he had no intention of revealing his inner joy, that he would
express nothing at all or at the very most a certain amount
of pity for this intrusive gentleman.

However none of this happens. The dark-haired man actually has apples in his bag and he really feels an immense
boyish joy over the beautiful day, his vacation, his tie, and
his yellow shoes. But if the other now chances to say, "Miserable business, this exchange rate," then the dark-haired man
will not act as his soul urges him to, he will not shout,
"Oh, nonsense, let's forget that, what does the exchange rate
matter to us!" Instead, he will look anguished and say with
a sigh, "Tch, tch, it's horrible, isn't it?"

It is a remarkable sight: these two gentlemen (like all of
us) apparently have no trouble at all in behaving this way,
in subjecting themselves to a monstrous compulsion of this
sort. They can act glum with a laughing heart, can pretend
coldness and repulsion when their souls cry out to communicate.

But you go on watching. If the soul does not lie in the

words, the demeanor, the tone of voice, it must exist somewhere, after all. And then you see that the blond man has
forgotten himself; feeling unobserved, he is gazing through
the car window at the pointed fir trees, and his glance is
free and untroubled, full of youth, yearning, and naïve,
ardent dreams. He looks entirely different, younger, less
complicated, more innocent, above all handsomer. The
other, however, the equally irreproachable and unapproach-
able gentleman, stands up and stretches out his hand to his
suitcase in the net above his head. He does this as though
he wanted to make sure of its being steady and in no danger
of falling, but the bag is perfectly all right and in no need
of steadying. In fact, this is not the young man's desire at
all, he simply wants to touch it, to assure himself that it is
there, to stroke it affectionately. For in that impeccably busi-
nesslike leather case there is, in addition to the apples and
his linen, something important, something holy, a gift for
his darling back home, a porcelain dachshund or the Cologne
cathedral in marzipan, no matter what, but it is of utmost
importance to this young man at this time, something to
build dreams on, to love and idolize, something that he
would really like to hold constantly in his hands and stroke
and admire.

During an hour's train trip you have now observed two
young, moderately well educated, average men of today;
they have uttered words, exchanged greetings and opinions,
nodded and shaken their heads, done a thousand little things,
talked shop, performed actions—and in none of all this have
their souls taken part, in no word, no glance; everything was
masked, mechanical, everything with the exception of the
one self-forgetful glance through the window at the distant
bluish woods and the brief, awkward reaching out for the
leather suitcase.

And you think: O timorous souls! Will you someday
break forth? Perhaps beautifully and intensely in a liberating experience, united with a bride, in battle for a belief,
in act and in sacrifice—perhaps suddenly and desperately
in a frantic release of the oppressed, concealed, and dark-

ened impulse of the heart, in a wild denunciation, in a crime, in a deed of violence! And I and all of us: how will we guide our souls through this world, will we succeed in helping them in the right course, in giving them a share in our gestures and our words? Will we resign ourselves to the crowd and submit to inertia, again and again caging the bird, again and again putting rings in our noses?

And the realization comes to you: whenever nose rings and gorilla hides are discarded, soul is at work. If it were untrammeled we would converse together like Goethe's characters and feel every breath as a song. Poor splendid soul, where you are, there is revolution, there is an end to decay, there is new life, and God. Soul is love, soul is the future; all else is only stuff, only matter, only a hindrance on which our divine power can exercise itself, shaping and destroying.

Further thoughts arise: Do you not live in an age when the new loudly proclaims itself, when the bonds of humanity are being rudely shaken, when violence strikes in monstrous fashion, death rages, despair cries aloud? And is not soul behind all these things as well?

Ask your soul! Ask her who means freedom, whose name is love! Do not inquire of your intellect, do not search backwards through world history! Your soul will not blame you for having cared too little about politics, for having exerted yourself too little, hated your enemies too little, or too little fortified your frontiers. But she will perhaps blame you for so often having feared and fled from her demands, for never having had time to give her, your youngest and fairest child, no time to play with her, no time to listen to her song, for often having sold her for money, betrayed her for advancement. Thus it has happened with millions, and wherever you look people wear nervous, tormented, angry faces, they have had no time except for the nonessential, for stock exchanges and sanitariums, and this painful state is nothing but a warning sign, an admonition in the blood. You will be neurotic and a foe to life—so says your soul— if you neglect me, and you will be destroyed if you do not turn to me with a wholly new love and concern. Nor is it by any means the weak and worthless who nowadays become sick and lose their capacity for happiness. Rather it is the good, who are the seed of the future; these are the ones whose souls are not at peace, who still withdraw simply out of timidity from this battle against a false world order but who tomorrow perhaps will take part in earnest.

From this vantage point Europe resembles a sleeper in a nightmare, striking out and injuring himself.

Yes, then you remember that once a professor said something like this to you, that the world was suffering from materialism and intellectualism. He was quite right, but he cannot be your physician any more than he can be his own. With him intelligence goes on discoursing to the point of self-annihilation. He will perish.

Let the world's course be what it may, you will always find a physician and helper, a new energy and future within yourself, in your poor, ill-used, tractable, indestructible soul. The soul has no knowledge, no judgment, no program. It has simply impetus, feeling, the future. The great saints and preachers followed it, the heroes and sufferers, the great generals and conquerors; the great magicians and artists followed it, and all those whose way began in the commonplace and ended on the holy heights. The way of millionaires is a different way and ends in the sanitarium.

Ants too wage war, bees have societies, pack rats collect treasures. Your soul seeks other paths, and when it is cheated, when you win success at its expense, no happiness blossoms for you. For "happiness" can be felt only by the soul, not by the intellect, the belly, the head, or the purse.

However, one cannot ponder and discuss this subject for long without hitting upon the saying that long since illuminated and expressed it definitively. It was spoken in ancient times and belongs among the few human utterances that are ageless and always new: "What shall it profit a man, if he shall gain the whole world, and lose his own soul?"

Artists and Psychoanalysis

1918

S INCE FREUD'S PSYCHOANALYSIS has aroused interest beyond the narrow circle of neurologists, since Freud's
pupil Jung has elaborated and in part published his *Psychology of the Unconscious* and his *Psychological Types,*
since, finally, analytical psychology has turned directly to
folk myth, to saga, and to poetry, a close and fruitful relationship has existed between art and psychoanalysis. Whether
one agreed completely and in detail with Freud's teaching or
not, his discoveries undeniably existed and they worked.

As was to be expected, artists in particular were quick to
take up this new and variously productive way of seeing
things. A great many of them, neurotics themselves, had a
personal interest in psychoanalysis. But over and above this,
artists displayed an inclination and readiness to concern
themselves with a completely renewed psychology, much
more so than professed scientists. The artist is always easier
to win over for a work of radical genius than is the professor. And so today the Freudian world of ideas is more frequently discussed and more widely subscribed to among the
younger generation of artists than among professional medical men and psychologists.

Now for the individual artist—provided he was not content to make the subject simply a new theme of coffeehouse
debate—the need to make artistic use of the new psychology
quickly arose. Or rather, the question was whether and how
much the new psychological insights could assist creative
endeavor.

I remember that about two years ago an acquaintance of
mine recommended to me two novels by Leonhard Frank,
saying that they were not only worthwhile stories but also

"a kind of introduction to psychoanalysis." Since then I have read many works of fiction in which evidences of preoccupation with the Freudian teaching have been clearly visible. I myself never had the slightest interest in modern academic psychology, but it seemed to me that in some of the writings of Freud, Jung, Stekel, and others, something new and important was being said; I read them with the liveliest sympathy and found in general that their conception of psychic events confirmed almost all my own surmises based on the poets and on my own observations. I saw explicitly formulated what already in part belonged to me as unconscious knowledge derived from presentiment and fleeting insight.

In its application to works of poetry as well as in the observation of daily life, the fruitfulness of this new doctrine was revealed at once. We had another key—not an infallible magic key but nevertheless a valuable new conception, a splendid new tool, whose usefulness and reliability were quickly demonstrated. In this connection I am not thinking about the individual historical literary attempts to turn a poet's life into the most detailed possible account of his illnesses. But the confirmations and corrections of Nietzsche's sensitive psychological presentiments were of the greatest value to us. The dawning knowledge and observation of the unconscious, the interpretation of psychic mechanisms such as repression, sublimation, and regression produced a clarity of formulation that was in itself enlightening.

Now if in a sense this made it convenient and easy for anyone to do psychology, nevertheless the usefulness of this science to the artist remained highly doubtful. Just as a knowledge of history does not enable anyone to write historical novels and botany and geology do not make landscape artists, just so the best scientific psychology could not help in the portrayal of human beings. In fact, you could see how psychoanalysts themselves constantly had recourse to the poetry of earlier preanalytical times for examples, sources, and confirmation. And so the fact was that analysis had recognized and given scientific formulation to what had always been known to poets; indeed, the poet proved to be the representative of a special kind of thinking that really ran counter to the analytical-psychological way of thought. He was the dreamer while the analyst was the interpreter of his dreams. And so was there anything left for the poet to do, however great his interest in the new psychology, but to go on dreaming and following the promptings of his unconscious?

No, there was no other course for him. He who had not been a poet before, who had not felt the inner structure and pulse of psychic life, could not be made into an interpreter of souls by any amount of analysis. All he could do was make use of a new system, could perhaps for a moment startle his audience, but could not in this way essentially increase his powers. The poetic comprehension of psychological processes remained then as before the business of the intuitive, not the analytical, talent.

This, however, does not settle the matter. Actually the path of psychoanalysis can significantly aid the artist too. Just as he is mistaken in carrying over the technique of analysis into works of art, by the same token he is right to take psychoanalysis seriously and to follow it. I see three sources of corroboration and encouragement that the artist can draw upon from analysis.

First of all, the basic confirmation of the value of fantasy, of fiction. If the artist looks at himself analytically he cannot fail to see that among the weaknesses from which he suffers are these: a doubt about his calling, a distrust of fantasy, an alien voice within him that agrees with bourgeois views and education and rates his whole activity as "only" a pretty fiction. But it is precisely analysis that emphatically teaches every artist that what he at times is inclined to regard as "only" a fiction is actually of the highest value, and reminds him loudly of the existence of fundamental psychological demands as well as of the relativity of all authoritarian standards and evaluations. Analysis justifies the artist in his own eyes. At the same time it throws open to him in analytical psychology a realm for pure intellectual activity.

These benefits of the method are, of course, available to anyone who simply studies it objectively. There are two other values, however, that are only open to one who tries out analysis thoroughly and earnestly in his own person, to whom analysis is not just an intellectual interest but becomes an experience. Anyone who contents himself with getting some clarification of his "complexes" and some information about his inner life in neatly labeled form forfeits the most important values.

Whoever has followed for some distance the path of analysis, the search for psychological causes in memories, dreams, and associations, retains as a permanent gain what may be called the "inner relationship to *his own unconscious.*" He experiences a warmer, more fruitful and passionate interchange between conscious and unconscious; he brings up into the light much that would otherwise remain "beneath the threshold" and waste itself in unregarded dreams.

And this in turn has an inner connection with the findings of psychoanalysis for ethics, for the personal conscience. Before everything else, analysis imposes an important basic demand, whose evasion or neglect brings instant retribution, whose goad penetrates very deep and inevitably leaves lasting marks. It demands a truthfulness toward oneself to which we are not accustomed. It teaches us to see, to recognize, to examine, and to take seriously exactly those things that we had been most successful in repressing in ourselves, the things that generations have repressed under continuing coercion. This at the very outset of analysis is a powerful, indeed a monstrous experience, a shock that reaches to the roots of one's own being. Whoever withstands this and presses onward sees himself more and more alone with every step, further separated from convention and accepted views, confronted by questions and doubts that have no limits. In return for this, however, he sees or surmises behind the collapsing theatrical scenery of tradition the inexorable image of truth arising, of nature itself. For only in the intensive self-examination of analysis can a portion of the individual's developmental history be actually experienced and transfused with the blood of feeling. By way of father and mother, by way of peasant and nomad, by way of ape and fish back into time, in no fashion can the descent, affiliation, and hope of mankind be so earnestly, so shatteringly experienced as in a serious psychoanalysis. What has been learned becomes visible, knowledge is transformed into heartbeats, and as the fears, embarrassments, and repressions diminish, the meaning of life and of personality emerges purer and more demanding.

Now no one is likely to find this stimulating, educative, goading power of analysis more beneficial than the artist. For his concern is not with the most comfortable adjustment to the world and its ways but rather with what is unique, what he himself means.

Among poets of the past some came very close to a knowledge of the essential principles of analytical psychology, most conspicuously Dostoevsky, who not only intuitively followed those paths long before Freud and his disciples but who already possessed a certain practical technique in this kind of psychology. Among the great German writers it is Jean Paul whose conception of psychological processes stands closest to those of today. Jean Paul is also the most brilliant example of the artist who through a profound and lively intuition has made his steady, close contact with his own unconscious a constantly productive spring.

In conclusion I shall quote a poet whom we usually number among the pure idealists, to be sure, but not among the strongly intellectual artists. It was Otto Rank who first discovered the following passage in a letter by Schiller and pointed it out as an astonishing premodern confirmation of the psychology of the unconscious. Schiller is writing to Körner, who had complained of a failure in productivity: "The cause of your complaints, it seems to me, is the compulsion that your intellect imposes upon your imagination. It seems to be a bad thing, disadvantageous to the creative activity of the soul, when the intellect examines too closely, as though at the very threshold, the ideas that stream toward it. An idea considered in isolation may seem very unpromising and even fantastic, but perhaps it will become more important through another idea that comes after it, perhaps in a certain combination with others that may appear just as absurd it can supply a very important connection: all this cannot be judged by the intellect unless it keeps hold of an idea long enough to examine its association with others. On the other hand, in a creative mind, it seems to me, the intellect has withdrawn its guard from the gates, the ideas rush in pell-mell, and only then does the intellect survey and criticize the whole assembly."

This is a classical statement of the ideal relationship between intellectual criticism and the unconscious. Neither by suppression of the material streaming out of the unconscious, out of uncontrolled fancy, dreams, and the byplay of the mind, nor by permanent surrender to the unshaped infinity of the unconscious, but rather through affectionate attention to these hidden sources, and only afterward through criticism and selection from that chaos—thus have all the great artists worked. If any technique can help fulfill this demand, it is that of psychoanalysis.

From My Diary

1918

LAST NIGHT I had a lot of dreams without being able to remember any of them clearly. All I am sure of is that the context and feeling of these dreams ran in two directions: some were concerned exclusively with all sorts of sorrow that befell me—the others with longing and striving to overcome this sorrow through complete understanding, through holiness.

Thus between suffering and contemplation, between despair and profoundest effort, my thoughts, wishes, and fantasies lashed themselves for hours against narrow walls, to the point of excruciating exhaustion, and at times were transformed into half-obscure bodily feelings: precisely circumscribed, most clearly differentiated states of sorrow, misery, and weariness of heart presented themselves palpably in pictures and harmonies, and at the same time from another region of the soul emerged impulses of greater spiritual vigor. Admonitions to be patient, to fight, to persevere on the road that has no end. A sob here was matched by a courageous forward stride there; a feeling of torment on one level was answered on another level by an exhortation, an urge, a self-realization. If there is any sense at all in dwelling on such experiences, bending attentively over the depths and abysses one bears within oneself, then this sense can only be disclosed if we try to follow the impulses of our souls as faithfully and accurately as possible—much further and much deeper than words can reach. Whoever tries to make a record of this does so with the same feeling one would have in attempting to discuss delicate and difficult personal matters in a foreign language of which one had but a smattering.

And so my condition and radius of experience was this: on the one hand endurance of great sorrow, on the other a conscious striving to master this sorrow, to achieve complete harmony with fate. This was approximately the judgment of my consciousness, or rather a first voice audible within my consciousness. A second voice, fainter, but deeper and more resonant, put the matter differently. This voice (which like the first one I heard clearly but far off in my sleep and dream) did not call the suffering wrong and my vigorous mental struggle for perfection right, but rather meted out right and wrong to both sides. This second voice sang of the sweetness of suffering, it sang of its necessity, it had no interest in mastering or eliminating it but only in deepening and illuminating it.

The first voice, roughly translated into words, said something like this: "Suffering is suffering, there's no argument about that. It hurts. It is painful. But there are forces that can overcome it. Well then, seek out those forces, cultivate them, put them to work, calm yourself by them! You would be a fool and a weakling to want to go on suffering and suffering forever."

But the second voice said something like this: "Suffering only hurts because you fear it. Suffering only hurts because you complain about it. It pursues you only because you flee from it. You must not flee, you must not complain, you must not fear. You must love. You know all this yourself, you know quite well, deep within you, that there is only a single magic, a single power, a single salvation, and a single happiness, and that is called loving. Well then, love your suffering. Do not resist it, do not flee from it. Taste how sweet it is in its essence, give yourself to it, do not meet it with aversion. It is only your aversion that hurts, nothing else. Sorrow is not sorrow, death is not death if you do not make them so! Suffering is magnificent music—the moment you give ear to it. But you never listen to it; you always have a different, private, stubborn music and melody in your ear which you will not relinquish and with which the music of suffering will not harmonize. Listen to me! Listen to me, and remember: suffering is nothing, suffering is illusion. Only you yourself create it, only you cause yourself pain!"

And so in addition to the suffering and the will to escape, there were also constant conflict and tension between the two voices. The first, the one closer to consciousness, had much to say for itself. To the dim realm of the unconscious it opposed its own clarity. On its side it had the authorities, Moses and the Prophets, father and mother, the school, Kant and Fichte. The second voice sounded farther off, as though emerging from the unconscious and from suffering itself. It did not create a safe island in the midst of chaos, it did not throw light into the darkness. It was itself dark, it was itself primal cause.

It is impossible now to describe how the two voices developed in concert. Each of the two original voices in fact divided, and each new secondary voice divided again but not so as to constitute two choruses standing opposite to each other, as for instance a brighter and darker, a higher and lower, a male and female, or whatever. No, rather each new voice contained something of *both* dominant voices, echoes of chaos and echoes of the formative will, day and night, male and female in new and unique combination. Each voice always had the diametrically opposed character to the voice whose child and offspring it seemed to be. A new secondary voice springing from the chaotic mother voice always sounded manlier and clearer, more purposeful, cooler, more sharply defined—and vice versa. But each was a mixture, each had been created out of yearning for the other principle.

Thus a polyphony and multiplicity emerged in which it seemed to me the whole world together with all its millions of possibilities was contained. Each possibility was counterbalanced by its opposite; the whole world seemed to be running its course in my dreaming soul to the accompaniment of constant muted pain. There were power and drive in its career, but also much friction, restraint, and agonizing limitation. The world revolved, it revolved beautifully and passionately, but the axle groaned and smoked.

As I have said, I know nothing more about what I dreamed.

The notes have disappeared, only the signature of the melodies and voices is recorded in my memory. All I know is I endured much that was bad, and at every new pain the valiant concept of freedom and redemption was kindled afresh. So here was presented an eternal process, a round of impulse and acceptance, of creation and endurance, of action and suffering—without end.

In witnessing this I was in distress. The whole had more the flavor of sorrow than of joy, and where the dream states took on bodily feelings, these were painful; my head ached, I was dizzy and faint.

Manifold were the events that befell me, and to each new experience or sorrow a new voice gave answer, and on each assault followed an inner exhortation. Examples emerged, among them I saw the Staretz Zossima of *The Brothers Karamazov* appear as model and teacher. But that primeval maternal voice, eternal and constantly re-formed, dissented each time, or rather, it did not dissent but gave me the feeling of a beloved being turning away from me and shaking her head in silence.

"Accept no examples!" this voice seemed to say. "Examples do not exist, they are something you simply make up for yourself out of pretense. To imitate examples is flummery. Right action comes of itself. Just suffer, my son, just suffer and drain the cup to the dregs! The harder you try to avoid it the bitterer the drink will be. The coward drinks his fate like poison or medicine, you must drink yours like wine and fire. Then it will taste sweet."

But it tasted bitter and all night long the wheel of the world rolled on, groaning and smoking on its axle. On the one hand was blind nature, on the other the seeing spirit— but the seeing spirit kept transforming itself into blind, dead, sterile things: into morality, into philosophy, into formulas; and blind nature kept constantly opening an eye here or there, a marvelous, moist soul eye, shy and bright. Nothing remained true to its name. Nothing remained true to its essence. Everything was "just" names, everything was "just" essence, and behind it all, life's sanctuary and the mystery of vocation receded farther and farther into new, more distant, more frightening mirror depths. So would my world roll on smoking, as long as the axle held.

When I awoke the night was almost past. I did not look at the clock—I was not wide awake enough for that—but for a short time I kept my eyes open and saw the pale morning light falling on the window sill, on the chair, and on my clothes. The arm of my shirt hanging loose and somewhat twisted challenged my pictorial imagination—nothing in the world is more fruitful and stimulating to our souls than twilight—a wavering spot of white in the darkness, a dissolving system of gray and black shadows against a misty background.

But I did not respond to the challenge of turning the dangling white form into a whirl of dancing girls, circling nebulas, snowy summits, or holy statues. I still lay under the spell of the long dream sequence, and my consciousness did no more than register the fact that I was awake and morning was near, that my head ached, and that I hoped I could fall asleep again. Rain drummed softly on the roof and on the window sill. Sadness, pain, and emptiness filled me; in flight I closed my eyes and crept back into the region of sleep and dreams.

However, I did not fully recover those dreams. I remained in a tenuous, fragile half sleep where I felt neither weariness nor pain. And now I had another experience, something like dream and yet not a dream, something like thought and yet not thinking, something like a vision, something like a momentary flooding of the unconscious with the bright beams of consciousness.

In my light morning half sleep I encountered a holy man. Half the time it seemed as if I myself were the holy man, thought his thoughts, had his feelings; and half the time I saw him as another person, separate from me, but penetrated by my understanding and most intimately known. It was as though I saw him and it was also as though I heard or read about him. It was as though I were telling myself about this holy man and as though he were telling me about himself; or as if he were living out something before my eyes that I experienced as my very own.

The holy man—no matter whether he was I or whoever— the holy man suffered a great sorrow. But I cannot write about this as though it had happened to anyone but myself, I experienced and felt it. I felt that my most precious thing had been taken from me, my children had died or were at that moment dying before my eyes. And they were not only my real, physical children with their eyes and foreheads, their little hands and voices—they were also my spiritual children and possessions that I saw there dying and deserting me, they were my very own most personal dearest thoughts and poems, they were my art, my thinking, the delight of my eyes and my life. More than this could not be taken from me. Nothing more grievous, more horrible could happen to me than that these dear eyes should grow dim and no longer know me, that these dear lips should no longer breathe.

This I experienced—or the holy man did. He closed his eyes and smiled, and in this mild smile there was all the suffering that can in any way be conceived, there was the admission of every weakness, every love, every vulnerability.

But it was beautiful and tranquil, this faint smile of pain, and it remained unchanged and beautiful on his countenance. Thus a tree looks in the autumn when the last golden leaves flutter down, thus the old earth will look when its remaining life disappears in ice or fire. It was pain, it was sorrow, deepest sorrow—but there was no resistance, no denial. It was agreement, resignation, obedience, it was knowledge and acquiescence. The holy man sacrificed and praised the sacrifice. He suffered and he smiled. He did not harden his heart and yet he survived, for he was immortal. He accepted joy and love and gave them away, gave them back—but not to a stranger, rather to the fate that was his own. As a thought subsides into memory and a gesture sinks into rest, so the holy man's children and all the possessions of his love subsided, faded away in pain—not lost, but gathered into his own inner depths. They had disappeared, not been killed. They were transformed, not destroyed. They had gone back into the depths, into the inside of the world and the inside of the sufferer. They had been life and had become symbols, in the way that everything is a symbol and at some time perishes in pain in order that, as a new symbol, it may wear a different dress.

Fantasies

1918

OCCASIONALLY IT IS INTERESTING and informative to try to watch the development of what is called a "train of thought," but which is usually much more a series of notions, images, and fantasies springing unbidden out of chaos. People actually "think" all day long (and all night long), but much of the time our notions do not enter consciousness but grow feeble and fall silent at the threshold. Psychoanalysis ascribes this to the "censor" of consciousness.

Yesterday morning a "train of thought" took its course in my mind while I was weeding the garden and entertaining the conscious hope that the morning mail would disturb me as little as possible in this activity—at a deeper, unconscious level, of course, it was just this that I wanted, to be definitely disturbed by the mail and to be faced with new tasks and new stimulation.

My "thoughts" began, so far as I can now recall, with the memory of a scientific review that explained all artistic gifts and accomplishments as a kind of sickness, and this in turn put me in mind of a conversation I had had the evening before with my wife.

Well then, I thought, if genius is madness, and if every endeavor of a poet or painter or composer is nothing but a desperate attempt to compensate on a different, more spiritual level for a lack in his personality, his life, his character, then the "normal" person, that is, the person free from such compulsions, is necessarily the ungifted person. Yes, the normal human being can and must have no sort of "gift" except the general one of being alive and the ability to keep himself alive as long as possible. For a moment I considered this with a shade of irony, with a certain malice toward the normal people I was offending by this point of view. Immediately, however, I knew it was only my own little joke, which would wilt and die momentarily, but that nevertheless behind the witticism—"the normal man is the ungifted man" —lay very serious and significant ideas.

All my life my world had been that of the poet, the man of imagination, who defends his own kind, his being, his talent, his spiritual needs—not without malice and not without secret fear—at the expense of the average person. But behind it all lay envy as well, and worry; I had known plenty of hours and days when I would only too gladly have been "normal" too. With this new thought my partisanship changed sides; I now tended to consider the normal person right and to regard the "gifted" individual critically, in fact with hostility.

From recent reading of various kinds, the idea of "politicizing the spirit" was familiar, and it was to this idea, which had always been profoundly repugnant to me, that I now felt drawn. Instead of regarding the average person with suspicion, as I had before, I began to examine the "man of imagination" under my microscope, and as point of departure I chose the question of politicizing the spirit. Proclamations and articles of very recent date occurred to me. Yes, by God, these "intellectuals" needed to politicize themselves! Even though poets were calling themselves "intellectuals"! Could one misunderstand and misinterpret oneself and one's task more completely or more foolishly? There was only one thing proper about all this, that the "intellectuals" felt a share of guilt for the war and for the misery of the world. Certainly they were implicated, indeed, deeply, vitally implicated, these magisterial "intellectuals." They had long since ceased to be poets, they were journalists and businessmen or sophists. And now they had come forward demanding the "politicizing of the poet"! As though their own guilt consisted in not having been hitherto political enough, in having given too little attention to the citizen, the law, the market place, to so-called reality! My God, it was just this dreary reality that was their world and their refuge; they had long since stopped doing the one thing the poet is brought into the world to do, the performance of a sacred duty toward that world which is more than real, which is eternal. That was why these people when they met together publicly never called themselves poets but rather "intellectuals," which is something like a lover describing himself as "a shareholder in the heart's stock." And that is why everything has now gone awry; their car being completely off the rails, they have hit on the idea of becoming political. If only there were enough of them, they thought, to form a great association, to gain representation in the Reichstag and in this way establish the "spirit" as a political vested interest alongside of industry and agriculture, then much would be gained.

After I had vented in this way a certain amount of spite and ill humor, I brought my thoughts back to the poet and his gifts. Why did poets exist? What did nature require of them? Why were they valued when after all the healthy and the normal were really the untalented?

On the road from fish, bird, and ape to the war-waging animal of our time, on the long road by which we hope in time to become men and gods, it could not have been the "normal" ones that had pressed forward from stage to stage. The normal ones were conservative, they clung to what was healthy and traditional. A normal lizard never hit upon the idea of trying to fly. A normal ape never thought of abandoning his tree and walking upright on the ground. The one who first did that, who first tried it, who had first dreamed about it, was a visionary and eccentric among apes, a poet, an innovator, and no normal ape. The normal ones, as I saw it, were there to maintain and defend an established way of life, to strengthen a race and species so that there might be support and vital provision for it. The visionaries were there in order to venture their leaps, to dream of the undreamed-of, so that perhaps sometime a land animal might emerge from the fish and an ape man from the ape.

And so the "normal" was really nothing ideal either but only a name for a function, the conservative, species-maintaining function. "Gifted" or "visionary" on the other hand was a name for the function of play and testing, of treating problems as games. One could be ruined by it, or go mad, or succumb to suicide. But in certain circumstances one could also invent wings, create gods. In short, while the normal saw to it that the species was maintained as it was, the task of the "visionary" was to see to it that the other and opposite possession of mankind, that is, its ideal, was also supported and was never lost. The life of mankind played back and forth between these two poles: holding fast to what had been attained, and throwing away what had been attained in order to strive for something more! That was it. And the poet's function was to act on the side of ideals, to create ideals, to have intuitions, to have dreams.

And that was the reason for the existence of that "reality" in which the poet could never believe, that ineffably important world of business, political parties, elections, foreign exchange, honorary titles, orders, routines, and so on. And if the poet became political, he was turning away from his human duty of prophetic dreaming and his service to the ideal; he was meddling into the business of the practical men who through election reforms and the like think they are achieving progress, whereas, limping along centuries behind the thoughts of the visionaries, they are simply trying to put to work on a small scale one or other of the details of their predecessors' intuitions and ideas. Thus a politician who strives for permanent peace is just one among a thousand ants working for the realization of an age-old dream. The creator of that dream, however, was the mind that some thousands of years ago first dreamed the mighty words: "Thou shalt not kill!"—a thought that had never existed in all the millions of years of earth's history and which since then has worked in mankind like yeast and will continue to work until some day it comes true, just as mankind has achieved upright stature and smooth skin.

Up to this point the train of thought had unreeled smoothly and effortlessly, streaming up out of the play of the unconscious, like air bubbles rising in a fountain. Now there was a small break, a connection of some sort had escaped me, I was suddenly disturbed, I saw the train of notions I had just entertained fluttering away insubstantially behind me and could no longer touch them. Instead I was confronted by a disagreeable feeling, a disagreeable idea that went something like this: Why have you thought of all this? These aren't thoughts, they are simply masks and disguises behind which a motive is in hiding! I felt that as a result of that conversation the evening before with my wife, a barb had stayed imbedded in me, and I needed to justify myself in my own eyes as a poet, for yesterday we had been speaking about this very thing, about how strange and really frightening it is that almost all artists are able to realize in their own lives little or nothing of the noble, splendid, ideal values that they set down in their works. So that is where the arrow had hit. It was simply to get rid of it that I had followed these hundreds of thought detours, not a hundredth part of which has been recorded here, regressing in lively fantasy to the ape and the lizard.

And now that I had removed the barb by finding the secret selfish source of my train of thought, I could smile and, unencumbered, go on dreaming a little further.

I dreamed that the ideal man would be constituted something like this: he would be a "normal" person who ordinarily has no need to raise repressions into the spiritual realm, who lives safely and happily in himself. But this man, undriven by need of virtue or inner compulsion to compensate for weakness through works of art, must be able voluntarily to arouse this need in himself. Now and again he would develop, as a game or luxury, special talents, special needs, perhaps only in the way one occasionally combs one's hair in a different fashion for a change. And he would come to know the bliss of dreaming, the torment of creation, the fear and ecstasy of giving birth, without knowing their curse; for he could come home from each such game satisfied, and by a simple act of the will would lay aside, as if on a shelf, the striving within himself, so that a new and different equilibrium resulted. This ideal person would sometimes write poetry, sometimes compose music, he would on occasion bring out from within himself his memory of the apes, at other times his intuition of future change and hope, and he would allow these to play as a trained athlete makes isolated groups of his muscles play, enjoying and testing them. All this would occur in him not compulsively or out of need but rather as it would in a very healthy, good-natured child. And, best of all, this ideal person would not resist so bitterly and bloodily as we poor fellows do a change in himself when some new demand of the ideal required it of him, but would be in absolute harmony with himself, with the ideal, with fate; he would change easily, he would die easily.

And here I was on uncomfortable ground again. I myself did not change willingly, I myself would not die easily. I knew, knew well and certainly, that every death is also a birth, but I did not know it completely, with my whole being; a mass of fibers within me rebelled against it, a part of me believed in death, a part was weakness and fear. And that was something I did not like to be reminded of. And so I was glad when the mailman rang the doorbell, and I immediately hurried to meet him.

On Poems

1918*

ONE DAY IN SCHOOL when I was ten years old, we read a poem in our primer called, I believe, "Speckbacher's Little Son." It told about a brave little boy who took part in a battle amidst a rain of bullets, picking up bullets for the grownups or carrying on some other sort of heroic activity. Our class was enthusiastic and when the teacher asked us with a touch of irony, "Now was that a good poem?" we all shouted emphatically, "Yes!" But he smiled and shook his head and said, "No, it is a bad poem." He was right; according to the taste and rules of the art of our time the poem was not good, not subtle, not genuine, definitely inferior. Nevertheless it had inspired in us boys a splendid surge of enthusiasm.

Ten years later, at the age of twenty, I would have had the confidence to declare at once after a first reading of any poem whether it was good or bad. Nothing simpler. One glance, the repetition half aloud of a couple of verses sufficed.

That was several decades ago and many poems have since passed through my hands and under my eyes, and today I am again completely uncertain whether or not to attribute value to a poem that is shown to me. Poems are often shown to me, mostly by young people want a "verdict" on them and hope to find a publisher. And the young poets are always astounded and disillusioned when they see that this elder colleague whom they had believed to be an experienced critic proves to have no experience at all but leafs through their poems uncertainly and does not trust himself to say anything about their worth. What I could have accomplished

* This is the 1954 version of a 1918 essay.

in two minutes with a feeling of assurance at the age of twenty has now become difficult or, rather, not difficult but impossible. Moreover, "experience" is the sort of thing that one imagines in youth must come of itself. But this is not so. Some people have a gift for experience, they acquire it from their schooldays if not from their mother's womb—and there are others, of whom I am one, who can live forty or sixty or a hundred years and in the end die without having properly learned or even glimpsed what "experience" is.

My certainty of judgment about poems at the age of twenty was based on the fact that at that time I loved a number of poems and poets very deeply, and I compared each book and poem almost exclusively with them. If it resembled them, it was good, otherwise it was of no account.

Today, too, I have my few poets whom I especially love, some of them the same ones as when I was young. But now I especially distrust poetry that instantly reminds me of the work of one of these favorite poets.

It is not my intention, however, to talk about poems and poetry in general, but only about "bad" poems, those that almost everyone, except the poet himself, at once regards as mediocre, paltry, unnecessary. In the course of time I have read not a few such poems, and earlier I knew with certainty that they were bad and why they were bad. Today I am no longer so sure about these matters. That certainty, that knowledge, like every habit and every knowledge, on some occasion revealed itself to me as ambiguous; it was at once boring, dry, and lifeless, it was full of holes; something in me rebelled against it, and in the end I saw it no longer as knowledge but as an outmoded attitude, an attitude that lay behind me and whose former value I could no longer grasp.

Today I often have this experience: with the unquestionably "bad" poems I often feel a desire to defend, indeed to extol, whereas the good, yes the best, often seem to me suspect.

It is the same feeling that one can sometimes have in the presence of a professor or an official or a madman: in general, one knows unquestionably that the distinguished official is an irreproachable citizen, a righteous child of God, a properly recognized and useful fellow human being, whereas the madman is simply a poor wretch, sick and unfortunate, whom one tolerates but deplores, since he has no value as a person. But then come days, or at least hours—perhaps when one has had more than usual to do with professors or with madmen—when suddenly the reverse is true: then you see in the madman a happy person, quiet and self-assured, a wise man, a favorite of God, a man of individual character who is contented and believes in himself—the professor on the other hand seems superfluous, mediocre, a figure of no character, personality, or substance, totally commonplace.

Something similar happens to me occasionally with bad poems. Suddenly they no longer seem bad, suddenly they have a fragrance, a uniqueness, a childlike quality; their obvious weaknesses and errors are especially touching, are endearing and delightful, and by comparison the most beautiful poem, which one ordinarily loves, seems a trifle pale and commonplace.

Moreover, since the influence of expressionism has spread, we can see something similar at work in many of our younger poets: as a matter of principle they no longer write "good" or "beautiful" poems. They consider that there are enough beautiful poems and that they themselves have certainly not been born and put into the world in order to turn out even more pretty verses, to continue the game of patience begun by earlier generations. Presumably they are quite right about this, and their poems sometimes even sound just as touching as used to be the case only with "bad" poems.

The reason is easy to find. In its origin a poem is something completely unequivocal. It is a discharge, a call, a cry, a sigh, a gesture, a reaction by which the living soul seeks to defend itself from or to become aware of an emotion, an experience. In this first spontaneous, most important function no poem can be judged. It speaks first of all simply to the poet himself, it is his cry, his scream, his dream, his smile, his whirling fists. Who would try to judge people's nighttime dreams by their aesthetic value, or our movements of hand and head, our expressions and way of walking by their expediency? The babe in arms that puts its thumb or toe in its mouth behaves just as intelligently and properly as the author who gnaws his penholder or the peacock that spreads its fan. No one of them does better than the others, no one is more in the right than the rest.

Now sometimes it happens that a poem, in addition to unburdening and freeing the poet, can also give pleasure to others, can move and touch them—that it is beautiful. Very likely this happens when what is expressed is something common to many, possibly to all. Though this is by no means certain.

Here, then, is the beginning of a vicious circle. Because "beautiful" poems make the poet beloved, a great quantity of poems come into the world that attempt nothing except to be beautiful, that pay no heed to the original primitive, holy, innocent function of poetry. These poems from the very start are made for others, for hearers, for readers. They are no longer dreams or dance steps or outcries of the soul, reactions to experience, stammered wish-images or magic formulas, gestures of a wise man or grimaces of a madman— they are simply planned productions, fabrications, pralines for the public. They have been made for distribution and sale and they serve to amuse or inspire or distract their buyers. So just this sort of poem finds approval. One does not have to project oneself seriously and lovingly into such poems, one is not tormented or shaken by them, rather one sways comfortably and pleasurably in time to their pretty, regular rhythms.

Now at times these "beautiful" poems can seem just as questionable and repugnant as anything else that is tamed and adjusted, like professors and officials. And sometimes when the proper world is completely odious to you, and you have an inclination to smash streetlights and set fire to the temples, on such days the "beautiful" poems all the way up to the holy classics strike you as a little bit censored, a little bit castrated, all too well approved, all too tame, all too auntlike. Then one turns to the bad ones; then no poem can be bad enough.

But here, too, disappointment lies in wait. The reading of bad poems is always a short-term pleasure; you quickly get enough of it. So why read? Cannot anyone make bad poems for himself? —Try it sometime and you will find that making bad poems actually gives much more pleasure than reading even the most beautiful ones.

The Brothers Karamazov, or The Decline of Europe

THOUGHTS ON READING DOSTOEVSKY

1919

*Nothing is outside, nothing is inside;
for what is outside, is inside.*

T O SET DOWN MY IDEAS on this subject in an agreeable or
even coherent form has proved to be beyond me. I seem
to lack the gift for it, and, besides, I feel it a kind of presumption for an author to construct out of a few notions, as so
many do, an essay that has an air of thoroughness and consistency, whereas after all it comprises only a few ideas and
a far greater amount of padding. No, I who believe in the
"decline of Europe," and especially in the decline of spiritual
Europe, have the least reason of all to strive for a form that
I would necessarily feel to be a masquerade and a lie. I say,
just as Dostoevsky himself says in the last book of *The
Brothers Karamazov:* "But I see I shall do better not to
apologize. I will do my best and the reader will see for himself that I have done what I can."

*   *   *

It seems to me that in the works of Dostoevsky, and in its
most concentrated form *The Brothers Karamazov,* what I
call to myself the "decline of Europe" is foretold and proclaimed with frightful clarity. That the young people of
Europe, and especially the youth of Germany, feel Dostoevsky to be their great writer, not Goethe, not even

Nietzsche—this fact seems to me decisive for our fate. Keep this in mind as you examine the most recent creative writing; you will find in all of it the influence of Dostoevsky, though the result often may be simply imitation and childish in its effect. The ideal of the Karamazovs, a primeval, occult, Asiatic ideal, begins to become European, begins to devour the spirit of Europe. This is what I call the decline of Europe. This decline is a turning back to Asia, a return to the mother, to the sources, to the Faustian "Mothers," and of course will lead like every earthly death to a new birth. It is only *we* who experience these phenomena as "decline," we contemporaries, just as the abandonment of an old beloved homeland brings only to the aged a feeling of grief and irremediable loss, whereas the young see nothing but what is new, what lies ahead.

*   *   *

But what sort of "Asiatic" ideal is this that I find in Dostoevsky and that seems to me to be in the process of conquering Europe?

Briefly put, it is a turning away from every fixed morality and ethic in favor of a universal understanding, a universal validation, a new, dangerous, terrifying sanctity such as the elder Zossima prophetically proclaims and by which Alyosha lives; such as Dmitri and even more Ivan Karamazov bring to completely conscious expression. With the elder Zossima, the ideal of righteousness still prevails; for him there are still good and evil, though he bestows his love by preference upon evil. In Alyosha's case this new kind of holiness has become far freer and more animated; he strides through all the filth and slime of his surroundings with an almost amoral unselfconsciousness and often he reminds me of that most noble vow of Zarathustra: "I once swore to renounce all repugnance!" But behold, Alyosha's brothers carry this idea even further, they pursue the same course with even greater determination, and it often seems, strangely enough, exactly as if the relationship of the brothers Karamazov slowly becomes reversed in the course of this thick three-volume work, so that all that is firmly established becomes questionable: the holy Alyosha becomes more and more worldly, the worldly brothers more and more holy, and it is precisely the most criminal and unrestrained brother, Dmitri, who becomes the holiest, most sensitive, most profound possessor of a presentiment of a new holiness, a new morality, a new humanity. This is very strange. The more Karamazovian things become—the more vicious and drunken, the more unrestrained and rowdy—that much nearer shimmers through these rough physical phenomena, these men and deeds, a new ideal; inwardly they become all the more holy, more spiritualized. And compared to Dmitri, drunkard, killer, man of violence, and the cynical intellectual Ivan, the honest highly respected types—the public prosecutor and the other representatives of society—become shabbier, emptier, more worthless, the greater their outward triumph.

*   *   *

And so the "new ideal," which threatens the European spirit at its root, appears to be an amoral way of thinking and feeling, an ability to perceive the divine, the necessary, the fated, even in what is most wicked and ugly, and also to pay it reverence and worship in this guise, yes, especially in this guise. The public prosecutor's attempt in his long speech to present this Karamazovianism with ironic exaggeration, and to expose it to the ridicule of the general public, actually does not exaggerate at all; it is really very tame.

This speech portrays from a bourgeois conservative point of view the "Russian man" who has since become a catchword. This dangerous, touching, irresponsible and yet remorseful, tender, dreamy, cruel, deeply childlike "Russian man" is still often called that today, although I believe he has long since been in process of transmutation into the European man. Just this is the "decline of Europe."

*   *   *

We must turn our attention for a moment to this "Russian man." He is far older than Dostoevsky but it was Dostoevsky who definitively described him to the world in all his terrifying meaning. The Russian man is Karamazov, he is Pavlovich, he is Dmitri, he is Ivan, he is Alyosha. For these four, however different they may appear, necessarily belong together, collectively they are Karamazov, collectively they are the "Russian man," the coming and already imminent man of the European crisis.

In passing, something highly remarkable should be noted: that is, how Ivan in the course of the story is transformed from a civilized person into a Karamazov, from a European into a Russian, from a standardized, historical type into unshaped material of the future! There is a legendary, dreamlike inevitability about this slipping away of Ivan from his original air of respectability, knowledge, coolness, and scholarly detachment, this gradual, hesitant, then wildly excited lapse of the apparently most solid Karamazov into hysteria, into Russianism, in Karamazovianism! It is he, the doubter, who toward the end has a conversation with the devil! This is something we shall discuss later on.

And so the "Russian man" (whom we have long since had in Germany too) is not to be adequately described either as a "hysteric" or as drunkard or criminal, or as poet and holy man, but only as the simultaneous combination of all these characteristics. The Russian man, the Karamazov, is at once murderer and judge, ruffian and sensitive soul, he is equally the complete egoist and a hero of total self-sacrifice. We cannot get at him from a fixed, moralistic, ethical, dogmatic —in a word, a European standpoint. In him good and evil, outer and inner, God and Satan are cheek and jowl.

This is the reason that from time to time these Karamazovs seem to need a supreme symbol adequate to their souls, a god who is at the same time the devil. Through that symbol, Dostoevsky's Russian man is transcribed. The god who is also the devil is the primeval demiurge; he is the one who existed before the beginning; he, the only one, stands beyond the opposites, knows neither day nor night, neither good nor evil. He is nothingness, he is the universe. He is indiscernible to us, for we can only perceive in terms of opposites, we are individuals bound to day and night, to warmth and cold, we require a god and a devil. Beyond the opposites, in the nothingness and the all, the demiurge lives alone, the god of the universe who knows neither good nor evil.

Much could be said about this, but it is really enough to have recognized the essence of the Russian man. He is man struggling to escape from the opposites, from characteristics, from morality; he is man in the process of disintegrating and withdrawing beyond the veil, beyond the principle of individuation. He loves nothing and everything, he fears nothing and everything, he does nothing and everything. He is once more primal stuff, the unformed material of souls. He cannot live in this form, he can only perish, he can only flash by.

*   *   *

This creature of the collapse, this dreadful ghost, is what Dostoevsky has conjured up. It has often been said that it is fortunate the Karamazovs were never completed, for otherwise not only Russian literature but Russia itself together with mankind would have blown up.

What has once been spoken, however, even though the speaker is not aware of the consequences, can never be taken back. What exists, what has been thought, what is possible, can never again be wiped out. Russian man has existed for a long time; he has been in evidence for a long time far beyond Russia, he controls half of Europe, and a part of the anticipated explosion has occurred in the last few years audibly enough. It is obvious that Europe is weary and wants to return home, that it wants to rest, wants to be reshaped and reborn.

*   *   *

Here two sayings occur to me, two sayings by a European who unquestionably could qualify for everyone as the representative of an old outworn Europe that has disappeared or at least fallen under suspicion. I mean Kaiser Wilhelm. One of them was a caption under a strangely allegorical picture, in which he exhorts the people of Europe to defend their "most holy possessions" against the rising danger from the East.

Kaiser Wilhelm was hardly an intuitive or a profound thinker; nevertheless, as the ardent devotee and guardian of an old-fashioned ideal, he had a certain native perception of the dangers that threatened that ideal. He was not a cultivated man, he did not like to read good books, and he spent most of his time at politics. And so that picture with its exhortation to the peoples of Europe was not inspired by reading Dostoevsky, as one might think, but probably because of a vague fear that the massive populations of the East might be brought into action against Europe through the ambition of Japan.

The Kaiser had only a very dim knowledge of what he was saying in that sentence or how monstrously right he was. He certainly did not know the Karamazovs, because of his aversion to good, profound books. But his feeling was uncannily correct. Exactly the danger he perceived did exist and came daily closer. It was the Karamazovs that he feared, it was the infection of Europe by the East, it was the reeling home of the weary mind of Europe to its Asiatic mother that he so greatly and so very rightly feared.

The second saying of the Kaiser's that occurred to me and had in its time made a frightening impression on me is this (I do not know whether it was actually said or only rumored): "That nation will win the war that has the better nerves." When I heard it at the very outset of the war, this remark impressed me like the faint advance warning of an earthquake. The Kaiser did not in the least mean it that way; instead he thought he was saying something very flattering to Germany. Quite possibly he had excellent nerves and so no doubt did his hunting companions and the generals who reviewed the troops. Also he knew the musty legends of a vicious and disease-ridden France and a virtuous populous Germany. But for others, for those who were knowledgeable or had intuitions and premonitions about tomorrow and the day after, for them that saying was terrifying. They knew that Germany did not by any means have better but rather worse nerves than her enemies in the West. And so those words from the leader of the nation sounded at that time like frightening and fateful hubris that would lead us blindly to destruction.

No, the Germans certainly did not have better nerves than the French, English, and Americans. At most they had better nerves than the Russians. For "having bad nerves" is the popular expression for hysteria and neurasthenia, for moral insanity, for all those evils that one can evaluate in various terms but, taken together, are precisely synonymous with Karamazovianism. Germany lay open to the Karamazovs and to Dostoevsky, more defenseless than any other European nation except Austria.

And so in his own way the Kaiser twice had a premonition of the decline of Europe and actually prophesied it.

*   *   *

Just how one should evaluate the decline of old Europe is a quite different matter, on which opinions differ widely. The convinced supporters of tradition, the loyal admirers of a noble, sacrosanct form of culture, the knights of established morality, all these can only seek to prevent Europe's decline or weep inconsolably as it occurs. For them it is the end—for others the beginning. For them Dostoevsky is a criminal—for the others a holy man. For them Europe and its spirit is something unique, soundly established, unassailable, secure, and continuing—for the others it is evolution, variability, continual transformation.

*   *   *

Now like everything else in the world the Karamazovian element—the Asiatic, chaotic, wild, dangerous, amoral element—can be evaluated positively as well as negatively. Those who simply reject this whole world, Dostoevsky, the Karamazovs, these Russians, this Asia, these fantasies about a demiurge, those who curse it and are filled with a nameless dread of it are now in a difficult position in the world, for Karamazov is more dominant than ever. But they are guilty of error in that they insist on seeing in all this only the factual, visible, material aspects. They see the approaching "decline of Europe" as a horrifying catastrophe with drumbeat and thunder, either as revolutions replete with slaughter and violence, or as a takeover by criminality, corruption, thievery, murder, all the vices.

All this is a possibility, it is present in Karamazov. But with the Karamazovs you never know what surprise they may have in store for you at the next moment: perhaps a lethal blow, perhaps a touching hymn of praise to God. Among them are Alyoshas and Dmitris, Feodors and Ivans. Indeed, as we have seen, they are not at all identifiable by their characteristics but rather by their readiness and ability at any time to assume any character.

*   *   *

For those who are fearful there should be no comfort in the fact that this unpredictable man of the future (though here he is in the present!) does good as well as evil and could establish a new kingdom of God as easily as a new kingdom of Satan. What is established or overthrown on earth is of little concern to the Karamazovs. Their secret lies elsewhere, and the worth and fruitfulness of their amoral being lies there too.

To be specific, these people differ from others, the earlier, organized, predictable, straightforward, honest people, principally only in that they live as much inwardly as outwardly, that they are constantly busied about their souls. The Karamazovs are capable of any crime but it is only by exception that they commit one; usually it suffices them to have thought of the crime, to have dreamed about it, to have calculated its possibilities. Here lies their mystery. Let us look for its formula.

Every organization of mankind, every culture, every civilization, every order rests on an agreement about what is permitted and what is forbidden. Man, on the road between the animal and the distant future of his race, always has a great deal to suppress within himself, to smother, to deny, in order to be a respectable fellow fit for society. Man is full of the animal and primeval world, full of vast, barely controllable instincts of a brutish, callous selfishness. All these dangerous instincts are there, always there, but culture, convention, civilization hide them. They are not on view. From childhood on, people are taught to recognize these instincts and to deny them, but every one of them comes to light sometime or other. They all stay alive, none is destroyed, none, in the long run, in all eternity, is transformed and ennobled. And each of these instincts is indeed good in itself, no worse than any other, but every age and culture chooses the instincts to fear more than others and to punish more severely. Now when these instincts reawaken as unresolved and only superficially and painfully controlled forces of nature, when these animals go on the rampage like beaten and oppressed slaves rising in revolt, with all the fury of their primeval nature, then the Karamazovs emerge. When a culture that attempts to domesticate mankind grows weary and begins to totter, then people in ever greater numbers behave strangely, become hysterical, have weird desires, act like youths at the age of puberty, or pregnant women. The impulses that stir in their souls have no names and from the point of view of the old culture and morality they have to be called bad, but they can speak with so strong, natural, and innocent a voice that all good and evil become problematical and every law is put in doubt.

Such are the brothers Karamazov; for them it is easy to see any law as a convention, to regard every upright man as a philistine and overrate every freedom and eccentricity; they are far too fond of hearkening to the many voices within their own breasts.

But from the chaos in these souls crime and confusion need by no means be the inevitable result. Give the emerging primal instinct a new direction, a new name, a new valuation and you have the root of a new culture, a new order, a new morality. For this is the way it is with every culture; we cannot kill the primal instincts, the animal in us, for we ourselves would die with them. But we can in some measure restrain and calm them, make them to some extent serviceable to the "good" in the way one harnesses an unruly nag to a good wagon. Only from time to time the luster of this "good" grows dim and tarnished, the instincts no longer really believe in it, do not willingly bear the yoke. Then the culture breaks down—usually slowly as, for instance, what we call the "classical" took centuries to die.

And before the old dying culture can be replaced by a new one, during that anxious, dangerous, painful stage, man has to look anew into his soul, see once more the animal rising within him, acknowledge anew the existence of primeval forces that are supramoral. Those condemned to this, chosen for this, those foreordained and ready are the Karamazovs. They are hysterical and dangerous, they can as easily become criminals as ascetics, they believe in nothing except the insane uncertainty of every belief.

*   *   *

Every symbol has a hundred interpretations, each of which may be right. The Karamazovs have a hundred interpretations and mine is only one of them. In this book, during a period of great upheavals, mankind has fashioned for itself a symbol, set up a picture in the way an individual in his dreams produces a copy of the instincts and forces battling and reaching an adjustment within him.

That a single human being could write *The Brothers Karamazov* is a miracle. Well, the miracle has happened and we are not required to explain it. There is, however, a need, a very profound need, to interpret the miracle, to read this writing as intensively as possible, from as many points of view as possible, insofar as possible in all its luminous magic. For this purpose my essay is a thought, a small contribution, a notion, no more.

Let no one think that I assume Dostoevsky himself was

aware of the various ideas and insights that I attribute to the book! Quite the contrary. No great seer and poet has ever been able to interpret his own views completely.

Finally I should like to suggest not only how this mythical novel, this dream of mankind, represents the threshold over which Europe is passing, the anxious, dangerous moment of hesitation between nothing and all, but also how the rich possibilities of what is new can be sensed and anticipated in it. In this respect the figure of Ivan is especially startling. We meet him as a modern, well-adjusted, cultivated man, somewhat reserved, disillusioned, skeptical, weary. But increasingly he grows younger, warmer, more significant, more Karamazovian. It is he who conjures up the "Grand Inquisitor." It is he who in the end is driven from a cool rejection of, indeed contempt for, the murderer, who is, he believes, his brother, to a deep feeling of involvement and self-accusation. He is the one too who experiences most vividly and remarkably the psychological process of coming to terms with the unconscious. (Everything turns on that! That indeed is the meaning of the whole decline, the whole rebirth!) In the last book of the novel there is an extremely odd chapter in which Ivan, returning home from Smerdyakov, finds the devil sitting in his house and converses with him for an hour. This devil is simply Ivan's unconscious, the aroused multitude of long-buried, apparently forgotten contents of his soul. And he knows this too; Ivan knows it with astonishing certainty and expresses it clearly. And yet he talks to the devil, he believes in him—for what is within is without!—he grows angry at him, seizes hold of him, even throws a glass at him, although he knows that the devil is within himself. Probably nowhere in all literature has a man's conversation with his unconscious been described more accurately and convincingly. And this conversation, this coming to terms with the devil (despite all vexation) is exactly the road the Karamazovs have been appointed to show us. In Dostoevsky the unconscious is still represented as the devil. Properly so, for to the tamed, cultivated, and moral eye we all have, the repressed material we carry within us is satanic and hateful. But perhaps a combination of Ivan and Alyosha would result in that higher, more fruitful conception which must form the foundation of the coming new age. Then will the unconscious no longer be the devil but rather the god-devil, the demiurge, he who always was and out of whom all things emerge. To assign good and evil is not the business of the eternal, of the demiurge, rather it is the business of man and his littler gods.

A whole chapter could be devoted to another, a fifth Karamazov who plays an uncanny principal role in the novel, although he is always half hidden. This is Smerdyakov, an illegitimate Karamazov. It is he who killed the old man. He is the murderer convinced of the omnipresence of God. It is he who also has to instruct the knowledgeable Ivan in the most divine and sinister matters. He is the least viable and at the same time the most knowing of all the Karamazovs. But I do not have the space to include that strangest one of all in these observations.

* * *

Dostoevsky's book is inexhaustible. All day long I could seek and find new aspects that all point in the same direction. One, a very fine one, yes, a charming one, occurs to me now: the hysteria of the two Hohlakovs. In these two figures we have the Karamazov element, the infection with all that is new, morbid, and bad. One of them, Mother Hohlakov, is simply sick. Her being is still rooted in the ancient and traditional, and her hysteria is just illness, weakness, stupidity. In her splendid daughter, however, it is not weariness that is transformed and expressed as hysteria, it is excess, it is the future. In the troubled period between childhood and sexual maturity, she develops her notions and visions much further in the direction of evil than her ineffectual mother, and yet with this daughter even the most repulsive, even the most wicked, shameless things have an innocence and power that point decisively toward a fruitful future. Mother Hohlakov is the hysteric ready for the sanitarium, nothing more. The daughter is the neurotic whose sickness is really the symptom of most noble but obstructed forces.

*   *   *

Well and good, but are these events in the souls of invented characters in a novel supposed to signify the decline of Europe?

Certainly. They mean it just as every blade of grass in the spring means to the inspired eye life and its eternity, and every falling leaf in November means death and its inevitability. It is possible that the whole "decline of Europe" will run its course "only" inwardly, only in the souls of a generation, in the reinterpretation of worn-out symbols, in the transvaluation of spiritual values. Thus the classical world, that first splendid coinage of European culture, did not come to grief with Nero or with Spartacus or the Germans, but "only" with the arrival from Asia of that seminal thought, that simple, ancient, homely thought which had long existed but at that time took the form of the teaching of Jesus.

*   *   *

Of course, you can if you like regard *The Brothers Karamazov* from a literary point of view as "a work of art." (If the unconscious of a whole period of time and section of the earth has been concentrated in the nightmare of a single prophetic dreamer and if the dream has burst out in a frightful rattling scream, then of course it is possible to assess this from the viewpoint of a singing teacher.) Unquestionably Dostoevsky was a highly gifted writer, despite the atrocities that are to be found in his books and from which a sound, uninspired writer like Turgenev, for instance, was free. Isaiah too was a quite gifted writer, but is that important? In Dostoevsky and especially in *The Brothers Karamazov* there are some of those almost greater than life-sized errors of taste that never befall artists but only occur when one is already dealing with the world beyond art. And yet here and there this Russian prophet steps forth as an artist too, as an artist of world rank, and it gives one an odd feeling to reflect that at a time when Dostoevsky had already written all his books, quite other authors were considered to be the great ones of Europe.

But now I am getting away from my subject. I wanted to say: the less of a work of art such a universal book is, the truer its prophecy is likely to be. Nevertheless the "novel" too, the story, the "creation" of *The Brothers Karamazov* expresses so much, says so much of significance that seems to me not arbitrary, not invented by an individual, as not to be a product of the imagination. For instance, to put the whole thing in a word, the main point of the novel is: the Karamazovs are innocent!

These Karamazovs, all four of them, father and sons, are dubious, dangerous, unpredictable folk; they have strange moods, strange consciences, and a strange lack of conscience; one is a drunkard, another a woman chaser, one an imaginative escapist, one a secret composer of blasphemous poems. They threaten great danger, these strange brothers, they pull people's beards, they cheat others out of their money, they threaten murder—and yet they are innocent, all of them together do nothing really criminal. The only ones guilty of homicide in this long novel that deals with almost nothing but homicide, robbery, and guilt, the only ones really guilty of murder are the public prosecutor and the jury, representatives of the old beneficent, established order, the irreproachable citizens. They condemn the innocent Dmitri, they jeer at his innocence, they are judges, they sit in judgment on God and the world according to their own code. These are the ones who go astray, the very ones who work a frightful injustice, who become murderers through narrowness of heart, through fear, through their own limitations.

This is no literary invention, nor is it a desire to be sensational on the part of a detective story writer (and Dostoevsky is that as well), nor is it the satirical wit of a clever author wishing to play the role of social critic in disguise. That's a role we know well and have distrusted for a long time! But no, with Dostoevsky the innocence of the criminal and the guilt of the judge are in no sense a cunning bit of plotting. They are so frightful, emerge and grow so secretly and in such deep soil that almost suddenly, almost in the last book of the novel, one stands for the first time face to face with this fact as though in front of a wall, as though confronted by all the whirling meaninglessness of the world, as though seeing all the sorrows and errors of mankind!

*   *   *

I have said that Dostoevsky is really not a writer, or is one only incidentally. I have called him a prophet. Hard to say what this really means—a prophet! It strikes me as something like this: a prophet is a sick man, just as Dostoevsky was really a hysteric, almost an epileptic. A prophet is an invalid of the sort who has lost the healthy, sound, beneficent instinct of self-preservation, which is the essence of all middle-class virtues. There must not be many of these men, otherwise the world would go to pieces. This sort of sick man, whether he is called Dostoevsky or Karamazov, has that strange, secret, morbid, divine capability, the possible existence of which Asiatics honor in every madman. He is a manic, he is a seer. This means that in him a people, a nation, or a section of the world has developed an organ, an antenna, a rare, especially sensitive, noble, vulnerable organ that others do not have, which in the case of all the rest, for their health and happiness, has remained vestigial. This antenna, this prophetic sense of touch, is not to be coarsely understood as a silly sort of telepathy or magic trick, although the gift can quite well manifest itself in these disconcerting forms. Rather the "invalid" of this sort transposes the events of his own soul into general terms applicable to mankind. Everyone has visions, everyone has imaginings, everyone has dreams. And every vision, every dream, every thought and inspiration a person has, may, on the way from the unconscious to consciousness, permit of a thousand different interpretations, each one of which may be right. The seer and prophet does not interpret his visions personally, the nightmare that presses upon him does not speak to him of personal illness, of his own death, but rather of the larger whole as whose organ, whose antenna, he lives. This whole may be a family, a party, a nation, it can as well be all mankind.

In Dostoevsky's soul what we usually call hysteria, a certain illness and openness to suffering, has served mankind as an organ, an indicator, a barometer. Mankind is on the point of taking notice. Already half of Europe, at least half of eastern Europe, is on the road to chaos; intoxicated with a divine madness it makes its way along the edge of the abyss and sings, sings drunken hymns the way Dmitri Karamazov sang. The citizen laughs indignantly at these songs, the holy man and seer listens to them with tears.

Thoughts on *The Idiot*
by Dostoevsky
1919

DOSTOEVSKY'S "idiot," Prince Leo Myshkin, is often compared to Jesus. This is easy enough to do. You can compare to Jesus anyone who has been touched by one of the magical truths, who no longer separates thinking from living and thereby isolates himself in the midst of his surroundings and becomes the opponent of all. Beyond that, the comparison between Myshkin and Jesus seems to me not exactly apt. Only one characteristic in Myshkin, an important one to be sure, strikes me as Jesus-like—his timid chastity. The concealed fear of sex and procreation is a characteristic that could not be wanting in the "historical" Jesus, the Jesus of the Gospels, a trait that is clearly part of his world mission and is not neglected in even so superficial a portrait of Jesus as Renan's.

But it is strange—little though I sympathize with the constant comparison between Myshkin and Christ—that I too see the two images unconsciously related to each other. It only occurred to me belatedly and in connection with a tiny matter. One day when I was thinking about the "idiot" I realized that my first thought of him always seems to be an apparently insignificant one. In the first flash of my imagination I always see him in one particular secondary scene of no importance in itself. I have exactly the same experience with the Savior. Whenever an association calls up the image of Jesus or I hear or see the word "Jesus," what leaps into my mind first is not Jesus on the cross, or Jesus in the wilderness, or Jesus the miracle worker, or Jesus risen from the dead, but Jesus in the garden of Gethsemane, tasting the last cup of loneliness, his soul torn by the woes of impending death and a higher rebirth. And as he looks about him for his disciples, in a last touching, childlike need of comfort, seeking a little warmth and human closeness, a fleeting comforting illusion in the midst of his hopeless loneliness—there are the disciples asleep! All of them together, the worthy Peter, the handsome John—all these good people about whom Jesus has again and again, intentionally and lovingly, deceived himself, with whom he has shared his thoughts, at least a part of his thoughts—as though they could understand him, as though it were possible in actual fact to communicate his ideas to these people, to awaken some related vibration in them, something like comprehension, something like a close relationship. And now in the moment of unbearable agony he turns toward these companions, the only ones he has; and he is now so openly and wholly human, so much the sufferer that he might come closer to them than ever before, find comfort and support in any silly word or halfway friendly gesture on their part—but no, they are not there, they are sleeping, they are snoring. This dreadful moment, I know not how, was impressed upon my mind in very early youth, and as I have said, if I think of Jesus, always and unfailingly the memory of this moment arises in my mind.

There is a parallel to this in Myshkin's case. If I think of him, the "idiot," likewise it is a moment of apparently lesser importance that first occurs to me and similarly it is a moment of incredible, total isolation, tragic loneliness. The scene is that evening in Pavlovsk, in Lebedev's house, when the Prince, a few days after his epileptic seizure and still recuperating from it, is being visited by the whole Yepanchin family, when suddenly into this cheerful and elegant though inwardly tense circle burst the fashionable young revolutionaries and nihilists. When the talkative Ippolit with the ostensible "son of Pavlishchev," when the "boxer" and the others rush in, this disagreeable, always repulsive and disquieting scene where these limited and misguided young people are so harshly and nakedly revealed in their helpless evil as though standing on an overlighted stage, where their every word inflicts a double pain upon the reader, first because of its impact upon the good Myshkin and then because of the cruelty with which it unmasks and lays bare the speaker—this is the strange, unforgettable, though in the novel not especially important or emphasized passage that I mean. On the one side society, the elegant worldly people, the rich, mighty, and conservative, on the other ferocious youth, inexorable, knowing nothing but rebellion and hatred for tradition, ruthless, dissolute, wild, incredibly stupid for all their theoretical intellectualism; and standing between these two groups the Prince, alone, exposed, observed by both sides critically and with the closest attention. And how does the situation end? It ends with Myshkin, despite the few small mistakes he makes during the excitement, behaving exactly according to his kind, gentle, childlike nature, accepting smilingly the unbearable, answering selflessly the most shameless speeches, willing to assume every fault and to search for every fault in himself—and his complete failure in this with the result that he is despised, not by one side or the other, not by the young against the old or the reverse, but by both, by both! All turn against him, he has stepped on everyone's toes; for an instant the most extreme social opposites in age and point of view are completely wiped out, all are united and at one in turning their backs with indignation and rage on the single one among them who is pure!

What is it that makes this "idiot" so impossible in the world of other people? Why does no one understand him, even though almost all love him in some fashion, almost everyone finds his gentleness sympathetic, indeed often exemplary? What distinguishes him, the man of magic, from the others, the ordinary people? Why are they right in rejecting him? Why must they do it, inevitably? Why must things go with him as they did with Jesus, who in the end was abandoned not only by the world but by all his disciples as well?

It is because the "idiot's" way of thinking is different from that of the others. Not that he thinks less logically or in a more childlike and associative way than they—that is not it. His way of thought is what I call "magical." This gentle "idiot" completely denies the life, the way of thought and feeling, the world and the reality of other people. His reality is something quite different from theirs. Their reality in his eyes is no more than a shadow, and it is by seeing and demanding a completely new reality that he becomes their enemy.

The difference is not that they prize power, money, family, state, and similar values and that he does not. It is not that he represents the spiritual and they the material, or however one wants to formulate it. This is not the point. For the "idiot" too the material world exists, he readily acknowledges the significance of these things even if he takes them less seriously. Nor is his demand, his ideal, a Hindu ascetic one, a dying to this world of apparent realities in favor of a spirit content in itself and confident that it alone is reality.

No, about the reciprocity of nature and spirit, about their necessary interaction, Myshkin would be quite able to reach an understanding with the others. But for them the coexistence, the equal validity of both worlds is a principle and an idea, for him they are life and reality! To make this clearer, let us try to put it somewhat differently.

Myshkin is different from others because as idiot and epileptic, and at the same time a very clever person, he has much closer and more direct relations with the unconscious than they do. For him the highest experience is that half second of supreme receptivity and insight that he has experienced a few times, that magical ability for a moment, for the flash of a moment, to be able to be everything, to empathize with everything, to sympathize with everything, to understand and accept everything in the world. There lies the essence of his being. He has not studied and accepted magic and mystical wisdom, not read and admired them, but (if only at very rare instants) actually experienced them. He has not only had strange and magnificent thoughts and inspirations but more than once he has stood on the magic threshold where everything is affirmed, where not only the most farfetched idea is true but also the opposite of every such idea.

This is the dread thing about this man, properly feared by the others. He does not stand entirely alone, not the whole world is against him. There are still a few people, very dubious, very threatened and threatening people, who at times understand him emotionally: Rogozhin, Nastasya. He is understood by criminals and by hysterics, he, the innocent, the gentle child! But this child, by God, is not as gentle as he seems. His innocence is by no means harmless, and people quite properly fear him.

The "idiot," I have said, is at times close to that boundary line where every idea and its opposite are recognized as true. That is, he has an intuition that no idea, no law, no character or order exists that is true and right except as seen from one pole—and for every pole there is an opposite pole. Settling upon a pole, adopting a position from which the world is viewed and arranged, this is the first principle of every order, every culture, every society and morality. Whoever feels, if only for an instant, that spirit and nature, good and evil are interchangeable is the most dangerous enemy of all forms of order. For that is where the opposite of order is, and there chaos begins.

A way of thought that leads back to the unconscious, to chaos, destroys all forms of human organization. In conversation someone says to the "idiot" that he only speaks the truth, nothing more, and that this is deplorable. So it is. Everything is true, "Yes" can be said to anything. To bring order into the world, to attain goals, to make possible law, society, organization, culture, morality, "No" must be added to the "Yes," the world must be separated into opposites, into good and evil. However arbitrary the first establishment of each "No," each prohibition, may be, it becomes sacrosanct the instant it becomes law, produces results, becomes the foundation for a point of view and system of order.

The highest reality in the eyes of human culture lies in

this dividing up of the world into bright and dark, good and evil, permissible and forbidden. For Myshkin the highest reality, however, is the magical experience of the reversibility of all fixed rules, of the equal justification for the existence of both poles. *The Idiot*, thought to its logical conclusion, leads to a matriarchy of the unconscious and annihilates culture. It does not break the tables of the law, it reverses them and shows their opposites written on the back.

The fact that this foe of order, this frightful destroyer, appears not as a criminal but as a shy, endearing person full of childlikeness and charm, a good-hearted, selfless, benevolent man, this is the secret of this terrifying book. Out of a profound perception, Dostoevsky has made this character a sick man, an epileptic. All representatives of the new, of the dreadful, of the uncertain future, all harbingers of an intuited chaos, are in Dostoevsky sick, dubious, overburdened. Rogozhin, Nastasya, later all four Karamazovs. All are represented as derailed, as exceptionally strange figures, but all in such a way that we feel for this derailment and mental illness something of that holy awe which Asiatics believe they owe to madmen.

What is remarkable and strange, important and fateful, is not that somewhere in Russia in the 1850's and '60's an epileptic of genius had these fantasies and created these figures. The important thing is that these books for three decades have become increasingly important and prophetic works to the young people of Europe. The strange thing is that we look at the faces of these criminals, hysterics, and idiots of Dostoevsky quite differently than we do at the faces of other criminals or fools in other famous novels, that we understand and love them so uncannily that we must feel in ourselves something related and akin to these people.

This is not due to accident and even less to the external and literary elements in Dostoevsky's work. However disconcerting any of his traits may be—you have only to think how he anticipates a highly developed psychology of the unconscious—we do not admire his work as the expression of profound insight and skill or as the artistic representation of a world essentially known and familiar to us; rather we experience it as prophecy, as the mirroring in advance of the dissolution and chaos that we have seen openly going on in Europe for the last several years. Not that this world of fictional characters represents a picture of an ideal future —no one would consider it that. No, we do not see in Myshkin and all the other characters examples to be copied; instead we perceive an inevitability that says, "Through this we must pass, this is our destiny!"

The future is uncertain, but the road that is shown here is unambiguous. It means spiritual revaluation. It leads through Myshkin and calls for "magical" thinking, the acceptance of chaos. Return to the incoherent, to the unconscious, to the formless, to the animal and far beyond the animal to the beginning of all things. Not in order to remain there, not to become animal or primeval slime but rather so that we can reorient ourselves, hunt out, at the roots of our being, forgotten instincts and possibilities of development, to be able to undertake a new creation, valuation, and distribution of the world. No program can teach us to find this road, no revolution can thrust open the gates to it. Each one walks this way alone, each by himself. Each of us for an hour in his life will have to stand on the Myshkin boundary where truths can cease and begin anew. Each of us must once for an instant in his life experience within himself the same sort of thing that Myshkin experienced in his moments of clairvoyance, such as Dostoevsky himself experienced in those moments when he stood face to face with execution and from which he emerged with the prophet's gaze.

Books on Trial

1919

Recently I had to sort out my books again, because circumstances forced me to give away part of my library. And so I stood in front of the bookcases, went step by step along the rows of books, and thought to myself, "Do you need this book? Do you love it? Are you sure that you will read it again? Would it pain you to part with it?"

Since I am one of those people who have never been able to "think historically," not even in those times when historical thinking was officially put far ahead of human thought, I began with the historical books and had little difficulty there. Handsome editions of memoirs, Italian and French biographies, court histories, diaries of politicians—away with them! Had the politicians ever been right? Has not a single verse by Hölderlin not been of more value than all the wisdom of the potentates? Away with them!

History of art came next. Pretty works by specialists on Italian, Dutch, Belgian, English painting, Vasari. Collections of artists' letters—discarding them didn't really hurt. Away with them!

The philosophers. Was it necessary to own Mauthner's dictionary? No. Would I ever again read Eduard von Hartmann? Oh no. But Kant? There I hesitated. You could never tell. And I let him stay. Nietzsche? Indispensable, together with his letters. Fechner? He would be a loss, and so remains. Emerson? Let him go! Kierkegaard? He's someone we'll still keep. Schopenhauer without question. The anthologies and collections, of course, looked pretty—*The German Soul—Book of Ghosts—The Ghetto Book—Germans Seen in Caricature*—does one need any of this? Away with it! Away with it all!

But now the poets. I won't talk about the moderns. But Goethe's correspondence? Part of it was rejected. What about all the volumes of Grillparzer? Must that be? No, it must not be. And all of Von Arnim? Oh, but that would cause me pain. He stays. Like Tieck, likewise Wieland. Herder was substantially plucked. Balzac was questioned, then retained. Anatole France gave me pause for thought. Toward one's enemies one is chivalrous; he was preserved. Stendhal? Many volumes but indispensable. Mann, without question. On the other hand, Maeterlinck was decimated. Four editions of Boccaccio's *Decameron*! Only one was left standing. Then the sections with the writers of eastern Asia. A few volumes of Lafcadio Hearn were dismissed, all others were left.

About the English writers many questions arose. So many volumes of Shaw? Some must go. And all of Thackeray? Half is enough. Fielding, Sterne, Dickens remain, even their trivia.

Of the Russians too almost all remain. With Gorky and with Turgenev there were hesitations and indecisions. Tolstoy's tracts were sharply reduced. From among the Scandinavians a few slid away. Hermann Bang remained, Hamsun remained, Strindberg remained. Björnson melted down, Geijerstam disappeared.

Who collects war literature? Some hundredweight are easily given away. I bought little of it, most simply flew into the house. I have not read a twentieth part of it. And what good paper there was as late as 1915 and '16!

Days later, when I was finished with the job, I realized for the first time how much my relationship to books had altered during these years, along with other things. There are whole categories of literature that I now cheerfully give away. There are authors whom it is no longer possible to take seriously. But what a comfort that Knut Hamsun is still alive! How fortunate that there is Jammes! And how nice it is to have cleaned out all the thick biographies of poets, with their boredom and their meager psychology. The rooms look brighter. Treasures remain behind and now they gleam far more brightly. Goethe stands there, Hölderlin stands there, all of Dostoevsky stands there, Mörike smiles, Arnim flashes audaciously, the Icelandic sagas outlast all troubles. Märchen and folk tales remain indestructible. And the old books, the books in pigskin with a theological look, which for the most part are so much dearer than all the new books, they too are still there. They are something that for once one doesn't mind being outlived by.

Variations on a Theme
by Wilhelm Schäfer

1919

WHEN PAINTERS judge a picture, not only do they place it in a good light, stand in front of it, step back and examine it from various angles, but many of them turn the picture around, hang it upside down with the sky at the bottom, and are satisfied only if the picture meets this last test too, if its colors continue even then to vibrate together magically and concordantly.

This has always been my approach to truths, of which I am a great friend. A good, a real truth, so it seems to me, must stand being inverted. When something is true, then it must be possible for its opposite to be true as well. For every truth is a brief formula for the appearance of the world seen from a certain pole, and there is no pole without its opposite.

An author very highly regarded by me, Wilhelm Schäfer, pronounced for me some years ago a dictum about the poet's task; he had invented it and later set it forth in one of his books. The saying impressed me, it was unquestionably good and true and it was splendidly formulated, something at which Schäfer is a master. For a long time it echoed in my mind, I have never really forgotten it, and it keeps turning up in my mind every now and then. That does not happen in the case of truths with which we are in absolute and complete agreement. They are quickly swallowed and digested.

The statement went like this: "It is not the poet's business to express what is simple significantly but what is significant simply."

I have pondered long and often on why the famous dictum (which I still continue to admire) did not quite content me but caused me a bit of uneasiness and dissatisfaction. I have analyzed it more than a hundred times through a series of related ideas. The first thing I discovered was a slight dissonance, a tiny error, a very minute crack in the clear crystal of this cleanly formulated dictum. "To express what is significant simply—not what is simple significantly"—that sounded like a perfect parallel, and yet it was not quite that. For the sense of the word "significant" was not precisely, not needle-sharply the same in the two halves of the sentence. The "significant" thing the poet was to say was unquestionably intended rationally and unambiguously; "significant" here meant approximately the same as "of unquestionable value." The other "significant," on the contrary, had an undertone of disdain. If a poet expresses what is "simple," what is obviously insignificant "significantly," he is doing something, in the sense of this dictum, that is really false, and the "significance" with which he characterizes his action is actually humbug and half ironical in intent.

And so it is strange that it took me so long to try coming to grips with the dictum by experimentally turning it upside down. Then it read: "It is not the poet's business to express what is significant simply but rather what is simple significantly." And behold, there a new truth stood before me. The inversion improved the sentence formally as well, for the word "significantly" now remained of equal value in both halves, instead of surreptitiously changing its meaning.

And suddenly I saw that for me the reversal of Schäfer's truth was even truer, was much more valuable than what he had actually said. Now everything was clear. Naturally Schäfer's dictum remained as true and beautiful as before —from his, Schäfer's, pole. From my opposite pole, however, the reversed dictum glowed with a wholly new power and warmth. Schäfer had said that it was not the poet's business to present something arbitrary and unimportant in such a way that it would appear significant but to select for presentation what was truly valuable and significant and to express this as simply as possible. My reversed sentence, however, meant: It is not the poet's business to decide whether this or that is significant and important; it is not his business to act in some sense as spokesman for future readers and to select from the confusion of the world and communicate to them only what is valuable, what is really important. No, on the contrary! The poet's real business is precisely to discover what is immense and eternal in every trivial thing, in every nothing, and to exhibit this treasure, this knowledge that God is everywhere and in everything, again and again, and to communicate it.

Thus I had found a formula for the meaning or the duty of the poet which for me, from my pole, was far truer and more valuable than the original dictum, although I too had once adjusted myself to that and agreed with it. No, the poet, in my deepest understanding of him, does not have the task of deciding between what is significant and insignificant on earth. He has, as I see it, exactly the opposite duty, the holy office of showing always that "significance" is only a word, that significance cannot be attributed to any one thing on earth but must be attributed to all things, that there are not things that one should take seriously and others that one should not. Schäfer, to be sure, had meant something different. The poet, in the sense in which he rejected him, is a man who through art and artifice makes a nothing, which is a nothing to him as well, into something apparently imposing, who inflates things into significance, who in fact engages in sham. I reject this sort of poet too. But I am at odds with Schäfer in that I do not believe at all in a dividing line between "significant" and "simple."

Starting with this idea, I found in the course of a few years more insight into a phenomenon of poetry and intellectual history that had always seemed to me somewhat dark and distressing and that had never been discussed to my satisfaction by our teachers and literary historians.

This strange phenomenon is the problematicist on one hand and the minor poet and idyllist on the other. There is a kind of poet whose works by no means enchant us but about whom an aura of greatness and weightiness hangs because he chooses the mighty material of humanity and deals with the huge problems of mankind. On the other hand, there is the so-called minor poet who never gives expression to a single great strong world-shaking thought, who never concerns himself about the origin and future problems of mankind but has preferred to sing and to fantasize about small fortunes, loves and friendships, the sorrow of mortality, about landscapes, animals, singing birds, and clouds in the sky, and such as he are very much loved by us and are read and reread again and again. There is always some embarrassment as to how one should place these poets and evaluate them, these simple souls who never really had anything overwhelming to say and yet are so dear to us! All the Eichendorffs, all the Stifters, all such poets belong together. —And on the other side in all their somber fame stand those great problematicists, those broachers of important questions, those Hebbels, those Ibsens (the few truly great poet-prophets I will not mention in the same breath: Dante, Shakespeare, Dostoevsky)—there stand those strange giants in whose works, it is admitted, the profoundest questions ring out, but who, taken all together, give us so little happiness.

Now those Eichendorffs and Stifters—and they are all simply poets who say what is simple significantly because they never notice the differences between the simple and significant, because they live on a quite different plane—see the world from a wholly different pole. And it is precisely these idyllists, these simple, clear-eyed children of God to whom a blade of grass can become a revelation, it is precisely they we call minor who give us the best. They teach us not a What but a How. In contrast to those thought-heavy great ones they are like good mothers compared to fathers, and how often do we have infinitely more need of a mother than of a father!

It always does one good to invert a truth. It always does one good when one inwardly hangs one's pictures upside down for an hour. Thoughts come more easily, inspirations spring up faster, our boat glides more gently down the stream of the world. If I were a teacher and had to keep school, if I had students who had to write essays and all such, I would from time to time take aside those with a capacity for it and say to them: Children, what we are teaching you is all very well. But from time to time try turning our rules and truths upside down for a change, just as an experiment, just for fun! Even if you reverse a word, letter for letter, there often emerges an astonishing source of instruction, fun, and good ideas.

Actually, in such a game a state of awareness arises in which labels fall away from things and they speak to us freshly and surprisingly. In such a mood the thin play of colors in an old windowpane becomes a Byzantine mosaic and a teakettle is turned into a steam engine. And it is just this mood, this willingness of the soul not to recognize the familiar world but to discover it as new and more significant, it is exactly this readiness that we find in those poets who speak of the significance of the insignificant.

On Reading Books

1920

W E HAVE AN INBORN TENDENCY to establish types in
our minds and to divide mankind according to them.
From the "characters" of Theophrastus and the four tem-
peraments our grandfathers talked about, to the most modern
psychology, this need for type arrangement can be traced.
Also everyone sorts the people around him into types according to their resemblance to characters that were important
to him in his childhood. Now however advantageous and revealing such categories may be, no matter whether they
spring from purely personal experience or from attempting
a scientific establishment of types, at times it is a good and
fruitful exercise to take a cross section of experience in another way and discover that each person bears traces of every
type within himself and that diverse characters and tem-
peraments can be found as alternating characteristics within
a single individual.

If I set forth the following three types, or better, three
stages, of book readers, I do not therefore mean that the
world of readers is comprised of only these three groups, or
that one reader belongs to this and another to that group.
Rather, each of us belongs at times to one group and at
times to another.

First of all, there is the naïve reader. Everyone reads
naïvely at times. This reader consumes a book as one consumes food, he eats and drinks to satiety, he is simply a
taker, be he a boy with a book about Indians, a servant girl
with a novel about countesses, or a student with Schopenhauer. This kind of reader is not related to a book as one person is to another but rather as a horse to his manger or
perhaps as a horse to his driver: the book leads, the reader

follows. The substance is taken objectively, accepted as reality. But the substance is only one consideration! There are also highly educated, very refined readers, especially of belles lettres, who belong entirely to the class of the naïve. These, to be sure, do not concentrate upon the material content; they do not evaluate a novel, for example, by the number of murders or marriages in the story, but they take the writer himself and the aesthetics of the book wholly objectively, they enjoy the writer's exaltations, they feel their way accurately into his attitudes toward the world, and they accept without reservation the writer's interpretations of his creations. What the material, setting, and action are to simple souls, the art, language, education, and intellectuality of the writer are to these cultivated readers. They take them objectively, as the final and highest value of a composition, just as the reader of Karl May accepted the exploits of old Shatterhands as true acts, as reality itself.

This naïve reader in his relationship to reading is not really a person at all, is not himself. He evaluates the events in a novel according to their suspense, their danger, their erotic content, their splendor or misery; or he may evaluate the writer instead by measuring him against aesthetic standards, which in the final analysis always remain arbitrary. This kind of reader assumes in an uncomplicated way that a book is there simply and solely to be read faithfully and attentively and to be judged according to its content or its form. Just as a loaf of bread is there to be eaten and a bed to be slept in.

However, since you may take a completely different attitude toward anything in the world, so you may toward the book. If one follows one's nature and not one's education one becomes a child again and begins to play with things; the bread becomes a mountain to bore tunnels into, and the bed a cave, a garden, a snow field. Something of this childlikeness, this genius for play, is exhibited by the second type of reader. This reader treasures neither the substance nor the form of a book as its single most important value. He knows, in the way children know, that every object can have ten or a hundred meanings for the mind. He can, for example, watch a poet or philosopher struggling to persuade himself and his reader of his interpretation and evaluation of things, and he can smile because he sees in the apparent choice and freedom of the poet simply compulsion and passivity. This reader is already so far advanced that he knows what professors of literature and literary critics are mostly completely ignorant of: that there is no such thing as a free choice of material and form. When the literary historian says: In such and such a year Schiller selected this subject and decided to treat it in iambic pentameters—then this reader knows that it was not open to the poet to choose either subject or iambics, and his enjoyment consists in seeing not the material in the hands of his poet but the poet in the grip of his material. From this point of view the so-called aesthetic values almost disappear, and it can be precisely the writer's mishaps and uncertainties that furnish much the greatest charm and value. For this reader follows the poet not the way a horse obeys his driver but the way a hunter follows his prey, and a glimpse suddenly gained into what lies beyond the apparent freedom of the poet, into the poet's compulsion and passivity, can enchant him more than all the elegance of good technique and cultivated style.

One stage further along we find the third and last type of reader. Once more it must be emphasized that no one of us need belong permanently to any one of these types, that each of us may belong today to the second, tomorrow to the third, the day after once more to the first stage. And so now to the third and last kind of reader. He is apparently the exact reverse of what is generally called a "good" reader. He is so completely an individual, so very much himself, that he confronts his reading matter with complete freedom. He wishes neither to educate nor to entertain himself, he uses a book exactly like any other object in the world, for him it is simply a point of departure and a stimulus. Essentially it makes no difference to him what he reads. He does not read a philosopher in order to learn from him, to adopt his teaching, or to attack or criticize him. He does not read a poet to accept his interpretation of the world; he interprets it for himself. He is, if you like, completely a child. He plays with everything—and from one point of view there is nothing more fruitful and rewarding than to play with everything. If this reader finds a beautiful sentence in a book, a truth, a word of wisdom, he begins by experimentally turning it upside down. He has known for a long time that for each truth the opposite also is true. He has known for a long time that every intellectual point of view is a pole to which an equally valid antipole exists. He is a child insofar as he puts a high value on associative thinking, but he knows the other sort as well. And so this reader is able, or rather each one of us is able, at the hour in which he is at this stage, to read whatever he likes, a novel or grammar, a railroad timetable, a galley proof from the printer. At the hour when our imagination and our ability to associate are at their height, we really no longer read what is printed on the paper but swim in a stream of impulses and inspirations that reach us from what we are reading. They may come out of the text, they may simply emerge from the type face. An advertisement in a newspaper can become a revelation; the most exhilarating, the most affirmative thoughts can spring from a completely irrelevant word if one turns it about, playing with its letters as with a jigsaw puzzle. In this stage one can read the story of Little Red Ridinghood as a cosmogony or philosophy, or as a flowery erotic poem. Or one can read the label "Colorado maduro" on a box of cigars, play with the words, letters, and sounds, and thereby take a tour through the hundred kingdoms of knowledge, memory, and thought.

But, it will be objected, can that be called reading? Is the person who reads a page of Goethe unconcerned about Goethe's intentions and meanings? If he reads it like an advertisement or like an accidental hodgepodge of letters, is he still a reader at all? Isn't the stage of reading that you call the third and last really the lowest, most childish and barbaric? For such a reader what becomes of the music of Hölderlin, the passion of Lenau, the will of Stendhal, the scope of Shakespeare? The objection is valid. The reader at the third stage is no longer a reader. The person who remained there permanently would soon not read at all, for the design in a rug or the arrangement of the stones in a wall would be of exactly as great a value to him as the most beautiful page full of the best-arranged letters. The one book for him would be a page with the letters of the alphabet.

So be it: the reader at the last stage is really no longer a reader at all, he doesn't give a hoot about Goethe, he doesn't read Shakespeare. The reader in the last stage simply doesn't read any more. Why books? Has he not the entire world within himself?

Whoever remained permanently at this stage would not read any more, but no one does remain permanently at this stage. But whoever is not acquainted with this stage is a poor, an immature reader. He does not know that all the poetry and all the philosophy in the world lie within him too, that the greatest poet drew from no other source than the one each of us has within his own being. For just once in your life remain for an hour, a day at the third stage, the stage of not-reading-any-more. You will thereafter (it's so easy to slip back) be that much better a reader, that much better a listener and interpreter of everything written. Stand just once at the stage where the stone by the road means as much to you as Goethe and Tolstoy, you will thereafter gain from Goethe, Tolstoy, and all poets infinitely more value, more sap and honey, more affirmation of life and of yourself than ever before. For the works of Goethe are not Goethe, and the volumes of Dostoevsky are not Dostoevsky, they are only an attempt, a dubious and never successful attempt, to conjure up the many-voiced multitudinous world of which he was the central point.

Try just once to write down one of those little sequences of ideas that drift through your mind in the course of a walk.

Or, apparently easier, a simple dream that you had during the night! You dreamed about a man who at first was threatening you with a cane but then bestowed a medal on you. But who was the man? You reflect, you find certain features of your friend in him, of your father, but there is also something different about him, something feminine; without your being able to say how, something about him that reminds you of a sister, of a beloved. And the cane with which he threatened you had a handle that reminds you of a walking stick you had when you went on your first hikes as a schoolboy, and then a hundred thousand memories burst in, and if you want to keep track of the content of this simple dream, even though only by shorthand and in key phrases, you can before you get it in order fill up a book, or two or ten books. For a dream is the opening through which you see into the content of your soul, and this content is the world, no more and no less than the world, the whole world from your birth up to today, from Homer to Heinrich Mann, from Japan to Gibraltar, from Sirius to the Earth, from Red Ridinghood to Bergson. —And to the extent that your attempt to write down your dream is related to the world that embraces that dream, so the work of an author is related to what he tried to say.

For almost a hundred years now scholars and amateurs have tried their hands at interpreting the second part of Goethe's *Faust* and have found the most beautiful and the most stupid, the profoundest and the most banal interpretations for it. But in every work of poetry, though perhaps hidden, there lurks under the surface that nameless ambiguity, that "overdetermination of symbols," as the newer psychology has it. Without having recognized this, be it only a single time, in all its infinite fullness and inexhaustible significance, you stand handicapped before every poet and thinker, you take for the whole what is a small part, you believe in interpretations that barely touch the surface.

The shiftings of the reader among the three stages are, as can be easily understood, possible for everyone in every field. You can occupy the same three stages with a thousand intermediate stages in respect to architecture, painting, zoology, history. In every case the third stage at which you are most yourself will put an end to your reading, will dissolve poetry, will dissolve art, will dissolve world history. And yet unless you intuitively know this stage, you will never read any book, any science or art except as a schoolboy reads his grammar.

A Poet's Preface
to His Selected Works
1921

A CONTEMPORARY POET, one of our popular storytellers, was invited to prepare a selection of his works and to explain in a preface the reasons that had led him to make this particular selection. After several weeks he sent his publisher the following

Preface

The suggestion that I undertake a popular selection of my writings has involved me in various labors and deliberations, principally the examination of all my writings to see whether this or that one had especial virtues to recommend its inclusion in such a special selection.

The criteria for the selection would be, first, that a work should have a respectable standing within its category; second, it should have a special position among my own works because it gave an expression of my own essential being that was clearer than others; and beyond this the form and attitude of the work would have to be successful, pleasing, well-proportioned. These would be the necessary considerations for a conscientious selection.

Of course a simpler way to go about it was perfectly possible: I could accept the popular voice as the voice of God and merely select those works that had already received approbation from readers. In that case my best books would be those that had been most kindly received by the critics and had sold the greatest number of printings. And yet if this voice of God were really valid, then I was with mathematical certainty a far more significant poet than many of our greatest masters whom I humbly revere. On the other hand, I was small and trivial when measured against the magnificent aggregate printings of certain contemporaries with whom it would be more hateful to me to be confused or compared than to fall among murderers. And so this method, after the briefest examination, was discarded and the laborious task still lay on my hands. I had at least to make a serious attempt to accomplish the impossible: to set up within myself a tribunal and to pass judgment on the public value or lack of it in my poetic efforts.

Two procedures were possible: I could either compare my stories with those of other established writers or—apparently easier—meticulously select those works that best represented me, my character, my varying views of the world, and those that most clearly expressed and justified my gift or vocation. Both ways had to be tentatively tried out before either could be chosen.

And so I experimented with the first by taking the works of established storytellers as my standard. The novelists of the first, the highest, rank—needless to say!—I left out of account; in my most ambitious hour it would never have occurred to me to compare myself with Cervantes or Sterne, with Dostoevsky, Swift, or Balzac. But a more modest, more respectful comparison, so I thought, with admired masters of the next though still very high order ought after all to be possible—though they exceeded me a hundred times, nevertheless it seemed to me there should be some emulative relationship discoverable. I was thinking about such honored and well-loved storytellers as Dickens, Turgenev, Keller. However I found no point of contact here either. Aside from the fact that these masters, too, stood far too high above me— there was something more that made comparison or even a standard of comparison impossible.

Whenever I tried to put any book of mine beside one of those esteemed works of greater writers, I felt that my work had nothing to do with theirs. I saw that I was trying to compare incommensurables. A common yardstick was lacking, a common denominator. After that, I very quickly discovered the truth about writing, a truth that was very humiliating.

My novels, it turned out, seemed to be comparable with the works of those earlier writers only in that they had in common the word "novel" or "tale" on the title page. In reality, however—this I suddenly saw with a chilling super-clarity— my novels were not novels, my novellas were not novellas. I was no storyteller at all, not by any means. And the fact that I had undeniably composed things that looked exactly like narratives, this was my most characteristic sin and weakness. I had been familiar with those splendid masters of narrative from childhood on and had spent much time reading them; it was there that my mimicry began, and at first I was not conscious of it at all, and later but confusedly. Only today have I become fully aware of it.

To be sure, I was not alone in my dilettantism and mimicry. Modern German literature of the past hundred years is full of novels that are not novels and poets who behave like storytellers but are not. Among these are great, brilliant writers whose ostensible novellas I passionately love despite everything—I need only mention Eichendorff. I stood close to those writers if only by virtue of my weaknesses. Narrative as disguised lyricism, the novel as a label borrowed for the attempts of poetical natures to express their feelings about themselves and the world, these were specifically German and romantic phenomena, and with them beyond question I felt related and involved. But there was something more. Writers like Eichendorff and many others had not, it appears, found it necessary to smuggle lyricism into the world under the false colors of the novel; they could produce excellent, undisguised, true lyricism and, thank God, had done so. But lyricism is not simply the composing of verses; lyricism is above all musicmaking. And that German prose is a marvelous, enticing instrument for music-making is something many poets have known and on this choice pleasure they have heaped glowing praise. Few, however, very few indeed, were strong or sensible enough to take advantage of temporarily borrowing the narrative form (part of that advantage being a larger public) and of thus proudly presenting their prose music to the world as Hölderlin did in *Hyperion* and Nietzsche in *Zarathustra.* —And so I too without really knowing it had played the role of storyteller as deceiver deceived. The fact that in this I had numerous and in part very good company did not exonerate me. About my narratives there could be no more doubt: no single one of them was good enough as a work of art to deserve so much as a mention. Pack up, my boy, and go home! From this point of view the notion of a selection of my writings had been judged and condemned.

Humbled by this insight, I tried the second road. Granted that my books were impure as works of art, that they were barbaric and unsuccessful from the start in their attempt to breathe life into incompatible forms, nevertheless they must retain their subjective, timely value as attempts at self-expression by a soul that felt, suffered, and quested in our time. The "selection" of my writings, therefore, could simply depend on which of them were the most sincere, the least mendacious, those that most clearly expressed my feeling, those in which truth and expression had been least sacrificed to imitation and falsity of form.

I began over again, and the weeks went by as I reread almost all my earlier writings, often with wonder and surprise, often with shame and groans. Some of them I had almost forgotten, but I remembered all of them as different from what they now appeared upon rereading. Much that had years and decades ago seemed to me very beautiful and effective now looked absurd and worthless. And all these stories were about myself, they reflected my chosen path, my secret dreams and wishes, my own bitter anguish! Even those books in which, when I wrote them, I had honestly thought I was portraying alien destinies and conflicts remote from myself, even these sang the same song, breathed the same air, interpreted the same destiny, my own.

None of all these narratives either came under consideration or did not come under consideration for the collection. There was nothing there to select. Writings in which I had

once (unconsciously, of course) been most stylized, most dis-
ingenuous and deceitful, precisely these—ugly and unsuccessful though I found them today—were the ones that
proclaimed the truth most loudly, revealed me most pathetically, when read with a sharpened eye. And precisely in those
writings which I had written long ago with the bitterest desire
for pure confession I now found strange, in part no longer
comprehensible evasions, concealments, and extenuations.
No, among these books there was not one that was not confession and a ringing desire to express my essential being,
but by the same token not one in which the confession was
complete and clean, not one in which the expression had
found its way to deliverance!

If I consider the sum of efforts, renunciations, sufferings,
and sacrifices that I have expended in the course of many
years in the production of these printed books and compare
that with the result as I see it today, then I could consider my
life as a failure and a waste. It may well be that on close
examination few human lives come out otherwise: no life
and no oeuvre can stand comparison with the demands of the
ideal. To judge the value or lack of it in one's whole life and
accomplishment is not the duty of any human being.

Now, however, there is no longer any occasion to allow my
Selected Works to appear. Before I embarked on this task the
idea gave me pleasure and at times I saw my collection, in an
agreeable wish-fulfillment way, arranged in front of me in
four or five handsome volumes. Now all that is left of those
volumes is this preface.

About Jean Paul

1921

I F I WERE TO BE CONFRONTED in an examination with the question: in what book of modern times does the German soul express itself most forcefully and characteristically, I would answer without hesitation—Jean Paul's *Flegeljahre* (*Unfledged Years*). In Jean Paul that secret Germany— which continues to live on though for several decades now a different, noisier, more hectic, more soulless Germany has been standing in its light—gave birth to its most character- istic, richest, and most bewildered spirit, one of the greatest poetic talents of all time, whose work presents a native jungle of poesy. And Germany with its astounding riches and its astounding forgetfulness has once more forgotten Jean Paul after a period when he was a popular author. Individual works by him, usually *Flegeljahre,* are still known here and there in families of good background; but beyond this he is known only to students of literature. In Germany, even now in the postwar years, there are complete editions of the *Thousand and One Nights,* of Voltaire and Diderot. There is, however, no complete edition of Jean Paul.

Jean Paul's real name was Johann Paul Friedrich Richter, and he was born on March 21, 1763, in Wunsiedel, the son of a schoolmaster and organist.

"Let no poet," he said on one occasion, "let no poet allow himself to be born and raised in a metropolis, but if possible in a village instead, or at most in a smallish town. The super- fluity and overstimulation of a big city are for the excitable child-soul like being nourished on dessert, brandy, and bath- ing in mulled wine. Life exhausts itself in him during his boyhood and after the maximum excitements he has nothing more to wish for but the smaller ones, those of the villages.

When I think carefully about what is most important for the poet—love—then I have to conclude that he is compelled to see in the city, beyond the warm tropical zone of his family, friends, and acquaintances, the larger cold, temperate, and arctic zones of unloved people; when he meets them he is as little able to feel any warm glow of love as the crew of a ship encountered by chance feels for the crew of the passing vessel. But in a village one loves the whole place, and no nursling is buried without his name and illness being known and sorrow felt for him; and this splendid sympathy for everyone in human form, which extends, of course, to strangers and beggars, exudes a concentrated love of man and the right impulse of the heart."

Two years after his birth the family moved to Joditz, where Jean Paul spent the greater part of his boyhood. Hungry for knowledge, ready to learn everything, he found no kind and interested teacher and had but little instruction. He relates how as a child he became aware for the first time of his own consciousness: "I can specify precisely the time and place when I witnessed the birth of my own self-awareness." His father, a decent enough man, seems to have done little to understand or assist him. He spent the last of his boyhood in Schwartzenbach and in 1779, the year his father died, Jean Paul entered the *gymnasium* in Hof. There the ardent young man met no people who were important to him, but he did encounter books and stormed into the kingdom of the mind. First of all, he drank in the literature of the Enlightenment, with understandable zest as befitted the gifted son of a pastor, and he developed that critical, revolutionary spirit that belongs to a proper youth, that sometimes sounds precocious and ill-tempered and in the case of Jean Paul too was not without bitterness. He filled many notebooks with sketches, essays, theses, plans, and is said to have written a novel too, or at least to have begun one. And soon he also made two or three friends, one of whom, Johann Richard Hermann, seems to have been a courageous, self-assured man; at any rate he is taken to be the prototype for those most manly and enterprising characters in Jean Paul's later writings, Schoppe, Leibgeber, and Gianozzo.

In the year 1781 the young poet went to Leipzig as a theological student and applied himself with the greatest zeal, though not to theology. He was attracted to almost anything else that had no taint of practical usefulness. He continued to write prodigiously; indeed few of our authors have so reveled in their own productivity as Jean Paul. In 1783, while an undergraduate, he began his career with the publication *Greenland Proceedings,* a book that exposed that critical-revolutionary spirit of adolescence in satirical, witty fashion, in impudent, often penetrating comments about everything in the universe, including sun, moon, and stars. On the other hand, only about a year later he wrote a *Devotional Handbook* in which he follows an Augustine course and reads himself a sermon; the critic has become a self-critic, the cynic a moralist. In late fall of 1784 young Jean Paul had to leave Leipzig because he literally had nothing to eat and had acquired a sackful of debts. Then for two years he remained miserably at home with his mother in Hof, in surroundings without stimulus or animation, sidetracked, sunk in himself, incapable of finding a footing in this crude world or commanding a place for himself. The brother of one of his schoolfriends finally took him in as a tutor in a village near Hof; he stayed there about two years, then found a place as a tutor in Schwartzenbach, and thus struggled along miserably from year to year, always close to starvation but always diligent in writing and usually surrounded by worshipful young ladies, whom all his life long he drew to himself with a special magic, although he was by no means a reliable love, despite his reputation as a great lover. He was much too fickle and faithless for that, and much too addicted to things of the mind and to friendship. Somewhere around 1790 his first important works were written and published, among them *The Little Schoolmaster Wuz.* And now rose rapidly, star after star, his whole bright heavens; there appeared *The Invisible Loge* and *Hesperus;* in 1794 *Quintus Fixlein;* in 1795 *Sie-*

benkäs, that marvelous book. Here, in the figure of Leibgeber, one of the poles of Jean Paul's character is for the first time clearly delineated.

In the year 1796 the young man of letters made a pilgrimage to Weimar, where he felt to some degree disillusioned, and indeed disillusionment was the constant fate of this demanding and insatiable soul who sought the ideal everywhere, and was fated everywhere to encounter the deathly smell of so-called reality. Only with women, with sensitive female readers, he often found great understanding, love, and admiration, but pleasant though this was he always soon had enough of it. Inadequacy, starvation of soul, drove him on. Now as a teacher, now as a writer, he made his living during these years in Hof, in Leipzig, in Berlin, in Weimar, in Meiningen, in Coburg. Soon becoming famous, honored, and patronized even by princes, he enchanted enthusiasts and horrified ordinary citizens by the life-style of a true eccentric who carries his heart on his tongue, never asks about labels and suchlike trash, offers this neighbor his heart or steps on that neighbor's toes, depending on the whim of the moment. He has often been reproached for his failure to adapt to the world, as though this were a sin and a weakness. It might be worth remembering that for someone disenchanted with life, for a poet and idealist at odds with reality, it constituted a very considerable achievement to maintain his poor hungry person alone in the face of the world and to remain defiantly true to his manners or lack of them, let the chips fall where they might. And it was thus he continued to act all his days.

Jean Paul was already a famous poet when he became engaged to the daughter of a high official in Berlin and married her; he had long since written *Siebenkäs* and therefore should have known how love and marriage go for people whose heads are in the clouds. Nevertheless he did it, and the marriage turned out just as unhappy and was borne just as decently as was to be expected of him. And once more works were produced, greater, more inspired, mightier works: his two masterpieces, *Titan* and *Flegeljahre.* Here lies the unmistakable high point of his life. The zenith was already passed when in 1804 he settled in Bayreuth, where he was accustomed to shut himself up in the famous Rollwenzelei* with his writing materials and a keg of beer and try to forget in the ecstasy of thought and creativity what was out of joint with the world. And a great deal was out of joint; aside from a few friendships and his correspondence, this life had no reality; it fell into two halves, one spent in a creative transport at his writing table, with beer, and the other wearing a gray, commonplace, sort of Siebenkäs face. Jean Paul never succeeded in bringing the two together and for this reason he is severely criticized by those same schoolmasters who nevertheless acknowledge his writings as works of genius. But none of these works would have been written if Jean Paul had had the good fortune to get on more easily with the world and with himself. They arose from this division, this lack; the empty place between here and there is quite literally the source of his whole productivity. During the years in Bayreuth Jean Paul wrote many more books, innumerable articles, prefaces, book reviews, speeches, essays, aphorisms, among them much that is precious, but that great spring had dried up, or so it appeared, his gigantic lust to create had become a compulsion to produce and only toward the end did something of the old power flame up again splendidly in the novel *The Comet,* which, however, was never completed. Jean Paul died on November 14, 1825.

Much has been written about Jean Paul. He who was once loved in all Germany as was hardly any other poet continued to be influential until the early years of our own fathers and mothers, and in almost every biography until after the middle of the last century there is some acknowledgment to Jean Paul, an account of enchantment, magic, seduction, or of vocation and consecration through him.

Perhaps the finest things that were ever said about the poet come from another great German, who has also been for-

---

* The Rollwenzelei was a rustic inn outside Bayreuth, owned and managed by a certain Frau Rollwenzel, where for the last twenty years of his life Jean Paul sat in the garden or inside and wrote most of his later works. [Ed.]

gotten now, who likewise continues today to have a subterranean influence and like Jean Paul himself will some day rise again and become popular and beloved when a hundred of the great of today and yesterday will have faded from memory—Josef Görres. For him, as for all the readers of Jean Paul, the greatest impression was and remained that of profusion, of superabundant riches. Some of his sentences about the poet are so beautiful that it would be a pity not to quote them here:

"Silvery, glistening white and pure as snowflakes, the ideas penetrate into the blue of the heaven he reveals to us, and under this heaven the earth lies like the calm surface of a sea: and he reaches down into the clear wave like Jamblichus and draws forth out of the fountainhead of earthy material heavenly Amor in the guise of a noble, beautiful, altogether adorable boy. But the capricious element will not always deliver up its treasure so easily, often it seems troubled and confused to its depths; the tritons emerge playfully on the surface, the mermaids sing their roundelays, dolphins juggle and dance, all the monsters of the deep hurry to the summons of the witches' dance, the crafty, strange-looking legions of fishes, thousand-armed polyps, starfish, annulated worms, and the conches locked in their porcelain towers: and as the poet hovers howling above this confusion, the sea draws itself upward in a waterspout, up to the thunderclouds, and the strange folk move up and down in this meteor that resembles the apostle's sack which extended from heaven to earth with all the animals and plants, and well satisfied the creator of this uproar strides like the giant of the Apocalypse whose legs are two pillars and whose head is the sun." And in another place in the same essay, *Romanticism and Its Echo,* are these words: "His works resemble that Indian picture of Govinda in which the god is riding on an elephant composed of many girls intertwined, and the fans of these bajaders are peacocks' tails and their hair extends into writhing madhavis, whose tendrils embrace the colossus in the form of brightly colored serpents and the eyes of these serpents bloom again in the form of water lilies in whose calyxes cobras sway and bright flamingos gleam in the shadows, but girls, flowers, and birds in turn are constituted of butterfly wings and pollen, colored seashells, variegated gems, electric flashes, and glittering light, and yet all this is bound together by the hidden magnet of art into a self-enclosed and living whole."

The picture of the stormy ocean bottom rising with slime and seashells, the picture of that sack in which the apostle was offered clean and unclean animals, the image of that Hindu god in which the whole of creation surges in perpetually changing form, each form with eternally changing significance, ever altering, ever bringing forth itself, where being and appearance, form and essence, dying and being born, come to mean the same, one changing into the other— all these images are very familiar to us again today, they could be found with equal ease in some work of Impressionism or in some scientific work, perhaps by Jung or Silberer, and all these pictures mean what present-day psychology calls the unconscious. This is the secret of Jean Paul's wealth of vision, of his profusion, of his tropical proliferation: his communication with the unconscious was accomplished easily and playfully, he needed only to penetrate a thin membrane and he stood on the primeval ground of memories, where earliest childhood and the primitive world of men and planets were recorded, in the primeval ground which contains all history, out of which all religions, all arts, have emerged and constantly re-emerged. And, to put the matter plainly at once (for naturally every poet draws on the unconscious), Jean Paul not only possessed this happy faculty, this dexterity in the play of inspiration, this constant presence of the apparently forgotten, but he was aware of it, he had apprehended the secret of this source, he expressed ideas that are in conformity with the present-day conceptions of psychoanalysis, and he knew, cared for, and studied that many-colored bridge between the conscious and the unconscious, the dream, more than any other poet, with the possible exception of Dostoevsky. Jean Paul had a profound intuition of what we of today seek under new images and with new theories as happiness, as perfection, as harmony of soul: an intuition of the balance of psychological functions, of a peaceful and fruitful coexistence of knowledge and intuition, thought and feeling.

If we examine Jean Paul's reputation as a poet today we find: in the judgment of the better-read historians and scholars he is considered an original, highly gifted, but chaotic and unbearably sentimental writer. If you contradict this judgment you will be reminded of the oceans of tears wept in Jean Paul's books, of the tumult and misery he depicts in men's souls, of the maiden figures he has created, composed of cobwebs and moonlight, hypersensitive, moved to tears by nothing. All this is true. Jean Paul greatly loved tears and delicate feelings and he was prolific in soft, sweet, noble, fairylike, tender female figures—but above all he loved the opposite, created the opposite. He created characters that are like aeolian harps, soft, passive, perpetually melting into emotion, and beside them he placed other characters of a hardness, coldness, harsh manliness, contempt for the world, and inner loneliness such as are to be found in few poets. And so Jean Paul is not sentimental? On the contrary, of course he is sentimental, and very likely he was unacquainted with that cowardly timidity of the younger writers of today at the signs of emotion, at the appearance of sensitivity! But he is also the opposite of sentimental, he is also a thinker, a scoffer, he is also a lonely Prometheus, aware of the impossibility of true understanding between human beings, enclosed in lonely greatness, cold and crushingly severe.

For Jean Paul is not an intellectual or an emotionalist, a thinker or an intuitive or a sensitive—he is all of these, just as every person has within him each of these potentialities. Jean Paul is the perfect example of a genius who has not cultivated a single specialty but whose ideal is the free play of all the powers of the soul, who would like to say yes to everything, enjoy everything to the full, love and experience everything. So we see the poet in each of his works (aside from a few small idyls such as *Wuz* or *Fibel*) unceasingly running back and forth between hot and cold, between hard and soft, between all the hundred poles and antipoles of his existence; and the hithering and thithering, the electrical discharge between all these poles is quite literally the life of his creations.

Now this recognition of Jean Paul's versatility seems to be a contradiction of what I said above about his lack of adaptation to the real world. I said above that he was a poor and constantly disillusioned enthusiast and now I say to the contrary that he was a quite uncommonly free spirit dancing lightly amid all the opposites. The contradiction between these two views is precisely the contradiction between poetry and life. Had Jean Paul been the person in life that he was as a poet, had he been able to master and apply in life the profound insights and deep knowledge of the innermost secret of living that he possessed as a poet, he would have been a model man, an exemplary person, an eminently happy individual, a son of the gods. But presumably then we would not have known about any of this, for then he would have had no reason to undertake the labor of all these complicated and extended works.

What Jean Paul could not do in life—acknowledge the opposites, say yes to everything, to dreams and also to the commonplace—this he attempted in his writing and progressed further in that direction than most German authors. In the process he became a great humorist, and his humor rests in no small part on the secret knowledge of himself, on his tacit recognition of the poet's own weaknesses, who is a lord god in his study, in daily life, however, a poor, nervous, distracted human being. The final realization that was perhaps possible on this path, the realization of the Self in the I, of the supratemporal in the temporal I, he nowhere expressed clearly in words, but as an intuition it is everywhere present in his works.

Our time, even though the guardians of the civil order would desperately deny it, stands under the sign of chaos. The "decline of the West" is actually taking place, only not in so crassly theatrical a fashion as the philistine imagines. It is taking place because every individual, insofar as he does not belong to the dying world, finds a chaos within himself, a world unregulated by any table of the laws, in which good and evil, beautiful and ugly, bright and dark are no longer separate. To separate them afresh, to divide them again, is the business of each individual. This is the reason that in the art and poetry of our day chaos and demiurge keep reappearing, for chaos requires to be acknowledged, demands to be experienced, before it can be incorporated into a new order.

It is therefore precisely for this period that Jean Paul has actually for the first time become wholly comprehensible. He to whom the thought of the polarity in all fields was so profoundly familiar has uncommon much to say to us today. He will not and should not be a "leader" for us, but a confirmer and also a comforter, for no poet preaches to us so penetratingly the fact that "the most important thing for the poet, love," suffers no diminution through the recognition of the opposites, that harmony between the divergent powers of the soul is a living and life-giving goal.

Exotic Art

1922

FROM THE END of the seventeenth century onward when
Chinese art, especially porcelain and embroidery, reached
France, it immediately became fashionable and was friv-
olously exploited in the contemporary "chinoiserie" of
eighteenth-century Europe. About the middle of the nineteenth century there came, this time from Japan, a new wave
of Asiatic art, also by way of Paris, whence it spread. In both
cases these were products of a late, already mannered, classical art and were precisely the kind of exoticism that, because
of its remoteness from nature and a certain world weariness,
was sure to appear least bizarre in Europe. The strikingly
receptive attitude of the Impressionist movement toward
Japanese woodcuts and printed cloth is of course well known.
The other arts of the Eastern countries did not exist for
Europe, at least not as art, but at best as ethnographic
specialties.

Since then, and with greatly accelerated tempo in the last
ten years, the exotics have been achieving influence in
Europe. Hardly had a new enthusiasm for Egypt on the part
of artists and amateurs reached its height, hardly had the
highly evolved sculptures of China, India, Siam, Java become
to some degree known among us when a new wave broke
over us: the genuine, wildly exotic African sculpture, the
wood carving and basket weaving from Oceania; the dancing
masks and the idols, the primitive erotic sculptures of African
tribes, the age-old demon figures of China have become
significant and important to us.

The victorious eruption (a splendid one cordially welcomed
by me) of painted skulls, hair-ornamented death masks, the
frightful chimeras of primitive people and times, into the

quiet, tepid, often boring temples of European art objects and philosophies of art, is visible proof of European decline—not, to be sure, the decline that the bourgeois newspaper reader pictures to himself when he becomes incensed at Spengler, but of that natural, healthy decline that is simultaneously the beginning of rebirth—the kind of decline that is nothing but the weariness of overspecialized functions of the soul in the individual, as it is in nations, and a first unconscious striving for the opposite pole. In times when such an atmosphere of collapse prevails, strange gods always emerge—and appear more like devils. What was formerly reasonable becomes senseless, what was formerly absurd becomes positive and hopeful, all distinctions and evaluations appear to be wiped out, the demiurge emerges, who is neither good nor evil, neither god nor devil, but simply creator and destroyer, the blind primeval force. This moment of apparent collapse is similar to the one that happens to an individual—a cataclysmic experience, a miracle, a conversion. It is a head-on encounter with paradox, the blazing instant when opposite poles touch, when boundaries fall, when standards melt. The process under certain circumstances makes morals and order disappear. The phenomenon itself, however, is the most enhancing that can be imagined.

This is how I feel about the incursion of exotic art from Brazil, from Benin, from New Caledonia, from New Guinea. It shows Europe its antitype, it exhales beginnings and fierce virility, it smells of jungles and crocodiles. It leads back to stages of life, to conditions of soul, that we Europeans apparently outgrew long ago. We will not re-enter them at the stage of the people of Oceania. But we will be inexorably forced to take up once more these devils and idols, not with our understanding and our sciences, but with our blood and hearts. What we in our art, our intellectuality and religions have won, cultivated, refined, and finally made so thin and tenuous—all our ideals, all our tastes—through them we have nourished one side of mankind at the expense of the other side, we have served a god of light and thereby denied the forces of darkness. And just as Goethe in his theory of colors celebrated darkness not as a nullity but as the creative antipole of light, so the artists and intellectuals of Europe now stand in astonishment (only not with Goethe's awareness) in front of the sculptures from Borneo and Peru and are forced to acknowledge, yes, to revere, what a short time ago were only horrors and specters. And suddenly one recalls how the men who were most potent in art in latter-day Europe, Dostoevsky and Van Gogh, possessed to an uncanny degree this wild fanatical trait, this smell of the forbidden, this kinship with crime.

We have long since started on the path; no majority decisions will roll back the wheel. Faust's path to the "Mothers." It is not convenient, it is not attractive. But it is necessary.

On Hölderlin

1924

A HUNDRED YEARS AGO lived a German poet who steadily attracted to himself the best of idealist youth, became their secret favorite and king, but was never much known to the many—Hölderlin. His work, a small volume of poems, in part of powerful hymnic rhythms, in part of tenderest lyrical reverie, sounded strangely beautiful, exciting, and tragic when considered together with his life. After a brief blazing youth, he lost himself in confusion, madness, and a suprapersonal, mythic realm. He was the prototype of the poet chosen by God and stricken by God, blazing up in superhuman purity, full of nobility and agonizing beauty, but he was also the prototype of a poet destined to suffer shipwreck in "normal life" and to leave the memory of a brief, brilliant blossoming of the spirit such as customarily occurs only in those who die young.

And now in the last few years this Hölderlin has been rediscovered by German youth. His warning cry to Germans has gained new and greater significance, and once more the star of this beautiful stranger shines forth brightly, in a time and atmosphere, to be sure, in which enthusiasm easily turns into a vogue. There actually was a Hölderlin vogue, and today this by no means easily accessible poet's books lie on many ladies' coffee tables next to Buddha's sermons and the pamphlets of Tagore. This vogue, which is already past its peak, had one good result: the philologists and publishers too have become interested in Hölderlin, so that now good and handsome editions of his works and letters are available. Two new Hölderlin editions must be mentioned here with appreciation: the five-volume edition which Zinkernagle is editing for the Insel

Verlag and which will soon be completed, and another in four handy volumes from the Lichtenstein Verlag in Weimar.

Even if Hölderlin, as I believe, is not wholly understood by those who in recent years have hoisted him rather noisily upon their shields, nevertheless it was no accident that he was remembered just at this time in the confused, eschatological mood of conquered Germany. It was not only the ecstasy of his flaming hymns, which in that revolutionary time incidentally acquired some qualities of a manifesto; it was above all the person of the poet, the air of noble idealism and exalted transcendence that produced so deep an effect in this period of profound corruption and hopeless commitment to material ends. For Hölderlin is not only a poet and his work and being are not identical with his written creations. He is more than that, he is the representative of a heroic type.

One of his very remarkable essays contains a thought in which the poet seems to have had an intuition of his own fate and to have recognized his own profoundest being. He says: "What is most important is that superior people should not cut themselves off too completely from what is inferior, nor the beautiful from the barbaric, but also they should not mix too much with either, they should recognize clearly and dispassionately the distance between themselves and others and out of this recognition work and endure. If they isolate themselves too completely, their effectiveness is lost and they perish in their loneliness." Here Hölderlin, who truly belonged among "the beautiful," had a profound insight. This sentence about distance and the need for it should not be taken as saying only that the nobler man must not isolate himself too rigorously from his more common fellow men. The sentence really shows its profundity only if we understand it from the inside as a demand that the noble person know how to recognize and tolerate not only what is common and naturally naïve in the outside world but also in his own soul. With this interpretation we are certainly not doing violence to Hölderlin's thought, for he was aware of the problem all his life and many times spoke about it; he recognized his danger, his one-sided membership in the class of the "sentimentalists," as Schiller puts it, and he suffered constantly from his lack of naïveté.

Translated into the vocabulary of present-day psychology, Hölderlin's demand would therefore run something like this: the noble person must not subject his instinctual nature too one-sidedly to the demands of the instinct-hating spirit, for every particle of our instinctual life that is not successfully sublimated brings us severe suffering by way of "repression." This was Hölderlin's personal problem, and he succumbed to it. He cultivated in himself a spirituality that did violence to his nature; his ideal was to put everything vulgar behind him, but he did not have the astounding tenacity of a Schiller, who in quite similar circumstances gave the clearest possible example of spiritual discipline of the will and thereby completely consumed and expended himself. "Sentimental" through and through like Schiller, his devotee and follower Hölderlin wore himself out with the demands he put upon himself; he struggled to be an example of spiritualization, and the attempt miscarried. And if we examine Hölderlin's poetry we find that precisely that Schilleresque spirituality, nobly though it became him, at bottom was imposed upon Hölderlin's real characters. For what we honor in his splendid poetry as unique and inimitable is neither its conscious mastery, lofty though that is, nor the "content" in ideas, but rather the completely original groundswell of music, of rhythmic and auditory mystery, often almost hidden by the influence of Schiller. This marvelous, mysterious, creative groundswell in many of Hölderlin's poems emanating from the unconscious is entirely at odds with his consciously cultivated ideal of the poet, and it was through the violence done to this secret and holy creative force that he came to grief. In a noble effort but at the expense of the profoundest values of his being, Hölderlin under Schiller's influence almost evolved into an intellectual.

These thoughts about the poet's individual psychology do not, however, fully explain Hölderlin's problem. His fate is above all a hero's fate, and such fates are supra-individual.

This is the reason we often see greatly gifted individuals come to grief from obstacles that lesser persons surmount with ease, and it is also the reason why the wholesome average intelligence has no difficulty in explaining gifted individuals as psychopaths either with or without the cooperation of psychoanalysis. To be sure, those heroes are among other things psychopaths. But far more important than this, they are heroes, they are humanity's honorable and hazardous attempts to ennoble itself, and their fate is shrouded in a heroic, tragic atmosphere even if the hero does not chance to meet a terrifying end. It was Hölderlin's lot to represent the tragic fate of the gifted man in thought-provoking fashion. The tragedy that runs with no less force through Schiller's life, for instance, in Hölderlin's case finds incredibly clear, incredibly moving expression. This distinguishes him, as real hero, in anyone's feelings, from all those poets whose being and image seem expressed for us completely in their works.

Postscript to *Novalis, Documents on His Life and Death** 1924

AMONG THE LIFE STORIES of remarkable men of intellect the ones that have always aroused the deepest interest in later generations have been those which clearly expressed the fact that genius is not simply a matter of intellectual development but at the same time and principally a biological matter. In modern German intellectual history the noblest figures of this sort are Hölderlin, Novalis, and Nietzsche. While Hölderlin and Nietzsche, after life had become impossible for them, withdrew into madness, Novalis withdrew into death, and not into the form of it that intrudes so often in the case of genius, suicide; rather he died by consciously consuming himself from within, a magical, early blossoming followed by an enormously fruitful death. —It is precisely from this strange end of the poet, from his positive, magical, extraordinary relationship to death, that his strongest influence radiates. And this influence is far deeper than the surface of our intellectual life permits us to imagine. In his own time Novalis was understood by only a few, and even later, yes, even today, his readers have been small in number. But every serious reader has caught fire from that marvelous, almost dangerously animated spirit, from the blazing intensity of that life. Intimate acquaintance with Novalis means for any perceptive spirit a deep and magical experience, that is,

* The book in question, *Novalis, Documents on His Life and Death*, appeared in 1925 in the series "Remarkable Stories and Persons," edited by Hesse for S. Fischer Verlag, Berlin.

the experience of initiation, of consecration into mystery. When I spoke of genius as a biological matter, I meant that the genius, the outstanding individual in his most successful form, almost always has a tragic life and moves in the pale light of imminent destruction—which has nothing to do with the philistine bourgeois theory that genius is always closely related to madness. No, genius, life intensified to the highest degree, so easily and quickly changes into an antipole, into death or madness, because in it human existence recognizes itself as a frightful mishap, as a great and daring but not wholly successful cast of nature. Genius, incontrovertibly recognized as the most desirable and noble fruit on the tree of man, is not in any wise protected by biological mechanisms, not to say propagated. It enters the world in the midst of a life for which it becomes guiding star and goal of desire, while at the same time it must suffer suffocation from that life. Such is the meaning of all those thousand stories and legends of genius early dead, of the gods' favorite prematurely snatched away.

This book brings us selected documents about the life and death of the poet Novalis, whose real name was Friedrich von Hardenberg. When we read of the early death of Novalis in the memoirs of the poet Tieck and the simple, touching recollections of Magistrate Just, we find in these reports the profound resonance of a great mysterious, holy experience. These men, Tieck and Just, felt that they had living and dying beside them a man who in many respects did not seem like themselves but at times rather like an angel of God and at other times like a specter. In any case, it was as if Novalis was a man destined to a remarkable fate.

Friedrich von Hardenberg was born in 1772 on his family estate and died in 1801. His bride had died a few years before at the age of fifteen, after which the idea of following her in death had become a cherished thought. He died of consumption, but what is the significance of that? Others have died at an early age from consumption, Novalis's own siblings suffered that fate, but only from Novalis, only from his grave, radiates that magic attraction; only he, instead of suffering death, entered into it like a banished king returning to his palace out of the grayness of a foreign land.

He left behind the most marvelous and mysterious work in the intellectual history of Germany. Just as his short, externally uneventful life strangely gives the impression of great abundance and seems to have exhausted every sensuous and every spiritual experience, so the runes of his work reveal beneath the playful, enchantingly flowery surface all the abysses of the spirit, apotheosis through the spirit, and despair of the spirit. Novalis lived out his fate consciously and trustingly, aware of its tragic aspect and yet superior to it, since a creative piety allowed him to hold death of small account.

His poetry remains, still read by only a few, still signifying to those few a gate into the realm of magic, yes, almost the gift of a new dimension. Some of his poems have actually become popular and even today at times are sung on Sundays by the congregations of Protestant churches. For through Schleiermacher some of Novalis's religious poems have found their way into church hymnals, and many a minister unsuspectingly delivers his official Sunday sermon hard by the perilous glow of those verses.

In addition to his poetry there remains the touching and rousing legend of his life as it affected a few of his friends. The purpose of the present book is to provide a good selection of the genuine documents concerning that life.

About Dostoevsky

1925

ABOUT DOSTOEVSKY there is nothing new to be said. Anything clever and appropriate that was to be said has been said long ago; new and witty in its time, it has now grown stale, whereas the well-loved and terrifying figure of the author seems constantly wrapped in fresh mystery and enigmas when we turn to him in an hour of need or contemplation.

The average person reclining on his couch and reading about Raskolnikov to derive an agreeable shudder from this world of specters is not the true reader of this author, no more than is the scholar and intellectual who admires the psychology in Dostoevsky's novels and writes praiseworthy monographs about his *Weltanschauung*. The time to read Dostoevsky is when we are miserable, when we have suffered to the limits of our capacity for suffering and feel the entirety of life as a single searing wound, when we breathe despair and have died the death of hopelessness. Staring from afar into life, bereft and crippled by misery and no longer able to understand life in its wild, beautiful cruelty, wishing to have no more to do with it, then we are open to the music of this terrifying and magnificent writer. Then we are no longer onlookers, no longer epicures and judges; we are fellow creatures among all the poor devils of Dostoevsky's creation, then we suffer their woes, and we stare fascinated and breathless with them into the hurly-burly of life, into the eternally grinding mill of death. But at the same time we can also catch Dostoevsky's music, his comfort, his love, and then we can first experience the marvelous meaning of his terrifying and so often hellish world.

In Dostoevsky's fictional works two forces grip us. Out of

the alternation and opposition of two elements and antipoles there grow the mythic depths and vast spaciousness of his music.

The one is despair, the suffering of evil, submission and nonresistance to the cruel, bloody harshness and ambiguity of all human existence. This death must be died, this hell must be traversed before the other, the heavenly voice of the master, can really reach us. The candor and bluntness of the admission that our existence and humanity are a miserable, doubtful, and perhaps hopeless affair—that is the prerequisite. We must give ourselves up to suffering, surrender to death, our eyeballs must congeal at the unconcealed, hellish grin of naked reality before we can perceive the depth and truth of that second, that other voice.

The first voice affirms death, denies hope, forgoes all the intellectual and poetic forbearance and reassurance with which we are accustomed to allow agreeable poets to soothe and deceive us about the danger and horror of human existence. But the second voice, the truly heavenly second voice of this writer, shows us on its other heavenly side a different element from death, a different reality, a different essence: the conscience of man. Let human life be all war and suffering, baseness and horror—in addition to that there is something else: man's conscience, his ability to put himself in opposition to God. There is no doubt that conscience leads us through suffering and fear of death to misery and guilt, but it also guides us out of unbearably lonely meaninglessness and into relationship with significance, with essence, with the eternal. Conscience has nothing to do with morality, nothing to do with laws, it can, in fact, come into desperate and deadly opposition to them, but it is incredibly strong, it is stronger than inertia, stronger than self-interest, stronger than vanity. To one in the deepest misery, in the last degree of confusion, it can always show a narrow path open, not back into this world dedicated to death but over and away from it to God. Hard is the road that leads man to his conscience. Almost all people all the time live counter to this conscience, they resist it, they are weighed down more and more heavily until they are destroyed by a suffocated conscience. But for everyone, at every moment, beyond suffering and despair lies open the calm road that makes life meaningful and death easy. Some people have to rage and sin against conscience until they have experienced all the hells and soiled themselves with all the horrors in order finally, sighing with relief, to recognize their error and experience the hour of transformation. Others live in perfect friendship with their consciences, rare, happy, and holy men, and whatever happens to them touches them only on the outside, never reaching their hearts. They remain always pure, the smile does not vanish from their faces. Such a one is Prince Myshkin.

These two voices, these two teachings, have I heard from Dostoevsky at those times when I was a good reader of his books, in those hours when despair and sorrow had prepared me. There is a musician I feel that same way about, whom I do not love at all times or always wish to listen to, just as I by no means always like to read Dostoevsky. It is Beethoven. He possesses the same knowledge of happiness, wisdom, and harmony, which are not, however, to be found along smooth roads, but rise resplendent only along paths close to the abyss. One does not grasp them smilingly but only with tears and in exhaustion and sorrow. In Beethoven's symphonies and quartets there are places where out of pure misery and lostness something infinitely touching, childlike, and tender blazes up, an intimation of meaning and knowledge about salvation. This is the kind of experience I find in Dostoevsky as well.

Our Age's Yearning
for a Philosophy of Life
1926-27

WITHIN THE LAST FEW DECADES, since the complete triumph of industrialization, the image of our earth's surface has been entirely altered and rearranged; every city and landscape in the world has suffered monstrous change; and a corresponding revolution has swept the souls and minds of men. In the years since the outbreak of the world war this development has been so rapid that today one can without exaggeration announce the death and destruction of that culture in which we older people were educated as children and which seemed to us at that time eternal and immutable. If physical man has not changed (something he is as little able to do within two generations as any other species of animal), nevertheless the ideals and fictions, the dreams and wishful thoughts, the mythologies and theories that dominate our spiritual life have been transformed completely. Things by nature irreplaceable have been lost and destroyed forever; unimaginable novelties are dreamed up in their place. Demolished and lost for the larger part of the civilized world are, above all, the two foundations of all orderly living: culture and ethics, religion and morality. Our lives are entirely lacking in propriety; there is no longer the traditional, established, unwritten agreement about what is proper and decent behavior between human beings.

A short trip in any direction will let you observe living examples of the decay of morality. But in those areas where industrialization is still in its early stages, where the tradition of the peasant and the townsman is still stronger than that of the modern businessman and factory worker, the influence and power of the churches still quite perceptibly have the upper hand, and in all such places we encounter more or less unchanged what used to be called tradition. In these "retarded" regions you still find the forms of intercourse, of greeting, of conversation, of social order, of festivals and games which have long since disappeared from modern life. As a feeble substitute for these lost traditions, what does our typical modern man have? He has fashion. Changing from season to season, fashion gives him the indispensable precepts for social life, tosses him the necessary stylish expressions, catchwords, dances, tunes—better than nothing, but nevertheless ephemeral, perishable, valueless. There are folkplays no longer, but instead the seasons' stylish entertainments; no folksongs any more, but last month's smash hit tune.

Now what custom does to cheer the outer forms of our lives, making easy our conduct according to tradition and convention, this for the deeper human needs is performed by religion and philosophy. In matters of usage and custom, in dress and conversation, in the worlds of sport and society, man does require a valid model formed by some ideal—be it only one day's ideal of a style—but these are not the only matters in which he requires guidance. In the deeper layers of his being he also needs to see some significance in what he is doing and striving for, some sense to his life and some meaning in his death. This religious or metaphysical need, as old and as important as the need for food, shelter, for love, is satisfied in quiet, culturally solid times by the Church and by the systematic philosophers. In times like the present, we see in general an impatience and disillusionment not only with the inherited religions but also with the academic philosophies; there is a huge demand for new formulations, new attributions of significance, new symbols, new foundations. The spiritual life of our time is characterized by the weakening of inherited systems, the frantic search for new interpretations of human life, the flowering of countless popular sects, prophets, and founders of congregations, the rank growth of the wildest superstitions. For even the least spiritual man, the most superficial, the most averse to thought, still has that primal need to recognize some meaning in his life, and when he no longer finds any, morality disappears and private life is characterized by wildly heightened egotism and profound fear of death. All these signs of the times are clearly to be read by anyone with eyes, in every sanitarium, in every madhouse, in the material that every day brings to every psychoanalyst.

But all life is a seamless fabric of ups and downs, decline and rebuilding, destruction and resurrection. And so in opposition to all the sinister and lamentable signs of the collapse of our culture, there are other more cheerful indications of a newly awakened metaphysical need, of the formation of a new spirituality, of a passionate struggle for a new interpretation of the meaning of our lives. Modern poetry is full of these signs, and modern art no less. Especially keenly felt is the need for a substitute for the disappearing cultural values, for new forms of religion and society. Naturally enough, there is no lack of tasteless and absurd substitutes, not to mention bad and dangerous ones. Seers and promoters abound, charlatans and quacks are taken for holy men, vanity and greed flourish in this new and promising domain—but these sad or laughable side effects must not deceive us. In itself this awakening of the soul, this wild flaring up of a new yearning for God, this fever stirred up by the war and privation is a phenomenon of marvelous power and passion that we cannot take seriously enough. The fact that around this mighty psychic tide of longing that is sweeping all nations there lurks a crowd of busy entrepreneurs, who make a trade of religion, must not mislead us about the greatness, value, and importance of the movement. In a thousand forms and gradations, from naïve belief in ghosts to genuine philosophical speculation, from primitive revivalist substitutes for religion to intimations of a true reinterpretation of life, the mighty tide sweeps over the earth, embracing American Christian Science and English theosophy, Mazdaism and the new Sufism, Steiner's anthroposophy and a hundred similar sects; it leads Count Keyserling around the world and to his experi-

ments in Darmstadt, brings to him as collaborator so serious
and important a fellow worker as Richard Wilhelm, at the
same time permits the rise of a whole army of necromancers,
sharpers, and buffoons. I do not venture to draw a line between what is still open to debate and what is obviously
completely grotesque. But alongside the founders of the always questionable modern secret societies, lodges, and
brotherhoods, the undismayed shallowness of American
fashionable religions, the credulity of determined spiritualists,
there are to be found other higher and even very high phenomena, marvelous achievements such as the Neumann translation and distribution of the sacred Buddhist texts, Richard
Wilhelm's translation of the great Chinese writers, the sudden,
splendid return of Lao-tse, who, unknown in Europe for
centuries, has appeared within three decades, in many translations into almost all European languages, and has taken
possession of European thought. Just as in the irritating confusion of the remarkable German revolution a few pure,
noble, unforgettable figures emerge, such as Landauer and
Rosa Luxemburg, so we can discern in the wild turbulent
flood of modern religious experimentation a number of noble
characters, theologians like the Swiss preacher Ragaz, figures
like Frederik van Eeden, a late convert to Catholicism, men
like Hugo Ball, unique in Germany, once a dramatist and one
of the founders of Dadaism, then a firm opponent of the war
and critic of the German war mentality, then a hermit and
author of the wonderful book *Byzantine Christianity*. And,
not to neglect the Jews, Martin Buber, who is showing modern
Judaism profounder goals and in his books has given back to
us again the piety of the Hasidim, one of the loveliest flowers
in the garden of religions.

"And now," many readers will ask, "where does all this
lead? What will the result be, the ultimate outcome? What
can we expect from it for the average person? Is it at all
likely that one of the new sects will become a world religion?
Will one of the new thinkers prove capable of constructing a
new philosophy on the grand scale?"

In many circles today these questions are answered in the

affirmative. In many followers of the new teachings, especially among the young, there is a cheerful, youthful air of victory, as though our epoch were destined to give birth to the Savior, to provide the world with new certainties for a new cultural period, new faiths, new moral orientations. That black destructive mood of many of the older dillusioned critics serves as antipole to this youthful credulity of the newly converted. And yet these young voices are pleasanter to listen to than those moody old ones—though the new believers could be in error.

It is only proper to greet with respect the will of our time, this powerful searching, these partly passionate and blind, partly thoughtful and audacious experiments. Should all of them be condemned to failure, they are nevertheless a serious striving toward the highest goals, and though none of them should last very long, nevertheless they fulfill for this time an indispensable task. They help, all these fictions, these religious structures, these new faiths—they help people live, they help them not only to endure this difficult uncertain existence but to value it highly and to sanctify it; and if they were no more than an ennobling stimulant or a sweet illusion, even so it would be no trifling matter. But they are more, infinitely more. They are the school through which the intellectual elite of this time must pass, for two tasks are required of every spirituality and culture: to give assurance and encouragement to the many, to comfort them, to bestow a meaning on their lives—and the second, more secret, no less important task is to make it possible for the few, the great spirits of tomorrow and the day after, to grow up, to provide their beginnings with protection and nourishment, to give them air to breathe. The spirituality of our time differs enormously from the one that we older people received as our inheritance. It is more chaotic, wilder, poorer in tradition, less well schooled, less methodical—but, all in all, this present-day spirituality, together with its strong tendency toward mysticism, is by no means worse than the more polite, better educated, traditionally richer but no stronger spirituality of that period in which obsolete liberalism and youthful monism were the predominating trends. For my own part, I must confess, the spirituality of the leading movements of today, from Steiner to Keyserling, is still a few degrees too rational, too lacking in daring, too unwilling to descend into chaos, into the underworld, and there give ear to Faust's "Mothers" and learn from them the longed-for secret doctrine of a new humanity. None of today's leaders, however clever and enthusiastic they may be, has the scope and profundity of Nietzsche, whose true heirs we have not yet shown ourselves capable of being. The thousand conflicting voices and paths of our time have, however, something valuable in common: an eager longing, a will to devotion, born of misery. And these are the prerequisites of everything great.

A Night's Work

1928*

THAT SATURDAY EVENING was important to me. I had lost several evenings during the week, two to music, one for friends, one through illness, and loss of an evening usually means the loss of a day's work for me, since I work best during the late hours. A long piece of writing I had been living with for almost two years had recently reached the stage where a book's essential significance is at stake. I well remember the time a few years ago (it was the same season of the year) when *Steppenwolf* was in just this dangerous and suspenseful state. In the art of writing as I practice it, there is no such thing as a really rational way of working, relying on will power and diligence. For me a novel begins to take shape at the moment I see a figure forming, one that can for a while be the symbol and bearer of my experiences, my thoughts, my problems. The appearance of this mythical person (Peter Camenzind, Knulp, Demian, Siddhartha, Harry Haller, etc.) is the creative instant out of which everything else emerges. Almost all the prose works of fiction I have written are biographies of souls; in all of them the center of interest was not in plot, complications, and suspense, but rather they are essentially monologues; that mythical figure, a single person, is examined in his relationship to the world and to himself. These works of fiction are called "novels." As a matter of fact, they are not novels at all, any more than their great models, holy in my eyes since my youth, Novalis's *Heinrich von Ofterdingen*, for example, or Hölderlin's *Hyperion*, are novels.

And so once more I lived through the brief, beautiful, dif-

---

* December 2, 1928, during the writing of *Narcissus and Goldmund*.

ficult, and exciting time in which a narrative passes its crisis, the time in which all the thoughts and moods that have a bearing on the "mythical" figure stand before me with the greatest sharpness, clarity, and urgency. The total material, the total mass of what has been experienced and thought, to which the emerging book is struggling to give form at this time (and the time does not last long!) is in a state of flux, of fusibility—now or never must the matter be seized and shaped, otherwise it is too late. With each of my books there has been such a time, even those that were never finished and published. With the latter I missed the harvest time, and suddenly a moment came when the figure and the problem of my narrative began to withdraw and to lose urgency and import, just as today *Camenzind, Knulp, Demian* no longer have any actuality for me. In this way on several occasions the work of many months has been lost to me and had to be thrown away.

Now this Saturday evening belonged to me and my work, and I had spent the greater part of the day preparing myself for it. Toward eight o'clock I got my supper out of the cool neighboring room, a jar of yogurt and a banana, then seated myself with my little desk lamp and picked up my pen.

I did not do so gladly, however necessary it might be. Since day before yesterday I had not looked forward to today's working hours, had, in fact, feared them. For my story concerning Goldmund stood at a ticklish point, almost the only place in the book where the events themselves hold the stage, where suspense is high. I feel the greatest repugnance for "exciting" events, especially in my own books; I have always avoided them so far as possible. This one, however, could not be sidestepped: Goldmund's experience that I now had to relate was not invented or unnecessary but belonged to the original and most important inspiration from which the figure of Goldmund had taken shape; it belonged to his substance.

For three hours I sat at my desk and tortured myself with *one* "exciting" page, trying to write it as simply, briefly, and unexcitingly as possible. I do not know whether I succeeded; often one can only see that much later. Then, very exhausted .

and downcast, I sat for a long time in front of the page I had covered with scribbles, tormented by familiar and inconclusive trains of thought. Were these nights of writing, this slow creation of a character that had begun as a vision almost two years ago—was this desperate, gratifying, irritating work really meaningful and worthwhile? Was it necessary that Camenzind, Knulp, Veraguth, Klingsor, and Steppenwolf should now be followed by another character, a new incarnation, a somewhat differently blended and variegated verbal incarnation of my own being?

This that I was doing, and have been doing all my life, was called in earlier times composing, and no one doubted that it was at least as valuable and made as much sense as traveling in Africa or playing tennis. Today, however, it is called "romanticism" with an unmistakable note of derogation. Why should romanticism be something inferior? Had not romanticism engaged the best minds of Germany—Novalis, Hölderlin, Brentano, Mörike, and all the German musicians from Beethoven through Schubert to Hugo Wolf? Many modern poets even use the silly though ironically intended description "Biedermeier" for what was once called poetry and then romanticism. By this they mean something "bourgeois," something very outmoded, elaborately and complicatedly sentimental, something that in our own splendid days appears stupid and fatuous, an occasion for laughter. They speak this way of everything that rises above the present-day level of mind and soul. As though the spiritual life of Germany and Europe for a century, as though the yearning and vision of Schlegel, Schopenhauer, and Nietzsche, the dream of Schumann and Weber, the poetry of Eichendorff and Stifter, had been passé, an outmoded fashion for us to jeer at, and happily long since extinct! But this dream had nothing to do with fashions, with charm and stylistic bagatelles, it was an examination of two thousand years of Christianity, of a thousand years of Germanism, and it had to do with the concept of mankind. Why was this today so little regarded, why was it considered ridiculous by the upper classes of our nation? Why were millions appropriated for physical fitness and also considerable sums for the routine training of our minds, and nothing left but impatience or laughter for any attempt at the education of our souls?

Was that mind from which the saying had come: "What shall it profit a man, if he shall gain the whole world, and lose his own soul?"—was that mind really romantic or even "Biedermeier"? Was it really obsolete, rejected, supplanted by something better, done for, and rendered laughable? Was "present-day life" in the factories, in stock exchanges, in stadiums and betting parlors, in big-city bars and dance halls, was this life really any better, richer, more intellectual, more desirable than the life of the people who had made the Bhagavad-Gita or the Gothic cathedrals? Certainly today's life and today's fashions have a right to exist, they are good, they mean change and an attempt at something new—but is it really proper and necessary to regard everything that has gone before, from Jesus Christ to Schubert and Corot, as stupid, old-fashioned, superseded, and ludicrous? Was this boisterous, wild, unbridled hatred for all and everything that preceded it really a proof of the strength of this new time? Was it not the deeply compromised, the fearful, who inclined to such exaggerated defensive measures?

And now for a night hour I allowed these questions once more to flood into my mind, not in order to answer them, for I have known the answer all my life long—rather in order to absorb their pain into myself and to taste once more their bitter savor. During this time I saw Knulp, Siddhartha, Steppenwolf, and Goldmund in front of me, my very brothers, my close kin, and yet not repetitions, all of them questioners and sufferers, and for me nevertheless the best that life has brought. I saluted them and accepted them and I knew once more that the ambiguity of my behavior would never deter me from going on with it. I realized once again that all the luck of the fortunate, all the records and all the health of sportsmen, all the money of financiers, all the celebrity of boxers would mean nothing to me if I had sacrificed for it even the tiniest part of my obstinacy and my passion. I also realized that the historical and intellectual bases for the worth of my "romantic" efforts did not matter at all, and that indeed I would go on playing my games and creating my figures even though all reason, all morality, and all wisdom spoke against them.

With this certainty I went to bed, strong as a giant.

A Virtuoso's Concert

1929

LAST NIGHT I attended a concert that was essentially different from the concerts I usually go to. It was a performance by a world-famous and fashionable violinist, that is, not only a musical event but also a sporting event, and most of all a social event. And so this concert turned out to be quite dissimilar to those in which music is the exclusive interest.

The program, to be sure, promised for the most part real music; it could almost have been the program of an ordinary musician. Beautiful pieces like the *Kreutzer* Sonata, Bach's *Chaconne*, Tartini's sonata with the devil's trill took up two-thirds of the concert. Then, however, toward the end, the program changed to compositions with pretty, promising titles, moonlight fantasies, and Venetian nights, by unknown composers whose names indicated nationalities that have not hitherto been conspicuous in music. In short, the third part of the program was strongly reminiscent of those you find displayed in the music pavilions at elegant spas. And the last several pieces had been composed by the great virtuoso himself.

I set out for this event full of curiosity. I had heard Sarasate and Joachim play the violin and in spite of a few misgivings had been enchanted by their playing. Of course, real music-making was something different, something completely different; it had nothing to do with virtuosity, and it demanded anonymity and piety in order to blossom. But on the other hand, ever since Paganini's time, the virtuosi had had for everyone, and for me too, the enchantment of the juggler and adept, that magic of the artistic Bohemian life. I too at the age of twelve, shortly after I had been given my first violin, had dreamed the dream of virtuosity, had in imagination stood before overflow crowds in huge concert halls, had made ten thousand happy with a smile, been greeted by emperors and decorated with gold medals, had traveled, lonely, famous, and homeless, from city to city, from one quarter of the world to another, beloved by women, envied by the public, a gifted and grateful dancer on the high wire of expertise and world fame. And so all this still went on; today once more, young boys would gaze with eyes aflame at the dazzling performer, teen-age girls would sigh, the galleries would thunder with applause. Good enough, I was pleased at this and expectant. And in fact it was all very fine.

Long before I had even reached the concert hall it was clear to me from many signs that the concert today was not going to be the sort of thing that my friends and I call music, not one of those quiet and dreamlike experiences in an unreal and nameless realm, but rather an event of the most overt public reality. The events of this evening did not run their course in a few more or less fanciful and impractical brains, but rather they set in violent motion motorcars, horses, purses, hairdos, and all the rest of reality. What was happening here was not alien to the world or mad, it was highly real and right, it had the same force as and similar setting to the great events of modern life: the sports stadium, the stock exchange, big celebrations.

It was hard to worm one's way through the milling crowds in the neighborhood of the concert hall and through the streams of automobiles. Once at the entrance to the hall, one could feel some pride of accomplishment, one had fought one's way through, triumphing over those behind, and had snatched a place for oneself in the sun. Even while I was on my way up the dusty street amid the hundreds of cars all struggling toward the concert hall, I learned new facts about the great man, his fame leaped at me, forced its way into my loneliness and made me, who do not go out in society or read the newspapers, the astonished possessor of interesting bits of information.

"Tomorrow evening," I heard it said, "he is going to play

again in Hamburg." Someone was doubtful: "In Hamburg?
How can he get to Hamburg by tomorrow evening, why, he
would have to be on the train right now." "Nonsense! He goes
by plane, of course, perhaps he has one of his own." And in
the cloakroom where I successfully continued my battle, I
learned from the lively conversation of my fellow strugglers
that the great musician had demanded fourteen thousand
francs for this evening and had got it. Everyone mentioned
this sum with awe. Some, to be sure, were of the opinion that
art should really not exist simply for the rich; agreement was
expressed with this, and it turned out that most of them
would have been glad if they had got their tickets at a
"normal" price but nevertheless all were proud that they had
paid so much. It was not possible for me to explore the
psychology of this paradox, for I had been given my ticket.

Finally everyone was inside and in his seat. In the aisles
between the rows of seats, in the corridors, in the next room,
on the stage, up close to the grand piano, extra chairs had
been placed and not one was empty. From time to time one
could hear from outside in the direction of the box office the
loud protests of those being turned away. The warning bell
rang, silence fell. And suddenly the great violinist strode in,
followed by a self-effacing young accompanist.

We were all immediately charmed. No, this was neither a
lovelorn gypsy swain nor a brutal moneygrubber, this was a
serious, sympathetic, ingratiating, and yet dignified gentleman of handsome appearance and distinguished manners.
He neither threw kisses nor played the part of world-disdain-
ing professor, he looked alertly at his public and knew exactly
what it was all about—that is, a battle between him and this
thousand-headed giant, a battle he intended to win and had
already half won, for it seldom happens that so numerous a
public, if it has paid high prices, afterward admits to disappointment.

We were all extremely well pleased with the virtuoso. And
then as he began to play the slow opening bars of the
Kreutzer Sonata, it became evident immediately that his
world fame was not undeserved. This agreeable man was

truly adroit in handling his instrument, he had a smoothness of stroke, a precision of touch, a strength and elasticity of tone, a mastery to which one willingly and happily yielded. He played the second movement a trifle fast, forcing the tempo a bit, but wonderfully well. The young man at the piano played a lively and sympathetic accompaniment.

The *Kreutzer* Sonata completed the first third of the program, and during the intermission the man seated in front of me counted up with his neighbor how many thousand francs the artist had already earned during that half hour. There followed Bach's *Chaconne,* very fine, but it was only in the third composition, the Tartini sonata, that the magnificence of the violinist became fully evident. This piece as played by him was in truth a miraculous work, astoundingly difficult and astoundingly well mastered, and it was in addition a very good solid piece of music. If the huge audience had perhaps followed Beethoven and Bach only out of respect and to please the violinist, they now began to respond and grow warm. The applause thundered, most correctly the virtuoso took his bows, at the third or fourth appearance he also granted a smile.

Then in the third part of the concert, we true friends of music, we purists of good music, got into some embarrassment, for now little by little the great public was courted, and what the good musicians Beethoven and Bach had failed to do and the talented Tartini had only halfway accomplished was splendidly achieved by these unknown, exotic, tango composers: the thousands of listeners caught fire, they melted and gave in, they smiled radiantly and wept tears, they groaned in ecstasy, and after each of these short bits of entertainment burst into intoxicated applause. The great man had won, every one of these three thousand souls belonged to him, all were his willing captives, letting themselves be stroked, petted, made happy, floating in a drunken enchantment. We few purists, on the other hand, inwardly defended ourselves, fought heroic, profitless battles, laughed resentfully at the trash being played but were unable nevertheless to keep from recognizing the mellowness of the virtuoso's stroke, the sweet-

ness of those tones, and now and then to grin at the magic of
a miserable but magically rendered passage.

The great enchantment had been achieved, for even we
disgruntled ones floated at least for a few instants on the
great wave, even we were seized now and then by the sweet
and lovely ecstasy. Once more we were boys coming from our
first violin lesson, once more we dreamed ourselves over the
mountainous difficulties, each one of us was for a wishful
moment the master, the magician, drawing hearts behind us
with an effortless stroke of the bow, conquering laughingly
and playfully that great monster, the crowd, drinking in the
applause, drinking in the intoxication of the masses, borne up
by it, smiling over it.

The thousands were aflame. They would not permit that
concert to end. They applauded, shouted, stamped. They
forced the artist to appear again and again, to play first one,
then another, then a third and fourth encore. He behaved
elegantly, took his bows, encore after encore; on their feet the
audience listened breathless, completely enchanted. Now they
believed they were the victors, these thousands, they believed
they had power over the man, they thought that through their
enthusiasm they could compel him to reappear constantly
and go on playing. However he gave exactly those encores
which, I suspect, he had agreed upon in advance with his accompanist, and when he had completed the last part of the
concert, not printed but reckoned for in the program, he disappeared and did not return. Nothing availed, the people had
to wake up, had to go away.

During this whole evening there were two persons inside
me, two listeners, two participants. One was an old music
lover with incorruptible taste, a purist of good music, who
frequently and gravely shook his head and in the last third
of the evening never stopped shaking it. He was not only
against the expenditure of this expertise on music of very
moderate worth, he was not only against these languishing,
entertaining, popular salon pieces—no, he was also against
this whole audience, against these rich people who were

never seen at the more serious concerts, who came here in their cars to hear this virtuoso as though to a horse race or to the stock exchange, he was against the shallow, quickly roused, and quickly quenched enthusiasm of all these teen-agers. The other person in me, however, was a boy, and he followed this hero of the violin, was one with him, vibrated with him.

In the course of the evening these two had much conversation and quarreling with each other. It would happen that the experienced music lover protested against the pieces played and that the boy in me was thereupon impelled to remind me that I myself once in an earlier time had written a novel in which a saxophone player gave some very pertinent answers to an irritated music critic.

And oh, how I wondered about the artist himself, that irreproachable magician! Was he at heart a musician who would have liked best of all to play nothing but Bach and Mozart and who very slowly and only after desperate resistance had accustomed himself not to thrust good music upon the people but to give them what they wanted? Was he a worldling smothered in success? Was he coldly calculating, knowing how to tickle people in exactly that delicate, sensitive spot between their tear glands and their purses, which makes tears and dollars fall like rain, if one but understands the magic? Or was he a humble servant of the art, too modest to permit himself a judgment of his own, willingly and helpfully playing his role, making no protest against fate? Or had he perhaps, after profound experience and reasoning, come to doubt the worth of music in modern life and the possibility of its being understood, and was his purpose to begin by leading men beyond all music once more back to the beginnings of the art, to the naked sensuous beauty of the tones, to the naked force of primitive feelings? It was too much for me to decipher. I am still puzzling over it today.

The Magic of the Book

1930

AMONG THE MANY WORLDS that man did not receive as a gift from nature but created out of his own mind, the world of books is the greatest. Every child, when he first draws letters on his slate and makes his first attempts to read, thereby takes the initial step into an artificial and highly complicated realm whose laws and rules of play are too much to learn and fully employ in any one lifetime. Without the word, without the writing of books, there is no history, there is no concept of humanity. And if anyone wants to try to enclose in a small space, in a single house or a single room, the history of the human spirit and to make it his own, he can only do this in the form of a collection of books. We have seen, to be sure, that preoccupation with history and the historical way of thought has its dangers, and in recent decades we have experienced a powerful revulsion against history in our feeling for life; but we have been able to learn through this very revulsion that the permanent renunciation of new conquests and acquisitions of intellectual territory will never bring back innocence to our lives and thought.

With all peoples the word and writing are holy and magical; naming and writing were originally magical operations, magical conquests of nature through the spirit, and everywhere the gift of writing was thought to be of divine origin. With most peoples, writing and reading were secret and holy arts reserved for the priesthood alone; it was a great and remarkable undertaking when a young man decided to acquire these mighty arts. It was not easy, it was reserved for the few, and had to be paid for with dedication and sacrifice. From the standpoint of our democratic civilizations, the spirit in those days was something rarer but also nobler and holier than today; toilsome roads led to it, it had divine protection and was not offered to everyone gratis. We can only dimly imagine what it was like in a hierarchic-aristocratic culture, in the midst of an illiterate folk, to possess the secret of writing! It meant distinction and power, it meant white and black magic, it was a talisman and magic wand.

Today all this is apparently completely changed. Today, so it seems, the world of writing and of the intellect is open to everyone; indeed he is forcibly initiated into it if he hesitates. Today, so it seems, being able to read and write is little more than being able to breathe or at most knowing how to ride horseback. Writing and the book have apparently been divested of every special dignity, every enchantment, every magic. In religious circles, no doubt, there is still the concept of the "holy" book based on revelation; but since the single, still really powerful religious organization in the Occident, the Roman Catholic Church, puts no great value on seeing the Bible distributed as reading matter, there are in reality no holy books at all except those of a small number of orthodox Jews and the members of a few Protestant sects. Here and there the requirement may still persist that, when taking an oath, the person swearing must place his hand on the Bible; this gesture however is only a chill, dead remnant of a once blazing power and for the average person contains, like the form of the oath itself, no magical force whatever. Books have ceased to be mysteries, they are accessible to everyone, so it seems. From a liberal, democratic point of view this is progress and is accepted as a matter of course; from other points of view, however, it is a devaluation and vulgarization of the spirit.

We need not allow ourselves to be robbed of the agreeable feeling of progress attained, instead we will rejoice that reading and writing are no longer the prerogatives of a guild or caste. Since the invention of the printing press the book has become an object of general use and luxury distributed in huge quantities. Large printings make possible low book prices and therefore every country can make its best books (the so-called classics) available to those in modest circum-

stances. Then too we will not grieve very much over the fact
that the concept "book" has lost almost all its former splendor
and that very recently the book seems to have sacrificed even
more of its worth and attractiveness in the eyes of the crowd
because of the cinema and the radio. And yet we need not
fear a future elimination of the book. On the contrary, the
more that certain needs for entertainment and education are
satisfied through other inventions, the more the book will win
back in dignity and authority. For even the most childish intoxication with progress will soon be forced to recognize that
writing and books have a function that is eternal. It will become evident that formulation in words and the handing on
of these formulations through writing are not only important
aids but actually the only means by which humanity can
have a history and a continuing consciousness of itself.

*   *   *

Today we have not quite reached the point where younger
rivals like radio, film, and so forth have taken everything
away from the printed book, but only that part of its function
which is dispensable. It is really hard to see, for example, why
popular novels without literary value but with situations,
images, excitement, and emotion have not been superseded
by picture sequences as in the cinema or by the spoken word
on the radio, or through some future combination of both,
thus saving thousands of people from squandering a great
deal of time and eyesight on such books. But the division of
creative labor that we cannot see on the surface is going on in
the secret area of the workshops, and in some cases was long
ago completed. Not infrequently we hear that some "author"
has abandoned books or theater to devote himself to films.
Here the necessary and desirable division has already occurred. For to think that "writing" and inventing films are
one and the same thing or even have much in common is a
mistake. In saying this I certainly do not intend to sing the
praises of the "author" and by comparison to underrate the
maker of films—nothing is further from my intention. But
the man who is engaged in communicating a description or a

narrative by means of the written word is doing something completely and fundamentally different from the man who undertakes to tell the same story by means of groups of people directed and photographed. The poet may be a miserable workman, the film-maker a genius, but that is not the point. What the crowd does not yet suspect and will perhaps not discover for a long time has already begun to be decided among the creators themselves: the fundamental distinction between the media through which an artistic goal is attempted. When this divorce is final, to be sure, there will still be sloppy novels and trashy films, whose creators are unstable talents, freebooters in areas in which they lack competence. But to the clarification of concepts and the relief of literature and her present rivals this separation will contribute much. Then the cinema will be no more able to damage literature than, for example, photography has hurt painting.

*　　*　　*

But let us return to our theme. I said above that "apparently" the book has lost its magic power today, that illiterates today, "so it seems," have become rarities. Why then "apparently"? Is it possible that the age-old magic still exists somewhere, is it ultimately possible that there still are such things as holy books, devilish books, magic books? Is it possible that the idea of "the magic of the book" does not completely belong to the past and to the realm of fairy tales?

Well, yes, that is how it is. The laws of the spirit change just as little as those of nature and it is equally impossible to "discard" them. Priesthoods and astrologers' guilds can be dissolved or deprived of their privileges. Discoveries or poetic inventions that formerly were secret possessions of the few can be made accessible to the many, who can even be forced to learn about these treasures. But all this goes on at the most superficial level and in reality nothing in the world of the spirit has changed since Luther translated the Bible and Gutenberg invented the printing press. The whole magic is still there, and the spirit is still the secret of a small hierarchically organized band of privileged persons, only now the band has become anonymous. In the past few centuries writing and books have become the common property of all classes—in very much the same way that the disappearance of regulations governing the dress of various classes has made fashion a common possession—only the creation of fashions, now as formerly, belongs to the few, and a dress worn by a beautiful woman of attractive figure and refined taste looks quite remarkably different from the same dress worn by the average woman. In the realm of the spirit, since it has become democratic, there has also taken place a very smart and deceptive shift: leadership has slipped out of the hands of priests and scholars to some place where it can no longer be called to account and made responsible, where, however, it can no longer legitimatize itself or appeal to any authority. For that stratum of writers and intellectuals which seems from time to time to lead because it shapes public opinion or at least supplies the slogans of the day—that stratum is not identical with the creative stratum.

There is no need to get too far into abstractions. Let us take a random example from modern intellectual and literary history. Let us imagine, for instance, an educated and well-read German of the period between 1870 and 1880, a judge, a doctor, a high school professor perhaps, or a private individual who loves books. What has he read, what has he known of the creative spirit of his time and people, where has he contributed to its contemporary and future development? Where today is the literature which at that time was recognized by the critics and by popular opinion as being good, desirable, and worth reading? There is hardly any of it left. And while Dostoevsky was writing his books and Nietzsche was regarded as an unknown or ridiculous eccentric in the rich and self-indulgent Germany of those years, German readers young and old, high and low, were reading, for example, Spielhagen and Marlitt, or at best the pretty poems of Emmanuel Geibel, which had printings to a number hardly rivaled by any lyric poet since then, and the famous *Trumpeter of Säckingen*, which even exceeded those poems in popularity and sales.

Examples could be produced by the hundreds. It is per-

fectly obvious: the spirit has apparently been made democratic and the intellectual treasures of a period apparently
belong to every contemporary who has learned to read, but in
reality everything important occurs in secret and is unrecognized, and there would seem to be somewhere under-
ground a secret priesthood or conspiracy, which from an
anonymous hiding place directs intellectual destinies throughout the earth, equipped with power and disruptive forces extending through generations, in order that public opinion,
happy in its enlightenment, shall notice nothing of this magic
which is carried on right before their eyes.

But in much narrower and simpler circles we can observe
every day how completely marvelous and like fairy tales are
the histories of books, how at one moment they have the
greatest enchantment and then again the gift of becoming
invisible. Poets live and die, known by few or none, and we
see their work after their death, often decades after their
death, suddenly rise resplendent from the grave as though
time did not exist. We saw in amazement how Nietzsche,
unanimously rejected by his people, after fulfilling his mission for a few dozen minds, became several decades too late a
favorite author whose books could not be printed fast enough,
or how Hölderlin's poems, more than a hundred years after
their composition, suddenly intoxicated our studious youths,
or how, from the ancient treasury of Chinese wisdom, suddenly after millennia the one and only Lao-tse was discovered
by postwar Europe; badly translated and badly read, Lao-tse
became a fashion like Tarzan or the fox trot; nevertheless he
was enormously influential on the productive level of our living minds.

And each year we see thousands and thousands of children
entering the first class, drawing their first letters, deciphering
the first syllables, and we see again and again that for a
majority of these children the ability to read quickly becomes
an ordinary matter of little value, while others from year to
year and decade to decade become more and more enchanted
and astounded by the use they can make of the magic key

that school gave them. For if today the ability to read is everyone's portion, still only a few notice what a powerful talisman has thus been put into their hands. The child proud of his youthful knowledge of the alphabet first achieves for himself the reading of a verse or a saying, then the reading of a first little story, a fairy tale, and while those who have not been called seem to apply their reading ability to news reports or to the business sections of their newspapers, there are a few who remain constantly bewitched by the strange miracle of letters and words (which once, to be sure, were an enchantment and magic formula to everyone). From these few come the readers. They discover as children a few poems and stories, a verse by Claudius, or a tale by Hebel or Hauff in the reader, and instead of turning their backs on these things after acquiring the ability to read they press forward into the realm of books and discover step by step how vast, how various and blessed this world is! At first they took this world for a little child's pretty garden with a tulip bed and a little fish pond; now the garden becomes a park, it becomes a landscape, a section of the earth, the world, it becomes Paradise and the Ivory Coast, it entices with constantly new enchantments, blooms in ever-new colors. And what yesterday appeared to be a garden or a park or a jungle, today or tomorrow is recognized as a temple, a temple with a thousand halls and courtyards in which the spirit of all nations and times is present, constantly waiting for reawakening, ever ready to recognize the many-voiced multiplicity of its phenomena as a unity. And for every true reader this endless world of books looks different, everyone seeks and recognizes himself in it. One gropes his way from children's tales and books about Indians to Shakespeare or Dante, another from the first schoolbook essay about the starry heavens to Kepler or to Einstein, a third from a pious child's prayer to the holy cool vaults of Saint Thomas or Saint Bonaventure, or to the sublime complexities of Talmudic thought, or to the springlike similes of the Upanishads, to the moving wisdom of the Hasidim, or to the lapidary and yet so friendly, so genial and merry teachings of ancient China. A thousand ways lead through the jungle to a thousand goals, and no goal is the final one; with each step new expanses open.

Then it becomes a matter of wisdom or luck whether such a true adept gets lost in the jungle of his world of books and smothers there, or finds his way, makes his reading experience into true experience, usable for life. Those to whom the magic of the world of books is completely denied think of it very much the way the unmusical think about music and are often inclined to deplore reading as a pathological and dangerous passion that makes people unfit for life. Naturally they are in some small measure right; although it would first have to be determined what is understood by "life" and whether life can only be thought of as the opposite of "mind," despite the fact that the great majority of thinkers and teachers from Confucius to Goethe have been really quite astoundingly active and capable men. Nevertheless the world of books has its dangers, well known to teachers. Whether these dangers are greater than the dangers of a life deprived of the wide world of books is something that I have not hitherto found time to think about. I am, you must know, a reader myself, I have been bewitched since childhood, and were I to have the experience of the monk of Heisterbach, I would be able to lose myself in the temple halls and mazes, the caves and oceans of the world of books for several centuries without noticing the shrinking of this world.

*   *   *

And in saying this I am not considering at all the constant increase in books thrust upon the world! No, every true reader could, even if not one new book were published, spend decades and centuries studying on, fighting on, continuing to rejoice in the treasure of those already at hand. Each new language we learn is an increase of experience—and there are amazingly many languages, many more than we were told about in school! There is in fact not just one Spanish or one Italian, or one German or even those three Germans, Old High German, Middle High German, and so on; oh no, there

are a hundred Germans, there are as many Germans, as many
Spanish languages, as many English languages, as there are
ways of thought and life-styles in each of these nations; yes,
there are almost as many languages as there are original
thinkers and poets. At the same time as Goethe, and unfortunately not properly recognized by him, Jean Paul was
writing his completely different and very German German.
And all these languages are essentially not translatable! The
attempts of outstanding nations (in this the Germans stand
at the very top) to assimilate all the world's literature in
translation—and in individual instances this has borne
splendid fruit—nevertheless have not been a complete success, and it is fundamentally impossible that they should ever
be. No German hexameters have ever been written that really
sound like Homer. In the last hundred years Dante's great
poem has been translated into German several dozen times—
with the result that the youngest and most poetically significant of these poetic imitators, recognizing the inadequacy of
all attempts to translate a language of the Middle Ages into
modern language, has invented for his German Dante a
language all his own, the German of a poetic Middle Ages de-
signed for this purpose, and we can only marvel at him for it.

But even if a reader acquires no new language, or for that
matter does not even acquaint himself with some new or
hitherto unknown literature, he can endlessly go on with his
reading, making finer distinctions, heightening, strengthening. For every thinking person each verse of each poet will
show a new and different face to the reader every few years,
will awaken a different resonance in him. When as a youth I
read for the first time, only partially understanding it,
Goethe's *Elective Affinities*, that was a completely different
book from the *Elective Affinities* that I have now read perhaps
for the fifth time! The great and mysterious thing about this
reading experience is this: the more discriminatingly, the
more sensitively, and the more associatively we learn to read,
the more clearly we see every thought and every poem in its
uniqueness, its individuality, in its precise limitations and see
that all beauty, all charm depend on this individuality and

uniqueness—at the same time we come to realize ever more clearly how all these hundred thousand voices of nations strive toward the same goals, call upon the same gods by different names, dream the same wishes, suffer the same sorrows. Out of the thousandfold fabric of countless languages and books of several thousand years, in ecstatic instants there stares at the reader a marvelously noble and transcendent chimera: the countenance of humanity, charmed into unity from a thousand contradictory features.

About Good and Bad Critics

NOTES ON THE SUBJECT OF
POETRY AND CRITICISM

1930

IT IS A RARE and always happy thing to find an individual born and endowed for a particular calling: the born gardener, the born doctor, the born educator. Even rarer is the born poet. He may seem unworthy of his gifts, he may rest content with his talent, never summoning up the seriousness, the courage, the patience and diligence necessary to make that talent effective—nevertheless he will always be enchanting, a darling of nature because of those gifts which no diligence, no faithful labor, no excellence of intention can ever replace.

Probably rarer than the born poet is the born critic, that is, one whose first bent toward critical activity comes not from diligence and scholarship, from assiduity and busyness, nor from a partisan spirit or vanity or malice, but rather from grace, from innate acuity of mind and analytical powers of thought, from serious cultural responsibility. Of course, this gifted critic may also have personal characteristics that adorn or distort his gift; he can be either kind or malicious, vain or modest, boisterous or quiet, he can nurture his talent or profligately waste it, but he will always have an advantage over the merely industrious, the merely learned—the grace of creativity. Obviously in the history of literature, especially German literature, there have been more born poets than born critics. In the single period between young Goethe and, let us say, Mörike or Gottfried Keller, we can name dozens of true poets. Between Lessing and Humboldt, however, the interval is harder to fill up with names of importance.

Whereas the poet, soberly considered, seems to be dispensable for his people and an exception and an oddity, the development of the press has made the critic a permanent institution, a man with a calling, a necessary factor in public life. Whether the need for poetic production, the need for poetry, exists or not, there seems to be an actual need for criticism; society needs publications that take upon themselves the intellectual mastery of contemporary events. We would burst into laughter over the notion of poetry offices or poetry appointments, but we find it perfectly natural that there are hundreds of steady, paid, critical positions on the newspapers. There would be no objection to this except that the genuine born critic is a rarity. Since no doubt the technique of criticism can be acquired, the handiwork can be taught, even though no increase of the genuine gift is possible, we see hundreds of well-paid critics plying this trade all their lives, a trade whose technique they may in some degree have mastered but whose inner meaning remains foreign to them—just as we see hundreds of doctors or merchants sketchily performing their superficially acquired professions without any inner feeling for them.

I do not know whether this situation means a disgrace to the nation; for a people with modest literary claims such as the Germans (among whom not one in ten thousand has really mastered his own language either in speech or in writing, and where one can become a university professor or even a minister of state without knowing German)—for such a nation it is presumably unimportant that there should be this sort of critical proletariat just as there is a medical and a pedagogical proletariat.

However, for the poet to be dependent upon very inadequate criticism is a great loss. It is a mistake to think that the poet shuns criticism, that out of artistic vanity he prefers any sort of stupid praise to true and penetrating criticism—quite the contrary: no doubt the poet seeks love, as every being seeks love, but to the same degree he seeks to be understood and recognized, and the commonplace joke of mediocre critics about the poet who cannot stand criticism springs from a muddied source. Every true poet rejoices at every true critic —not because he can learn very much about his art from him, for that is impossible, but because it means a highly important illumination and corrective to have himself and his work seen objectively, weighed in the balance of his nature and culture, put in his proper place according to his gifts and accomplishments, instead of being left, with his work misunderstood (no matter whether overvalued or under-valued), in a paralyzing limbo of unreality.

Incompetent critics (who are aggressive because of their uncertainty, because they have always to judge values they cannot feel in essence but can only investigate theoreti-cally and mechanically from outside) like to reproach poets with vanity and hypersensitivity about criticism, even with enmity toward the intellect in general, until in the end the bewildered reader is no longer able to distinguish between the true poet and the idiotic, long-haired poetaster repre-sented in the newspapers and magazines. I myself have more than once made an attempt with critics of the second order (naturally not in my own interest, but on behalf of authors who seemed to me to be neglected) not to influence their judgment but by providing factual information to encourage them to come to a judgment, and not a single time have I encountered genuine openness to impartial examination, indeed in general no zeal whatsoever for matters of the spirit. The answer of these professional men always consisted in a gesture that unmistakably meant, "Leave us in peace! Don't take this stuff so damn seriously. See here, we have more than enough of this miserable slave labor; what would become of us if we were to examine every essay we wrote under a magnifying glass?" In short, the critic of the second or third rank behaves toward his profession with the same lack of love and responsibility as the average factory worker does toward his job. He has adopted one of the critical pro-cedures in favor when he was young and learning his trade, he has chosen the method of smiling at everything with mild skepticism or praising everything with wild superlatives, or one of the other ways of evading his real business. Or (and this is what happens most often) he does not attempt a literary criticism at all but concentrates instead simply on the derivation, opinions, or politics of the author. If the author belongs to an opposing party, then he is rejected either by contradiction or by ridicule. If he belongs to the critic's own party he will be praised or at least treated with consideration. If he belongs to no party at all, then he is often ignored, for after all there is no power behind him.

The result of this situation is not only disappointment for the poet but a systematic distortion of the mirror in which the people believe they can observe the state and development of the intellectual and artistic life of their time. As a matter of fact, we find enormous differences between the picture the press gives of our intellectual life and that life itself. Often for many years at a time we find names and books seriously and thoroughly discussed, works that have not the slightest influence on a single level of society, and we find authors and works passed over in silence that have a powerful influence on the life and temper of the times. There is no technical or economic field in which the public would be satisfied with such capricious and irresponsible reporting of the news. An average newspaper contains much more factual and carefully written material in its sports and business sections than in its literary supplements, though fine exceptions to this rule occur from time to time.

The true critic by vocation may have various faults and bad habits, nevertheless his criticism will be more pertinent than that of his most respectable and conscientious colleague who lacks the creative quality. Above everything else, the true critic will have an infallible feeling for genuineness and quality of language, whereas the run-of-the-mill critic easily confuses what is original with what is imitative and at times is even taken in by fraud. The genuine critic can be recognized by two important hallmarks: in the first place, he likes a good and lively style, he is on intimate terms with his own language and does not misuse it. In the second place, he feels under no need or compulsion to suppress his subjective view, his individual style, but on the contrary brings it to the clearest possible expression so that the reader can make use of it in the way one uses a yardstick: without sharing the critic's subjective values and preferences, the reader is easily able to deduce the objective values from the critic's reactions. Or, to put it more simply, the good critic is so completely personal and expresses himself so clearly that the reader knows or feels precisely with whom he is dealing and through what sort of lens the light has fallen that meets his eye. Therefore it is possible that a gifted critic may all his life long reject a poet of genius, make fun of him or attack him, and the reader may nevertheless, from the critic's reaction, form a correct impression of the poet's essential quality.

On the other hand, the principal weakness of the poor critic is that he has little personality or is unable to express it. The strongest words of praise or condemnation on the part of the critic remain ineffective if they are spoken by someone you cannot see, someone who does not know how to show himself to us, someone who remains a nonentity. It is precisely the incompetent critic who often pretends to objectivity, as though aesthetics were an exact science; he distrusts his personal instincts and conceals them through impartiality ("on the one hand—but then on the other") and neutrality. In a critic, neutrality is almost always suspect and a lack—a lack, that is, of intensity of intellectual experience. The critic should not hide his passion, in case he has any, but make a point of sharing it. He should not act as though he were a measuring machine or a ministry of culture but should stand up for his own opinions.

The attitude of the commonplace author to the commonplace critic is something like this: they do not really trust each other—the critic doesn't, as a matter of fact, think much of the author, nevertheless he is afraid that the fellow may possibly turn out to be a genius. The author feels that he is not understood by the critic, that neither his value nor his faults are understood, but he is glad at least not to have encountered an expert who might have annihilated him, and he hopes eventually to get on good terms with the critic and so gain his support. This shabby tradesman's relationship obtains between the average German author and the average German critic, and in this respect there is no difference between the radical press and the conservative press.

A true poet, however, hates nothing more than to be on friendly terms with this average critic, with this uncomprehending article-writing machine. Instead he tries to provoke such critics, he prefers to be spat upon and torn to pieces by them rather than to be slapped on the back. But when he encounters a real critic, even though he be a declared opponent, he always has a kind of feeling of esprit de corps. To find oneself recognized and diagnosed by a powerful critic is the same thing as being examined by a good doctor. That is something quite different from having to listen to the claptrap of a quack! Perhaps you are terrified, perhaps you are hurt, but you know that you are being taken seriously even if the diagnosis should turn out to be a death sentence. And at bottom one never really believes in death sentences.

Conversation between Poet and Critic

POET: I still say there was a time when criticism in Germany was on a higher level than today.

CRITIC: Please cite examples.

POET: All right. I'll mention Solger's essay on *Elective Affinities* and Wilhelm Grimm's review of Arnim's *Bertold*. Those are beautiful examples of creative criticism. The spirit that produced them is hard to find today.

CRITIC: What spirit do you mean?

POET: The spirit of awe. Tell me honestly, do you consider that criticism on a level with those two is possible among us today?

CRITIC: I don't know. Times have changed. A counter question: Do you consider compositions in the class of *Elective Affinities* or of Arnim's work possible for us today?

POET: Aha, so you believe that as poetry goes so goes criticism! You mean that if we had a true poetry today no doubt we would also have true criticism. That's worth considering.

CRITIC: Yes, that's what I mean.

POET: May I ask whether you know the essays by Solger and Grimm?

CRITIC: Frankly, no.

POET: But the *Elective Affinities* and *Bertold,* you know them?

CRITIC: The *Elective Affinities,* yes, of course. Not *Bertold.*

POET: And yet you believe that *Bertold* is superior to our present-day literature?

CRITIC: Yes, I believe that, out of respect for Arnim and even more out of respect for the poetic power that the German spirit possessed at that time.

POET: But then why don't you read Arnim and all the other real writers of that time? Why do you busy yourself all your life long with a literature that you yourself consider inferior? Why not say to your readers, "Look here, this is real poetry, forget about today's rubbish and read Goethe, Arnim, Novalis!"

CRITIC: That's not my job. Possibly I neglect to do it for the same reasons that you neglect to write masterpieces like *Elective Affinities.*

POET: A good reply. But how do you explain the fact that at that time Germany produced such poets? Their masterpieces were unasked-for offerings, no one demanded them. Neither *Elective Affinities* nor *Bertold* was read by their contemporaries, nor are they much read today.

CRITIC: At that time the populace was not much interested in poetry, nor is it today either. That's the way our nation just happens to be. Perhaps all nations are. In Goethe's time there were lots of pleasant books of entertainment and they were read. Today it is just the same. The books of light entertainment are read, they are reviewed, they are not taken very seriously either by reader or critic, but they fulfill a need. The writers of light literature are read and

paid and so are their critics. People read them and forget
them very quickly.

POET: And the true poems?

CRITIC: We assume that these are written for eternity. The
present therefore feels no obligation to take notice of them.

POET: You should have been a politician.

CRITIC: That's right, and that's what I wanted too. I should
have preferred taking over foreign policy. But it just happened that when I joined the paper there were no political
assignments open; all they had to give me was the review
section.

Choice of Subject Matter

The phrase "choice of subject" is popular with many critics;
for some, indeed, it is indispensable. The average critic, if he
is a newspaperman, finds himself confronted by a mass of
material thrust upon him from outside which he has to deal
with. He envies the poet for his apparent freedom of creation
if for nothing else. Besides, the daily reviewer has to handle
almost exclusively light literature, imitation poetry, and a
skillful novelist can, to be sure, with a certain capriciousness
and careful calculation, choose his material, although his
freedom too is much restricted. The popular novelist, for
instance, is free to choose the scene of his book; following
the fashion of the moment he will place his new novel at the
South Pole, or in Egypt; he will have it deal with questions
of politics or sports, he will discuss current social problems,
moral problems, and legal problems in his books. Behind
this contemporary façade, however, even the slyest imitation
author will unroll the history of a life that corresponds to his
own deepest, most firmly established convictions, he will not
be able to overcome a preference for certain characters, for
certain situations, and an indifference toward others. Even in
the trashiest novel a soul is revealed, the author's, and the
worst writer, who is unable to give a clear representation of
a single figure or single human situation, will nevertheless
always succeed in one thing about which he has never

thought: in his sorry productions he will inevitably lay bare his own ego.

Now in true works of literature there is no choice of subject at all. The "subject," i.e., the principal figures and the characteristic problems of the novel, is never chosen by the author; instead the subject is really the primal subject of all poetry, it is the poet's vision and the adventures of his soul. The poet can draw back from his vision, he can flee from a life and death problem, he can leave unused a genuine subject through incapacity or inconvenience. But to "choose" his subject is something he can never do. Never can he take material which from rational or purely artistic considerations he considers suitable and popular and give it the appearance of having come to him through grace, make it seem as though it had not been carefully planned but had been experienced in his soul. Of course true poets too have often attempted to choose subjects, to command poesy: the results of these attempts are always extremely interesting and instructive to their colleagues; as works of literature they are stillborn.

To put it briefly: if someone asks the author of a true work of literature, "Wouldn't you have done better to choose a different subject?"—it is exactly the same as for a doctor to ask a patient suffering from pneumonia, "Wouldn't you have done better to choose a cold instead?"

The So-called Flight into Art

You hear it said: The artist must not flee from life into art.

Now just what does that mean? Why shouldn't the artist do that?

Seen from the artist's point of view, is art anything but an attempt to make good the inadequacies of life, to fulfill in poetry the unfulfillable wishes, to fulfill the unfulfillable demands—in short, to sublimate the unacceptable aspects of reality?

And why should one always put the above idiotic question only to artists? Why shouldn't you ask the statesman, the doctor, the boxer, or the swimming champion to make a satisfactory settlement of his personal problems before taking flight into the tasks and satisfactions of his profession?

That "life" must inevitably be harder than art seems to be an axiom among the minor critics.

And now just take a look at the far too many artists who constantly and successfully take flight out of art into life, who paint such miserable pictures, write such miserable books, but are such charming people, such genial hosts, such admirable heads of families, such noble patriots!

No, if a man believes he is an artist, I would rather see him fight his battle and hold his ground where the tasks of his calling lie. There may be much truth (or rather half-truth) in the assumption that every triumph of a poet's work is paid for by sacrifices in his private life. No work is accomplished otherwise. It is a silly and untenable assumption that art is born from superfluity of happiness, contentment, and harmony. Since every other sort of human accomplishment comes into being only through necessity and under heavy pressure, why should art be an exception?

The So-called Flight into the Past

Another "flight" that is in ill favor today with reviewers is the so-called flight into the past. Let a poet write something that is remote from the world of fashion or of sport, let him rise from questions of the moment to questions of humanity, let him seek either a period of history or a poetic, timeless realm beyond history, and the accusation is instantly brought against him that he is "fleeing from" his own time. Thus Goethe fled to Götz and to Iphigenia instead of enlightening us about problems in Frankfurt or among the burgher families of Weimar.

The Psychology of the Half-Educated

It is a well-known fact that the crassest atavisms have the greatest need to disguise themselves as modern and progressive. Thus literary criticism in a period of the most benighted barbarism disguises itself in the panoply of psychoanalysis.

Need I make preliminary obeisance to Freud and his achievements? Is it necessary for me to grant Freud the right to examine any other genius in the world with the aid of his special techniques? Need I call attention to the fact that when Freud's teaching was still a subject of controversy I helped to defend him? And must I now specifically ask the reader not to see an attack on Freud's genius or on his psychological and psychotherapeutic accomplishments if I find the misuse of basic Freudian principles by worthless critics and turncoat philologists ridiculous?

Together with the propagation and elaboration of the Freudian school of thought, which continues to make significant contributions both to psychological research and to the treatment of neuroses and which for years has received almost universal recognition—along with the spread of this teaching among the masses and the increasing penetration of Freudian methods and terminology into other intellectual fields, there has developed a highly undesirable, indeed, repulsive by-product: the pseudo-Freudian psychology of the half-educated, a kind of dilettante criticism which examines literature by methods that Freud used for the examination of dreams and other unconscious material.

The result of these "researches" is that these men of letters trained neither in medicine nor in psychology not only succeed in recognizing the poet Lenau as emotionally disturbed, which was no discovery in any case, but also reduce his great accomplishments, as well as those of other poets, to a common level with the dreams and fantasies of any other neurotic. On the basis of a poet's work, his complexes and favorite fantasies are examined and he is assigned to this or that class of neurotic, and a masterpiece is explained by attributing it to the same causes that produced Herr Muller's agoraphobia or Frau Meier's nervous stomach. Attention is systematically diverted from the poetry, systematically and with a kind of vindictiveness (the vindictiveness of the ungifted toward the spirit), the poems are degraded to symptoms of psychic illness, the critic in interpreting the works falls back upon the grossest errors of rationalizing and moralizing from biographical facts and leaves behind a heap of ruins on which the plucked contents of great works of poetry lie amid blood and filth. And all this hubbub seems to be perpetrated with the sole intention of proving that Goethe and Hölderlin were simply human beings, just as Faust and Heinrich von Ofterdingen were quite ordinary souls with quite ordinary instincts, simply tricked out in prettily stylized masquerade.

Nothing is said about what constitutes the real achievement of these works; man's highest achievements in individuation are reconverted into formless matter. Nothing is said about the rather remarkable fact that the same state that neurotic Frau Meier turns into a nervous stomachache is transformed into works of high art by certain other individuals. No regard is paid to this phenomenon, no attention is paid to what has been produced, to the unique, precious, inimitable, but instead only to the formless, crude material. We need no such tedious, repetitious researches to know that the physical experiences of poets are very much the same as those of everyone else. And about the thing we would so much like to know, about the breath-taking miracle that now and again in a creative individual the commonplace turns into world drama, the ordinary is translated into a shining marvel —about this nothing is said, attention is directed elsewhere. Among other things it is a sin against Freud, whose genius and degree of differentiation has for some time been a thorn in the flesh of those of his followers devoted to oversimplification. The concept of sublimation, established by Freud himself, has long since been forgotten by these semi-disciples who have sought refuge in literature.

Now whatever the possible biographical and psychological value of such analyses of a poet's work may be (it is possible, of course, that something may be gained in these secondary departments, though nothing can be added to the understanding of the works of art), nevertheless it is very meager and very dubious. Whoever in the course of his life has either undergone a psychoanalysis himself or conducted one on another person or even shared as a participating confidant, such a person knows what an amount of time, patience, and toil is demanded and how artfully and persistently the looked-for first causes, the origins of the repressions, seek to hide themselves from the analyst. He knows, too, that in order to penetrate to these causes, patient attention to the uninhibited expressions of the soul is required, a careful examination of dreams, of errors in action, etc. Were the patient to say to his analyst: "Dear sir, I have neither time nor inclination for all these sessions, but I am handing you this package which contains my dreams, wishes, and fantasies insofar as I have written them out, partly in printed form; take this material and be so kind as to decipher from it what you need to know" —how heartily the doctor would laugh at this naïve patient! To be sure, a neurotic may paint pictures or write poems, and the analyst will examine these too, will try to make use of them—but to try to read a person's unconscious psychic life and his earlier psychic history from such documents, this would seem to any analyst highly naïve and a dilettante act of presumption.

Well, these half-educated interpreters of the poets actually pretend to readers even less educated than themselves that it is possible to construct an analysis out of just such documents. The patient is dead, there is no danger of his confronting them, and so they can go ahead and fantasize at will. It would be entertaining to see the result if a skillful writer subjected these pseudoanalytical interpretations of poets to an analysis of his own and revealed the very primitive motives that inspire these zealous pseudo-psychologists.

I do not believe that Freud himself ever takes these works of his illegitimate disciples seriously. I do not believe that any serious practitioner or researcher of the psychoanalytical school reads their essays and monographs. Nevertheless—an explicit rejection of this dilettante activity on their part would be welcome. The bad thing, of course, is not the publication of these apparently profound revelations about the geniuses of earlier times, these apparently razor-sharp interpretations of works of art in monographs and books, or that all this has given rise to a new field of literature, which, to be sure, is little read but in which ambitious authors can gather laurels. The disagreeable part is what those amateur analysts, the daily reviewers, have learned from it, a new way of simplifying their task by giving it the appearance, the pretense, of being somehow scientific. Suppose that in the work of an author who is unsympathetic to me I detect traces of complexes and neurotic involvements, then I denounce him to the world as a psychopath. Presently, of course, the world will get tired of this. The time will come when the word "pathological" will lose its present meaning. Relativity is bound to hold good in the realm of sickness and health just as elsewhere, and people will become aware that the sick of today may be the healthy ones of tomorrow and that staying healthy is not always the most infallible symptom of health. But for a person of high intellect endowed with delicate, vulnerable senses, a superior, highly talented person, it might be oppressive, in fact horrible, to live in the midst of today's conventions about good and evil, about what is beautiful and ugly. This simple truth will also be discovered someday. Then Hölderlin and Nietzsche will be moved back again from the category of psychopaths into that of geniuses, and it will be realized that we stand today, without having advanced or achieved a single thing, exactly where we were before the advent of psychoanalysis and that we must make up our minds that the arts must be pursued by their own means and systems if one wishes to advance them.

My Belief

1931

I HAVE NOT ONLY occasionally made a confession of belief in essays, but once, a little more than ten years ago, attempted to set forth my belief in a book. The book is called *Siddhartha* and its religious content has been frequently examined and discussed by Hindu scholars and Japanese priests but not by their Christian colleagues.

The fact that my faith in this book bore a Hindu name and had a Hindu face is no accident. I have encountered religion in two forms, as child and grandchild of upright pious Protestants and as a reader of Hindu revelations, among which I place at the top of the list the Upanishads, the Bhagavad-Gita, and the discourses of the Buddha. Nor was it any accident that in the midst of a genuine, living Christian atmosphere I experienced my first religious stirrings in Hindu form. My father and my mother and her father as well spent their whole lives in the service of the Christian mission to India, and although it was only one of my cousins and I who realized that there is no order of precedence among religions, nevertheless my father, mother, and grandfather had not only a rich and fairly thorough knowledge of Hindu forms of belief but also a sympathy, though only half admitted, for those forms. I breathed and participated in spiritual Hinduism from childhood just as much as I did in Christianity.

On the other hand, I encountered Christianity in a unique and rigid form, decisive in my life, a meager and transitory form now outdated and almost extinct. I encountered it as pietistically tinged Protestantism, and the experience was deep and strong: the lives of my grandparents and parents were entirely controlled by the Kingdom of God and stood in its service. That men should see their lives as a loan from

God, and try to live them not on egoistic impulse but as
service and sacrifice to God, this chief experience and inheritance of my childhood has strongly influenced my life. I
have never taken the "world" and worldly people quite seriously, and I do it less and less with the years. But however
grand and noble this Christianity as lived by my elders was—
as service and sacrifice, as community and commitment—the
confessional and in part sectarian forms in which we children
came to know it were very early questionable in my eyes and
in part completely intolerable. There are many verses spoken
and sung that even at that time offended the poet in me, and
as my first childhood came to an end I was by no means
ignorant of how much persons like my father and grandfather suffered and agonized because they did not have, like
Catholics, a firmly established creed and dogma, an approved
ritual, a genuine, true Church.

The fact that the so-called Protestant Church did not exist,
that rather it had fallen apart, into a great number of small
established churches, that the history of these churches and
their overlords, the Protestant princes, was no nobler than
that of the despised Popish Church, that, furthermore, almost all true Christianity and true devotion to the Kingdom
of God were not to be found in these boring by-way churches,
but in even more obscure, though for that very reason inspired and active, conventicles of more dubious and transitory form—all this was no secret to me in my fairly early
youth, although in my father's house the established churches
and their traditional forms were always mentioned with
reverence (a reverence which I felt was not wholly genuine
and early grew doubtful of). And as a matter of fact during
my whole Christian youth I did not derive any sort of religious
experience from the Church. The personal family meditations
and prayers, my parents' conduct of life, their royal poverty,
their open hand for misery, their brotherliness toward fellow
Christians, their concern about the heathen, the whole inspired heroism of their Christian lives clearly got its nourishment from reading the Bible and not from the Church, and
the divine services on Sunday; the Confirmation class and

instruction in the Catechism brought me no sense of religious feeling.

Now in comparison with this narrow and pinched form of Christianity, with these somewhat mawkish hymns, these generally so boring ministers and sermons, the world of Indian religion and poetry was frankly far more inviting. Here no such oppressive narrowness, no smell of the sober gray paint of pulpits or of pietistic Bible hours; my imagination had room, I could welcome without resistance the first messages that reached me from the world of India and they have continued all my life to have their effect on me.

Later on, my own personal religion often changed in form, never suddenly in the sense of a conversion but always slowly as growth and development. The fact that my Siddhartha puts not knowledge but love ahead of everything, that he rejects dogma and makes the experience of unity the central point, may be interpreted as a swinging back toward Christianity, yes, as a truly Protestant characteristic.

The Chinese spiritual world did not become known to me until later than the Hindu one, and this produced new developments; the classical Chinese concept of virtue, which allowed me to see Confucius and Socrates as brothers, and the hidden wisdom of Lao-tse with its mystic dynamism influenced me greatly. A later wave of Christian influence came through my association with certain Catholics of high spiritual rank, especially my friend Hugo Ball, whose relentless criticism of the Reformation I could acknowledge without, however, becoming a Catholic. At that time I also saw something of the business and politics of the Catholics, and I perceived how a character of the purity and greatness of Hugo Ball was made use of by his Church and its political representatives, now for propaganda purposes according to expediency, now dropped, now repudiated. Obviously this Church too was no ideal place for religion, obviously here there were also at work the struggling and pretension, the quarreling and the rude push for power, obviously here too Christian life preferred to withdraw into privacy and concealment.

And so in my religious life Christianity plays by no means the only role, but nevertheless a commanding one, more a mystic Christianity than an ecclesiastical one, and it lives not without conflict but nevertheless without warfare beside a more Hindu-Asiatic-colored faith whose single dogma is the concept of unity. I have never lived without religion and could not live for a single day without it, but all my life long I have done without a church. The separate churches divided by creeds and politics have always seemed to me, and most of all during the World War, like caricatures of nationalism, and the inability of the Protestant sects to achieve a supra-denominational unity was to me always an accusatory symbol of German inability to unite. In earlier years such thoughts prompted me to look with some awe and a certain degree of envy toward the Roman Catholic Church, and my Protestant yearning for an enduring form, for tradition, for a manifestation of the spirit even today aids me in retaining my reverence for this greatest cultural structure of the West. But this admirable Catholic Church is in my eyes only worthy of this reverence at a distance, and as soon as I approach, it has a smell, like every human institution, a strong smell of blood and power, of politics and secrecy. Nevertheless occasionally I envy the Catholic his opportunity of saying his prayers before the altar instead of in a narrow room, and making his confession through the orifice of the confessional instead of always simply laying it bare to the irony of his lonely self-criticism.

Gratitude to Goethe*
1932

O F ALL GERMAN POETS, Goethe is the one to whom I owe
most, the one who has preoccupied me most, oppressed, encouraged, and forced me to follow him or to rebel.
He is not by any means the poet I have loved and enjoyed
most, against whom I have had the least resistance—oh no,
others are ahead of him there: Eichendorff, Jean Paul, Hölderlin, Novalis, Mörike, and others as well. But none of these
beloved poets has become a serious problem for me or a significant moral stumbling block; with none of them have I had
to wage battles and arguments, whereas with Goethe I have
constantly been forced to hold imaginary conversations and
engage in conflicts of ideas (one of them is recorded in
Steppenwolf, one from among hundreds). For this reason I
would like to try to show what Goethe has meant to me and
under which aspects he has generally appeared to me.

I learned to know him when I was still a boy, and his
youthful poems, together with *Werther*, won me completely.
To surrender myself to Goethe the poet was easy, for he
brought with him the fragrance of youth, together with the
fragrance of forest, meadow, and wheat field, and in his
language, beginning with the counselor's wife, all the profundity and playfulness of folk wisdom, the sounds of nature
and men at work, and in addition a high degree of music.
This Goethe the pure poet, the singer, the eternally young
and naïve, has therefore never been a problem for me and
has never grown pale in my eyes.

On the other hand, while I was still young, I came upon a
different Goethe: the great author, the humanist, ideologue,

* Written at the request of Romain Rolland for the Goethe
number of the magazine *Europe*.

and educator, the critic and programmatist, the Weimarian man of letters, Goethe the friend of Schiller, the art collector, the founder of newspapers, the author of countless essays and letters, Eckermann's autocrat, and this Goethe too became enormously important to me. In the beginning I admired and honored him too without reservation and defended him against my friends, even for those documents which seemed to have been written in a chancellery. If now and then he appeared a bit middle-class, a bit commonplace, somewhat official, and too much at variance with Werther's wildness, the format was nevertheless always handsome and the intended goal a lofty one, the noblest of all goals: to make possible and to establish a life ruled by the spirit, not just for himself but for his nation and his time. Even in its failures, it was an attempt to master knowledge completely, and every form of human experience in his time, and to put them to the service of a high personal spirit, yes, beyond that into the service of a suprapersonal spirituality and morality. Goethe had set up for the elect of his time a model of humanity, an example which it became the goal of men of good will to simulate or to approach.

In Goethe the poet, there was much to enjoy but nothing to learn. What he could do was unique and unteachable. Therefore he became neither a model nor a problem for me. On the other hand, the man of letters, the humanist and ideologue Goethe soon *did* become an important problem for me; no other writer except Nietzsche has preoccupied me to such an extent, attracted me so and pained me so, compelled me to such heated arguments. Part of the way, Goethe the man of letters seemed to be walking parallel with Goethe the poet and to be almost the same person, but suddenly they were far apart, contradicted each other and broke off relations. If the poet was more sympathetic and brought greater enjoyment, nevertheless Goethe the man of letters had to be taken very seriously and could not be evaded. This I felt when I was twenty years old, for his was the grandest and obviously the most successful attempt to base a German life on the spirit. Moreover, his was a completely unique attempt to form a syn-

thesis of German genius with reason, to reconcile the man of
the world with the stormer of heaven, Antonio with Tasso,
the irresponsible musical-Dionysiac enthusiast with the apostle of responsibility and moral duty.

Obviously this attempt was not wholly successful. Indeed,
it could not succeed! Nevertheless it had to be repeated again
and again, for to strive for the highest and the impossible—
just this seemed to me to be the hallmark of the spirit. Goethe
in his own life and works was not completely able to unite
the naïve poet with the shrewd man of the world, the soul
with reason, the worshipper of nature with the extoller of
the intellect; here and there a wide crack appeared, here and
there painful, yes, intolerable conflicts arose. At times reason
and virtue hung about the poet like an oversized peruke on
his head, and not infrequently his naïve genius was smothered in a stiffness that rose from his striving after awareness
and restraint.

And in addition Goethe does not seem to have succeeded in
establishing himself as an example and leaving behind him
anything like a real school or teaching. Even those poets and
writers who tried most zealously to follow his example did
not attain the desired unity and in fact remained far behind
their model. One example among many was Stifter, a much-
loved poet of the first rank, who in his marvelous *Indian
Summer* occasionally emits, exactly like a little Goethe, philistine commonplaces about art and life in a wooden language,
passages that startle one because they can appear so close to
others of enchanting beauty. The model was unmistakable,
and one silently reminded oneself that in *Wilhelm Meister*
too the most marvelously poetic pages stood beside exactly
similar hopeless aridities.

No, Goethe had not been so entirely successful, and at
times for this very reason he was extremely annoying and
painful to me. But was he in the end, as those naïve Marxists
who had not read him would have it, no more than a hero of
the middle class, one of the creators of an unimportant,
short-lived, now long since outmoded ideology?

I might have set him aside then and let the matter rest on

a note of disappointment, but that was exactly what I could not do! Just this was the marvelous, beautiful, and also tormenting thing: one could not get free of him, one had to join in his assaults, suffer with him in his failures, find his duality within oneself!

This in itself was winning and important: that he did not content himself with little goals, that he sought the greatest, that he erected ideals that could not be attained. Compelling, however, beyond everything else was the insight that increased in me year by year that Goethe's problem was not his alone, and not that of the middle class alone, but that it was the problem of every German who was serious about the spirit of the written word. One could not be a German writer and avoid Goethe's example and his attempts, whether they failed or not. Other men of letters might have been far more brilliant in representing the spirit of their time in words, Voltaire, for example, might have given his century and his social class a sharper and more complete portraiture. But was not Voltaire for that very reason out of date, was he anything more to us than a memory, the name of a great virtuoso? Did we still have any emotional and responsible interest in his efforts and opinions? No. But Goethe had not wilted with his age, he still mattered to us, he was still uncannily contemporary.

Thus for many years I tormented myself with Goethe and allowed him to become a disturbance in my inner life, him and Nietzsche. Had not the World War come, I would have continued to think the same thoughts a thousand times and endure the same alternations. But the war did come and with it the old problem of the German writer; the tragic fate of the spirit and the word in German life appeared more painful to me than ever. The complete failure of those tribunals which Goethe had helped to build became apparent. An irresponsible writing rabble appeared on the scene, partly drunk with enthusiasm, partly, too, simply bribed, a very patriotic but stupid, mendacious, and coarse writing rabble, unworthy of Goethe, unworthy of the spirit, unworthy of the German people. Even famous scholars and authors were suddenly writing like noncoms; it not only seemed as though every bridge between spirit and people had broken down, it seemed as though the spirit no longer existed at all. (It is not my task here to investigate how far this phenomenon was not purely German but a hallmark of many or all of the countries at war; for me it was important in its German form, and in its German form it challenged me to fight. My duty was not to discover whether France and England had been abandoned by the spirit and to warn them against the sins against the spirit increasing daily, but rather to do this on my own home ground.)

Here the problems of Goethe in my life seemed to cease for a prolonged period. The problem was now no longer Goethe but war, and when the war came to an end the problem was Europe, and today the situation in all the countries of Europe is that the small minority of those who think have recognized precisely what the problems and demands of the hour are, whereas collective officialdom and the politicians continue to fight close to the edge of the abyss for the motley banners of long-dead ideals.

It was war, and for the moment Goethe was shunted aside, whereas the regulation of human life through the spirit, which was Goethe's great problem, was the single burning problem in the world. We men of letters, insofar as we were not corrupted or simply intoxicated by war, found ourselves compelled to examine minutely the foundations of our lives and to become clear, little by little, about our own responsibilities. My own spiritual concerns were at white heat. But even in the midst of the war there were from time to time arguments with Goethe, and occasionally the actual conflict suddenly conjured up his figure, which once again became a symbol to me. During the first stage of the war the spiritual and ethical problem that had made my life a torment was the apparently insoluble conflict between spirit and love of one's fatherland. At that time, if one had been willing to believe the official voices, from great scholars to newspaper columnists, then the spirit (that is, truth and service to the truth) was the immediate and deadly enemy of patriotism. A patriot, according to public opinion, would have nothing to do with truth, was in no way obligated to such frivolity and chimera; or rather, the spirit was permitted within the boundaries of patriotism just so far as it could be misused—to support the cannon. Truth was a luxury, and lies in the service of the fatherland were permitted and extolled. I could not make this patriot's morality my own, however much I loved Germany, for I saw in the spirit not a chance tool or weapon of war, and I was not a general or chancellor but a servant of the spirit. At that time and in this connection, then, Goethe confronted me once more. The patriots who were then trying to exploit every resource of the nation in the cause of the war very soon discovered that Goethe was unusable for this purpose; he was no nationalist, and a few times he had even ventured to tell his people some very unpalatable truths. From the summer of 1914 Goethe and with him many other great minds fell very low on the intellectual exchange, and in order to fill out the empty spaces (for great minds were needed for the disgusting business of "cultural propaganda") other names were discovered and plastered on the billboards, names that were better adapted to the justification of nationalism and the war: the most successful of these exhumations was Hegel.

When at that time Romain Rolland in one of his articles about the war discovered in me a political ally and described my standpoint as "Goethean" the word struck me as a piercing reminder: it recalled Goethe to me as the star of my youth, and it strengthened in me all that was holy; at the same time I was not unaware of the fact that from the official German point of view the description "Goethean" was neither more nor less than a term of abuse.

That stage too has passed. And it turns out that even the war, that violent eruption into our lives, was not able to separate me from Goethe or to make him a subject of indifference.

Why was that? Was Goethe ultimately even more than the partially frustrated writer and ideologue, was he not even a little more than simply the poet of genius and lord of language? Why must one keep going back to him, even after

so many arguments, so many disagreements with him on
important matters?

When I try to get to the bottom of this, then another Goethe
rises before my eyes, less clearly outlined, half visible, mysterious: Goethe the wise. However clear and endearing the
picture of Goethe the magic poet seems to me, however dis-
tinctly I believe I see Goethe the man of letters and educator
—behind these figures, shining through them, stands still that
other figure. For me this is the loftiest figure of Goethe, and
in it the contradictions are reconciled; it does not wrap itself
in one-sided Apollonian classicism, nor in the dark spirit of
Faust in search of the "Mothers"; rather it consists precisely
in this bipolarity, in this being nowhere and everywhere at
home. Single sayings and verses of this mysterious wise man
are to be found especially in the works of his old age, in
poems, in the late parts of *Faust,* in letters, in the "Novelle."
But the same mature, already suprapersonal Goethe looks out
at us, once we know him, from much evidence and proof of
his manhood and youth. He was always present, he simply
hid himself for long periods. He is timeless, for all wisdom is
timeless. He is impersonal, for all wisdom transcends the
person.

This wisdom of Goethe's, which he himself often kept
hidden, which often seemed lost to him, is no longer middle-
class, is no longer storm and stress or even classicism or even
Biedermeier, it is indeed hardly still Goethean, but instead
breathes the same air as the wisdom of India, China, Greece,
is no longer will and no longer intellect but piety, awe, the
willingness to serve—Tao. Every true poet has a spark of it,
neither art nor religion is possible without it, and certainly it
emanates from the smallest poem by Eichendorff, but in
Goethe's case it expressed itself a few times in such magical
words as are not to be found in every nation or in every
century. It stands high above all literature. It is nothing but
reverence, nothing but awe at life, it wants simply to serve
and knows no pretensions, no demands, no rights. It is that
wisdom of which the sagas of all noble peoples speak, that
once was present at the time of the great rulers and to which

the rulers and their servants proved disloyal, and going back
to it is the only way to reconcile earth once more with heaven.

To me, who have a special love for the classical Chinese
authors, it seems that Goethe too has a Chinese aspect. For
this reason it gives me special pleasure to know that on
several occasions Goethe became immersed in Chinese literature and that a small and marvelous group of poems of his
old age (written in the year 1827) bears the superscription:
"Chinese-German Times of the Year and Times of the Day."
In more modern literature we do not have many expressions
of this primeval wisdom. In Germany it has but seldom found
expression in words; Germany is more mature, more pious,
and more wise in its music than in its words.

The fact that Goethe, through and beyond his activity as a
poet and as a man of letters, rose by degrees to this highest
point, to the peace above the maelstroms, it is this that has
drawn me back to him again and again, that has impelled me
to study many even of his dubious or unsuccessful writings.
For there is no nobler spectacle than the human being who
has become wise and has thrown off the limitations of the
temporal and personal. And when we know a person who we
think has attained this, then he embodies for us an interest
beyond comparison with anything else on earth. And when
we have moments of doubt about all faith, all wisdom, then
it can be a very real comfort to follow the steps of a wise man
and to see how human, how weak, how inadequate he too
could be at times.

I have to conclude from many indications that the youth of
Germany today barely knows Goethe. Presumably their
teachers have spared them this. But if I were in charge of a
school or high school, I would forbid the reading of Goethe
and keep him in reserve as the highest reward for the best,
maturest, and worthiest students. They would discover with
amazement how directly he confronts the reader of today with
the great question of today, the question of Europe. And they
would find, in the spirit that can save us and in the readiness
to serve that spirit by every sacrifice, no better guide and
comrade than Goethe.

A Bit of Theology

1932

FROM THE THOUGHTS and notes of several years I have decided today to try to bring into relationship two of my favorite concepts: that of the three stages of human development known to me, and that of two types of human beings. The first of these ideas is important to me, holy, in fact; I consider it the simple truth. The second is purely subjective and I do not, I hope, take it more seriously than it deserves; however, now and again it does me good service in my observations of life and history. The path of human development begins with innocence (paradise, childhood, the irresponsible first stage). From there it leads to guilt, to the knowledge of good and evil, to the demand for culture, for morality, for religions, for human ideals. For everyone who passes through this stage seriously and as a differentiated individual it ends unfailingly in disillusionment, that is, with the insight that no perfect virtue, no complete obedience, no adequate service exists, that righteousness is unreachable, that consistent goodness is unattainable. Now this despair leads either to defeat or to a third realm of the spirit, to the experience of a condition beyond morality and law, an advance into grace and release to a new, higher kind of irresponsibility, or to put it briefly: to faith. No matter which forms and expressions the faith assumes, its content is always the same: that we should certainly strive for the good insofar as we are able, but that we are not responsible for the imperfections of this world or for our own, that we do not govern ourselves but are governed, that, above our understanding, is God or "It" whose servants we are and to which we may surrender ourselves.

I have expressed this in European, almost Christian

fashion. Indian Brahmanism (which, if one includes its opposite wave, Buddhism, is probably mankind's highest
achievement in theology) has many categories that can be
interpreted quite similarly. There the sequence of stages is
something like this: the naïve person controlled by fear and
greed longs for deliverance. The means and path to this are
yoga, education in controlling the instincts. No matter
whether yoga is carried on as a wholly physical and mechanical penitential exercise or as the highest form of spiritual
training, always its meaning is: education in contempt of the
world of appearances and the senses, attention to the spirit,
the atman, which dwells within us and is one with the world
soul. Yoga corresponds exactly to our second stage; it is a
striving for deliverance through works. It is regarded with
awe and overvalued by the populace. The naïve person always
inclines to see a penitent as a holy man and one who has attained deliverance. Yoga, however, is only a stage and ends
in despair. The Buddha legends (and a hundred others)
represent all this in clear pictures. Only when yoga yields to
grace, when it is recognized as ambition, as busyness, as
eagerness and hunger, when he who is awakening from the
dream of pseudo-life recognizes himself as eternal and incorruptible, as spirit of spirit, as Atman, does he become the
uninvolved observer of life and can at will act or remain
passive, enjoy or refrain, without his ego being in any way
involved. His ego has become entirely Self. This "enlightenment" of the holy men (identical in meaning with Buddha's
Nirvana) corresponds to our third stage. Once more in Lao-
tse one finds the same series of stages, though in somewhat
different symbolism. His "way" leads from striving after
righteousness to striving no longer, from guilt and morality to
Tao, and for me the most important spiritual experiences are
connected with the fact that gradually and with pauses of
years and decades I found the same interpretation of human
life among the Hindus, the Chinese, and the Christians, I was
confirmed in my intuition of a central problem, which I found
expressed everywhere in analogous symbols. These experiences supported more strongly than anything else my belief

that mankind has a meaning, that human need and human searching at all times and throughout the whole world are a unity. It is unimportant from this point of view whether we regard, as many do today, the religious-philosophical expression of human thinking and experience as something outmoded, an exercise of an epoch now outdated. It does not matter to me if what I am here calling "theology" is transient, a product of one stage of human development that someday will be superseded and left behind. Art too and even speech are perhaps means of communication that are appropriate only to certain stages in human history and they also may become obsolescent and replaceable. But at each stage nothing will be so important to men, it seems to me, in their search for truth, nothing will be so valuable and comforting as the realization that beneath the division in race, color, language, and culture there lies a unity, that there are not various peoples and minds but only One Humanity, only One Spirit.

Once more in outline: the way leads from innocence into guilt, out of guilt into despair, out of despair either to failure or to deliverance: that is, not back again behind morality and culture into a child's paradise but over and beyond these into the ability to live by the strength of one's faith.

At any stage, of course, a step backward may ensue. It would be rare, however, for one who has become awakened to relapse from the realm where good and evil hold sway, back into innocence. But it happens very often that one who has already had the experience of grace and deliverance will fall back once more to the second stage and again be the victim of its laws, of fear, of forever unfulfillable demands.

Thus far I can recognize the stages in the evolution of a human soul. I know them from my own experience and from the evidence of many other souls. Always, at every point in history and in all religions and life-styles, these typical experiences occur in the same stages and sequence: loss of innocence, concern about righteousness under the law, followed by despair in a fruitless struggle to overcome guilt through works, or by knowledge and final emergence from hell into a changed world and into a new form of innocence. Mankind has sketched for itself a hundred times in magnificent symbols this course of development: that which is most familiar to us begins with Adam in paradise and ends with Christian redemption.

It is true that many of these symbolic representations show us stages of development that are even higher: to Mahatma, to God, to the pure existence of spirit unencumbered by the nothingness of matter and immune to the torments of change. All religions know these ideals, and there is one ideal that has often appeared to me as the best: the perfect individual free from pain, immaculate, immortal. But whether this ideal is anything but a noble dream, whether it ever was translated into experience and reality, whether a human being ever actually became God, about this I know nothing. About those principal stages in the soul's history, however, I do know; I know about them, and everyone who has experienced them knows that they are realities. Now whether those dreamed-of even higher stages of human development exist or not, it is nevertheless a welcome thing for us that they are present as dreams, as ideals, as poetry, as longed-for goals. If they were ever really experienced by human beings, then these persons have remained silent about them and by their very essence they are incomprehensible and incommunicable to one who has not been touched by them. In the sacred legends of all religions there are hints of such experiences that sound convincing. In the false teachings of small sects and false prophets we find frequent descriptions of them, but the accounts bear all the earmarks of hallucination or conscious fraud.

But it is by no means only those mystical final stages and possibilities of experience of the soul that elude understanding and unambiguous communication. Even the earlier and indeed very earliest steps on the path of the soul are comprehensible and communicable only for one who has experienced them in his own person. Anyone still living in his first innocence will never understand confessions from the realms of guilt, despair, deliverance; they will sound just as nonsensical to him as the mythologies of foreign peoples do to an untraveled reader. On the other hand, everyone understands the typical experiences of the soul that he himself has had, recognizes them infallibly and instantly when he encounters them in the reports of another—even in those cases where he has to translate them out of a foreign and unfamiliar theology. Every Christian who has had a genuine experience himself invariably recognizes the same thing in the cases of Paul, Pascal, Luther, Ignatius. And every Christian who has come a bit nearer the center of faith and therefore has outgrown the realm of simply "Christian" experience always finds among the adherents of other religions, only in a different symbolic language, all the basic experiences of the soul, with all their typical characteristics.

To describe my own, originally Christian, spiritual history and systematically to derive from it my personal form of faith would be an impossible task; all my books are an attempt to do that. For some of my readers these books have a perfectly definite meaning and worth: they find in them the confirmation and clarification of their own most important experiences, victories and defeats. Their number is not great, but in general there are not a great many people who have spiritual experiences. The majority never become fully human, they remain in their primeval condition, childishly below such conflicts and developments; the majority perhaps never come to know even the "second stage," but remain in the irresponsible animal world of their instincts and infant dreams, and the saga of a condition beyond their twilight, of good and of evil, of doubt concerning good and evil, of an emergence from misery into the light of grace, sounds ludicrous to them.

There may be a thousand fashions in which individuation and the spiritual history of a human being can be achieved. The path of this history, however, and the sequence of its steps are always the same. —To observe how this invariably rigid path is encountered in so many different ways by dif-

ferent types of men, struggled and suffered over, is probably
the most rewarding passion of the historian, the psychologist,
and the poet.

Among our attempts to understand this colorful picture
book and to get hold of it rationally and divide it up systematically, there stands at the top of the list the age-old effort to
divide and arrange mankind by types. If I too in my own way
and according to my own observation now attempt to present
two fundamentally opposed basic types of human beings and
accordingly two basically different ways in which the un-
changing path of man can be experienced, I am well aware in
doing so that every presentation of so-called basic types of
people is simply a game. There is not a limited or unlimited
number of permanent types into which people can be divided:
nothing can be more damaging to a philosopher than the
literal belief in any theory of types. There is, however, a
classification of types—constantly made use of unconsciously
by people—as a game, as an attempt to handle the mass of
our experience, as a feeble means of ordering the events of
our world. Even the small child presumably distinguishes
people around him according to types whose originals are his
father, mother, and nurse. Out of my experience and reading
I have arrived at a division of people into two principal types,
which I call men of reason and men of piety. For me, the
world divides itself according to this very crude system. But
naturally, on the basis of a mere device, the division lasts only
an instant, thereafter to fall once more into an impenetrable
puzzle. I have long since given up the belief that we are
granted more by way of knowledge and insight into the chaos
of world events than the apparent order revealed in a happy
instant, the occasionally encountered happy experience when,
for a second, chaos presents itself as cosmos.

If in such a happy moment I apply my formula "reason or
piety" to world history, then at that instant humanity consists
for me simply of these two types. I believe I know to what type
each historical figure belongs, and also I believe I know this
precisely about myself: that is, that I belong to the species of
the pious, not to that of the rational. But in the next instant,

when that pleasant mental excitement is over, the nicely ordered world collapses once more into meaningless confusion and what I had just thought I saw so clearly, that is, to which of my two types Buddha or Paul or Caesar or Lenin belonged, I now do not know at all; and, unfortunately, I am no longer at all certain about myself. Just now I knew with assurance that I was a man of piety—and now I discover trait by trait the signs in me of the man of reason and, with a special clarity, the disagreeable traits.

It is the same with all knowledge. Knowledge is action. Knowledge is experience. It does not last. Its duration is an instant. —I shall now try, avoiding any attempt to be systematic, to give a rough sketch of the two types that provided me with the pattern for my mental game.

The man of reason believes in nothing so much as human reason. He considers it not a pretty gift but the absolute highest.

The man of reason believes he possesses within himself the "meaning" of the world and of his life. He projects the semblance of order and efficiency of a well-organized individual into the world and history. Therefore he believes in progress. He sees that the men of today can shoot better and travel faster than those of earlier times, and he will not and dare not see that opposed to these advances there are a thousand regressions. He believes the man of today to be a higher evolvement than Confucius, Socrates, or Jesus because the man of today has developed certain technical capabilities to a higher degree. The man of reason believes that the earth was given to men for exploitation. His most feared enemy is death. He avoids thinking about the transcience of his life and activity and when he cannot avoid the idea of death he opposes death with a redoubled energy and seeks refuge in acquisitive activity: for possessions, for knowledge, for laws, for a rational mastery of the world. His belief in immortality is faith in that progress; because he is an active link in the eternal chain of progress he believes that he is fully protected against annihilation.

The man of reason is occasionally inclined toward hatred

and irritation at the pious man who does not believe in this progress and is a deterrent to the realization of the rational ideal. One has only to remember the fanaticism of revolutionaries or the expressions of the most violent impatience from all progressive, democratic, rational, socialistic authors against disbelievers.

The man of reason seems more assured of his faith in the daily life than the pious man. In the name of the goddess of reason he feels justified in giving orders, organizing, exerting power over his fellow man, on whom he thinks he is simply bestowing favors: hygiene, morality, democracy, etc.

The man of reason strives for power if only in order to accomplish "the good." His greatest danger lies here, in striving for power, in misusing it, in love of giving orders, in the exercise of terror. Trotsky, who finds it utterly unbearable to see a peasant beaten, allows hundreds of thousands to be slaughtered without scruple, for the sake of his idea.

The man of reason easily falls in love with systems. Since these reasonable men seek and gain power they can not only despise and hate the pious man, they can persecute him, bring suits against him, they can kill him. They assume the responsibility of holding power and applying it "for the good," and all means to this end are to them justified, up to and including guns. The man of reason can at times fall into despair at seeing nature and what he calls stupidity remain so strong. —Sometimes he finds it hard to endure the fact that he has to prosecute, punish, and kill.

His transcendent moments are those when, in spite of all evidence to the contrary, he feels strong within him the faith that, after all, reason is essentially one with the spirit that created and governs the world.

The man of reason rationalizes the world and does violence to it. He inclines always to grim earnestness. He is an educator.

The man of reason is always inclined to distrust his instincts.

The man of reason always feels uncertain in the face of nature and of art. Sometimes he looks down on them contemptuously, sometimes he overvalues them superstitiously. It is he who pays millions for old masterpieces or establishes reservations for birds, wild animals, and Indians.

The basis of the pious man's faith and attitude toward life is reverence. This expresses itself in two principal characteristics: a strong sense of nature and a belief in a suprarational world order. The pious man treasures reason, to be sure, as a precious gift, but does not see in it an adequate means of understanding the world, still less of mastering it.

The pious man believes that the human being is an ancillary part of the earth. He finds refuge, when horror of death and mortality seizes him, in the faith that the creator (or nature) is striving toward a goal even through these terrifying means, and he sees no virtue in forgetting the thought of death or struggling against it but rather in a trembling but reverent surrender to a higher will.

He does not believe in progress, since his model is not reason but nature, and since in nature he can perceive no progress but only a living out and self-realization of infinite forces without any perceptible final goal.

The pious man inclines occasionally toward hatred and impatience at the men of reason; the Bible is full of crude examples of uncontrollable impatience against unbelievers and their worldly ideals. Yet in rare exalted moments the pious man also experiences the lightning of that spiritual feeling that gives him the faith to believe that all the fanaticism and wildness of the rationalists, all wars, all persecutions and enslavements in the name of higher ideals, in the end must also serve God's purpose.

The pious man does not strive for power, he recoils from using force upon others. He does not like to command, and this is his greatest virtue. On the other hand, he is often too tepid in his zeal for worthy ends, he easily leans toward quietism and omphaloskepsis. Often he is glad to hug his ideals and be content, without exerting himself for their realization. Since God (or nature) is after all stronger than we are, why should he try to interfere?

The pious man readily falls in love with mythologies. He is

able to hate or despise but he does not persecute and kill. Never will Socrates or Jesus be the prosecutor and slayer, always the sufferer. On the other hand, the pious man often lightheartedly assumes no less grave responsibilities. He is answerable not only for his lukewarmness in working toward high ideals, he is answerable too for his own destruction and the guilt that his enemy incurs in slaying him.

The pious man mythologizes the world and in so doing often does not take it seriously enough. He always inclines a little toward playfulness. He does not educate his children but regards them as blessed. He is always inclined to distrust his intelligence.

The pious man always feels himself comfortably at home in the presence of nature and of art; on the other hand, he is uncertain about education and knowledge. Sometimes he despises these as stupid stuff and is unjust to them, sometimes again he overvalues them superstitiously. To take an extreme case of collision: let us say that a pious man is caught up in the reason-machine and unwillingly takes part either in a lawsuit or a war on the orders of the men of reason and is lost—in such a case both parties are always at fault. The man of reason is guilty because there are such things as death penalties, prisons, wars, guns. The pious man, however, has done nothing to make all this impossible. The two legal actions in which more clearly and symbolically than in any other a pious man was put to death by men of reason, the trial of Socrates and of the Savior, show moments of a terrifying ambiguity. Could not the Athenians and Pilate have easily found, without sacrifice of their own prestige, an attitude that would have allowed them to discharge the accused? And could not Socrates as well as Jesus, instead of making their accusers guilty through a certain heroic ferocity and dying in order to triumph over them—could they not without too much difficulty have prevented the tragedy? Certainly. But tragedies are never prevented; they are not unhappy accidents but the collisions of opposing worlds.

If what I have written constantly opposes the "pious man" to the "man of reason," the reader must always bear in mind the purely psychological meaning of these labels. Naturally the "pious" have been just the ones who on occasion have wielded the sword, and the "men of reason" have bled (during the Inquisition, for example). But by the pious I naturally do not mean the priest and by the men of reason those who take joy in thought. When a Spanish court of Inquisition burned a "freethinker," it was the inquisitor who was the man of reason, the organizer, the man of power; his victim was the man of piety.

Moreover it is, of course, far from my intention, despite a certain crudeness in my system, to deny efficiency to the man of piety or genius to the man of reason. Genius flourishes in both camps, as do idealism, heroism, and a readiness for sacrifice. The "men of reason" Hegel, Marx, Lenin (ultimately Trotsky) I consider all to be geniuses. On the other hand, a pious man opposed to force, like Tolstoy, nevertheless made the greatest sacrifices for material ends.

In general it seems to me that one characteristic of the man of genius is that although he represents an especially favored exemplar of his type, at the same time he bears within him a secret longing for the opposite pole, a silent respect for the opposing type. The mere calculator is never a genius, just as little as the mere man of moods. Many exceptional men seem to oscillate between the two basic types and to be mastered by profoundly opposing gifts which do not stifle but strengthen each other; among the many examples of this belong the pious mathematicians (Pascal).

And so, just as the pious genius and the genius of reason know each other very well, secretly love each other, are attracted to each other, so too the highest spiritual experience of which we human beings are capable is always a reconciliation between reason and reverence, a recognition that the great contradictions are one and the same thing.

Final Reflections

Now if in conclusion we apply the two schemes to each other—the scheme of the three stages of human development to the two basic human types—we shall find, of course, that the meaning of the three stages is the same for both types. But we shall also discover that the dangers and hopes of the two types are different. The condition of childhood and natural innocence will be represented by the two types similarly. But the very first step in human development, the entrance into the realm of good and evil, is different for the two. The pious person will be more childlike, he will leave paradise with less impatience, more reluctance, to experience the consciousness of guilt. By way of recompense, however, in the next stage he will have stronger wings on his way from guilt to grace. He will in general pay as little attention as possible to the middle stage (called by Freud "civilization and its discontents") and will withdraw from it as much as possible. With his essential feeling of being an alien in the realm of guilt and discomfort, the ascent in some circumstances to the next stage of release is made easier. Sometimes, however, the infantile retreat into paradise, into the irresponsible world without good or evil, will be easy for him and he will succeed in making it.

For the man of reason, on the contrary, the second stage, the stage of guilt, the stage of culture, of activity and civilization, is quite literally home. His childhood does not seriously encumber him, or for long; he likes to work, he gladly bears responsibility, and neither has he homesickness for his lost childhood nor does he especially long for freedom from good and evil, although this experience is something that he too can desire and can achieve. More easily than the man of piety he succumbs to the belief that things can be settled through the tasks imposed by morality and culture. It is harder for him than for the man of piety to reach the stage of despair, to see the defeat of his efforts, the negation of his righteousness. On the other hand, once despair has set in, it will perhaps be less easy for him to surrender to the temptation of fleeing into the primitive world of irresponsibility.

At the level of innocence, the pious and the reasonable fight each other like children of varied gifts.

At the second level the two opposing poles, now having become conscious, fight each other with the violence, passion, and tragedy of enemy governments.

On the third level the warriors begin to recognize each other no longer as strangers but as being dependent upon each other. They begin to love each other, to long for each other. From here the road leads toward possibilities for humanity whose realization has not yet been glimpsed by human eye.

On Reading a Novel

1933

RECENTLY I READ A NOVEL, the work of a gifted author with a certain reputation; an attractive, youthful work that interested me and in a number of places gave me pleasure, although it dealt exclusively with people and things that in real life interest me very little. The story is about people living in big cities, and they are passionately engaged in filling their lives to the brim with "experiences," with pleasures and sensations, because otherwise life would be valueless, neither worth living nor worth writing about. There are many such novels, and occasionally I read one because, as a country character living a retired life, I like once in a while to find out about my contemporaries, especially about the lives of those contemporaries from whom I find myself cut off by a great abyss, people who are strangers to me, whose passions and opinions have in my eyes the magic of the marvelous, exotic, and incomprehensible; in short, the life of the pleasure seekers and cosmopolitans. For the life of this class I have more than the playful interest that a European may have in elephants and crocodiles; I have a very well founded and legitimate curiosity. It is not, in fact, a secret to me that however quietly one may remain on one's country acres, nevertheless one's life and well-being are influenced by those people in the big cities—and how greatly and inescapably influenced they are! For there in that confusion, in that atmosphere of harried, impulse-ridden, and therefore unpredictable life, decisions are made about war and peace, about markets and foreign exchange, not by men but by the fashion, by the stock exchange, by the mood, by the "Street." What the cosmopolitan calls "life" is carried on almost exclusively at that level, and what he means by "life" in addition to politics is business and society, and by society in turn he means almost exclusively the part of his life that is devoted to a search for sensation and pleasure. That metropolis whose life I do not share and which is foreign to me makes decisions about many things that are of a certain importance to me. Nor am I unaware of the fact that among the readers of my books the larger part are city dwellers, although in no way do I write or am able to write for them, since I know them only from a great distance and take the little that I have seen of the outer aspects of their lives with about as much seriousness as I do my own wallet or the momentary form of our government: precious little, that is.

I have no value judgments to make about the metropolis or about the novels that deal with it. It is true that I would have more sympathy and personal interest in reading books about more serious and exemplary characters. But I myself am a writer and I have known for a long time that the authors who "choose" their material are no novelists, and are never worth reading, and so the material of a novel can never be the subject of a value judgment. A novel can deal with the most splendid material of world history and be worthless, and it can deal with a nothing, a lost pin or burnt soup, and be a genuine work of literature.

And so I read the novel by that author without any particular respect for his material; respect for material is what the author ought to feel, not the reader. On the other hand, the reader ought to have respect for the writing, for the author's skill, and ought to judge a work of literature, disregarding its subject matter, first of all for the excellence of its workmanship. I am always prepared to do that and in fact I incline more and more to rate the quality of the handiwork above the content in ideas and emotions. For after some decades of living and writing I have made the discovery that it is easy to imitate ideas and emotions or to pretend to have them, but that this is not true of excellence in handiwork. So I read this novel with sympathy and with a colleague's respect, not understanding everything, smiling at only a little of it, and really respecting a great deal. The hero of the book is a young writer who is hindered in his profession by the fact that he lives a life of self-indulgence with his friends and also has to devote himself to the ladies, whose passion for him is his source of inspiration. He feels great repugnance toward the metropolis, society, the search for sensation, journalistic reporting; he has an intuition that all hardness of heart and cruelty, all exploitation, all war have their roots here. But our hero is not strong enough to turn his back resolutely on this world; instead he escapes by going around in circles—trips, constant alternation of pleasures, love affairs.

This, then, is the material. It entails the description, among other things, of restaurants, trains, hotels, the sum of dinner checks, etc., and these things no doubt have their own interest. But now I came to a place that brought me up short. The hero arrives in Berlin and puts up at a hotel, in room number 11, to be exact, and as I read this (professionally interested and eager as a colleague to learn from every line) I think, "Why does he need this precise information of the room number?" I wait, I am convinced that 11 will turn out to have some meaning, perhaps even a very surprising, pleasing, and ingenious one. But I am disappointed. The hero returns a page or two later to his hotel—and now suddenly he has room number 12! I go back and read the passage again; I was not mistaken, first it was 11, then it was 12. And there is no joke involved, no game, no attraction or mystery, it is simply an oversight, an inaccuracy, a bit of carelessness in the handiwork. The author wrote 12 once and 11 once, he did not read his work through again and obviously did not read the proofs, or he read them with exactly the same indifference and carelessness with which he wrote the numbers: because, of course, little things don't matter; because literature, for God's sake, is not a schoolroom where one is called to account for mistakes in thinking and writing; because life is short and the metropolis demanding and leaves the young author little time for his work. Granted, and granted too is my respect for the author's dislike of irresponsible, carelessly written, sensational newspaper articles, for the superficiality and irresponsibility with which the metropolis rides over everything! But suddenly from that number 12 onward, the author no longer possesses my full confidence, suddenly he has to reckon with my distrust, suddenly I begin to read with extra-close attention and I recognize the carelessness with which he wrote that 12 in other places as well, and I remember other instances that I read day before yesterday, still with full confidence. And suddenly the whole book loses its inner weight in responsibility, in genuineness and substance, all on account of that silly number 12. Suddenly I have the feeling: this pleasant book was written by a city dweller for city dwellers, for the day, for the moment; he is not very serious about it, and therefore he is not serious either about the heartlessness and superficiality of the metropolis, no more serious than a pamphleteer with a happy inspiration.

While I am thinking about this, a similar petty reading experience from years ago comes back to me. A young author already well known had sent me a novel with the request that I give him my opinion. It was a novel of the time of the French Revolution. In it, among other things, a summer was described, a summer of severe drought and heat: the country was parched, the peasants were in despair, the harvest was blighted, there was not a green blade of grass in the land. But a few pages later the hero or heroine during this same summer was walking through this same country and rejoicing in the laughing flowers blooming in a luxuriant wheat field! I wrote the author that this forgetfulness and carelessness had spoiled the whole book for me. He was unwilling to enter into a discussion on this point, since life was too short for that and he was already deeply immersed in other pressing works. He simply replied that I was a narrow-minded schoolmaster and that in a work of art, after all, the thing that mattered was not bagatelles of this kind. Fortunately not all young authors share this belief. I regretted my letter and have never since written a similar one. But to think that truth, accuracy, charm, neatness are not important in a work of art, especially in a work of art! How lucky that even today there are still young poets who know how to present certain bagatelles with charm and with the precisest miniature work, with a graceful playfulness which, like the art of acrobats, owes its grace to rigorous practice and conscientiousness in execution.

Still I may be a carper, an old-fashioned Don Quixote of artistic morality. Do we not all know that ninety percent of all books are written rapidly and irresponsibly and read in just the same way, and that day after tomorrow all this printed matter, including my own carpings, will be waste paper? So why take small matters so seriously? And why be unjust to an author who writes pretty things for the day by reading him as though he had intended to write for eternity?

It is too late for me to change my opinion on this subject. This is the beginning of every decline: to consider it a matter of course to take large matters seriously and neglect small ones. To exalt mankind and mistreat one's servants, to hold fatherland or church or party holy and do one's daily work badly and carelessly—here corruption begins. There is only *one* means of preventing this: to set aside for the time being in one's own mind as well as in conversation with others all the so-called serious and holy subjects such as political convictions, philosophy of life, patriotism, and so forth; on the other hand to take seriously all the small and smallest things, to turn one's attention to the task of the moment. Anyone who has his bicycle or his gas heater repaired by a mechanic does not demand from the mechanic either love of humanity or belief in the glory of Germany but competent work, and by that and that alone he judges the man and is right in doing so. Why should a work, just because it is called a work of art, not need to be precise and competent? And why should we be willing to overlook the "small" mistakes in handiwork because of some beautiful intention? No, instead we will do the opposite, we will reverse the spear. In other fields as well, fine airs and views and programs are often spears that surprise us when reversed, if only because they turn out to be of cardboard.

From a Diary
July, 1933

T HE NEWS FROM GERMANY (most recently proposed legis-
lation on Reich citizenship, etc., the honoring of
Rathenau's murderers, and other revolting berserkeries)
frightens me now and then, but you get used to such things,
and at this point a little more or less cruelty and hysteria
doesn't seem so very important. What has me permanently
troubled is not my own critical attitude toward the German
regime, which is probably not so very different from that of
most foreigners, but my failure to understand the "positive"
and "vital" elements that so many well-meaning Germans
seem to see in the new regime, and how they can subscribe to
this "revolution" that so frightened them at first, in short, my
failure to understand the present form of patriotism in Germany. Why—the question is interesting but also painful—
have quiet, serious, nonpartisan individuals (I am thinking of
Otto H. and certain others) now come out in favor of this
revolution? Why do they accept it as a state of war and
emergency? And why, either in the role of collaborators or of
victims, do they give it their support? If the "revolution" is
merely reaction and white terror, if, as many indications
argue, it is indeed animated not by mere naïveté but by a
pathologically obstinate blindness and fear of criticism, if in
other words it is inherently wrong and hostile to all spontaneous, organic life, then there can be no point in saying, as
Otto H., for instance, has said in a letter to me: "If this
enormous exertion, this great mustering of our people should
also flag and fail, then everything will collapse; this must not
be allowed to happen." No, whatever collapses would be no
loss, and even if quantities of good blood and of sincere German love and idealism are lost, it is better that they should be

lost than that they should uphold an organization that is fundamentally evil and diabolical. And to me, who am not a political man, the whole mentality of the Third Reich seems evil and diabolical, though I am willing to grant the possibility of sincere delusion in any of its supporters or even leaders. It strikes me as most significant that the Protestant Church has lost no time in espousing this movement and seems prepared to offer its unconditional services as a German, Germanic, no longer Roman or even Christian organization, to the bearers of high-sounding titles and fine uniforms. Here everything objectionable in Protestantism, from Luther's servility to princes to the idolization of pure dynamics in the more recent theology, joins to form a special brand, the German and Protestant brand, of blind nationalism. This fits in with the self-adoration of the present-day German, with his rapt admiration for the "tragic," "Faustian" soul, by which he means that he, the elect and at the same time the outcast among nations, is destined to transcend the petty barriers of mere reason and mere morality and achieve overwhelming greatness by unleashing his instincts and satisfying his desires. The theology of the National-Protestant churchmen supports this role with a dogma of *"peccandum est,"* which if possible is even more ingenious than the dogma that glorified the war of 1914. I am alarmed then by two questions: why, in large part, even the decent, trustworthy, and far from cowardly people of the Reich applaud and participate in this new form of the warmongering, flag-waving patriotism whose shipwreck they lived through only a few years ago? And secondly: may it not be that this mindless but powerful variety of organized instinctual life, this method of leadership by shouting, this steamroller that crushes the people and reduces them to uniformity—may it not be that this mechanism (in fascist, in socialist, or in some other form) is the organ by which in the present moment of history the nations want to be and must be governed? Because I am still enough of an intellectual and Christian to recognize that all forms of power without exception, the striving for power and the exercise of power, are things of this world, that they partake of instinct and never of the spirit, even if a thousand "spiritual" arguments are invoked to justify them. The Napoleons will always rule and the Christs will always be put to death—and yet in abjuring the Christian-European customs, forms, and restrictions of a thousand years and under a thin veil of ideology subscribing almost without reserve to a doctrine of sheer power, the Third Reich, like the Soviet Union, is something new, something specific to our times, something that is strong because it has broken with ideas that were decaying. What the Soviets and Hitler have broken with is primarily the Christian convention; in that they are identical. I am not saying that Bismarck and Metternich were true Christians as opposed to the "anti-Christian" leaders of the Third Reich. The conventions of humanity, justice, and international morality were breaking down even then, but an effort was made to observe them, whereas now they are simply thrown overboard. It seems plausible to suppose, for example, that if in 1914 the Germans had gone into the war not with the crumbling old conventions but with the brutal, ruthless new ideology that rejects all Christianity, etc., as stupid sentimentality, and if the decaying old morality had still been in force among its enemies— the Germans, for all the overwhelming power aligned against them, would have conquered the world. But as it happens, they did not win the war, they lost it, and if there were another such war today, they would lose it again. Thus, even from a purely biological point of view, the new ideology seems to be of doubtful value. A segment of history—the war, the political history leading up to it—has been expunged from the memory of the people by primitive magic, and a new method of wielding power and controlling the masses has been learned from Bolshevism. Neither of these novelties is as novel as is widely supposed. They cannot suffice to maintain so vast an ideological edifice—even if we don't expect too much of an ideology. After all, German history did not begin with the sudden irruption of the devil disguised as the Peace of Versailles into the innocent paradise of Germania, nor, considered in purely rational terms, can the ravings about blood and race be compared with Marxism. God knows, I am no lover of this Marxism and its threadbare rationality, but to bear comparison with the Soviet Union the Third Reich would need something more than the swastika and blue eyes.

But such rational considerations are not the whole story. Underneath them I sense, in the swastika and the fanatical pogrom atmosphere of the Reich, powers that cannot be confuted with reason, and since I sense their existence, but cannot approve or accept them, they torment me . . .

In the face of the suprarational and subrational processes at work in the people my heart contracts in anguish much as it did in 1914, but today the "great times" touch me much less directly, I feel far removed from them. I have not forgotten what I then said in criticism of myself and my people; in all rational matters my mind and conscience stand firm and self-assured. Today for this very reason I feel no need to speak, to take a public position, to come out with criticism or to engage in opposition. It is a matter for self-reproach that my heart does not participate in the soul-stirrings of my people, but as to whether these stirrings are good or evil I have no doubt. I cannot share the hope of many well-meaning persons that the present movement may save Germany from collapse; I believe it would be better for the crash to come sooner than later. Both the falsification of history that characterizes these leaders and the savage methods with which they erase, prohibit, and suppress everything they are afraid of, especially all truth and criticism of themselves, condemn the whole undertaking out of hand—but, it must be admitted, only for those who consider it "from outside" and "objectively." It is a different matter for those who experience it biologically as an ecstatic upsurge. Many of the letters I receive from Germany were written as though in high fever, exactly like the letters of August 1914, ardent, ecstatic, drunk, letters of hate and frenzy. Other voices are less frequent, because no one dares to write openly from the Reich, because everyone is terrified of spies, secret police, and informers. But when from time to time a letter does speak more openly, or when a sober-minded German comes to us in Switzerland, we hear tones of suffering, indignation, or resignation that strike a chord in my whole being. Once again my heart is there among the oppressed and chastised, the maltreated, the imprisoned, the Jews, the banished. Not that I concur without reserve in the attitude of the refugees! I can join their party no more than any other. Actually the Third Reich has not molested me thus far, none of my books has been pilloried, none of the newspapers has closed its columns to me, I have been receiving my royalties, which to be sure are very much reduced because hardly anyone buys a book any more.

Carlo was our guest for three days, and his friend Kleinknecht, the young prosecuting attorney, visited us twice, a good sort. Both surprised me by the serenity, not to say callousness, with which they look on recent political developments, make fun of Hitler and everything else, but show no inclination to stir a finger, either for or against. Then I see that my detachment from current affairs is not as great as I sometimes think. I feel a kind of obligation to engage in opposition, but to do so would be to neutralize myself and my work even further. I see no way of engaging in active opposition because basically I do not believe in socialism. Consequently my opposition to the Third Reich is no different from my opposition to every other Reich, to every state and all rule by violence—the opposition of the individual to the mass, of quality to quantity, of the soul to matter . . .

Memories of
Klingsor's Summer
1938

*K*lingsor's Last Summer and the narrative *Klein and Wagner*, which appeared in the same volume with it, were written in the same summer, a strange and unique summer for the world and for me. It was in 1919. The four years of war were at an end, the world seemed shattered into fragments, millions of soldiers, prisoners of war, ordinary citizens were returning home after years of rigidly uniform obedience to a freedom that they feared as well as longed for. The war, that great ruler of the world, was dead and buried; an altered and impoverished world waited emptily for us released slaves. Everyone had ardently longed for this world and for the chance to move about freely in it, and everyone felt a little fearful of release and freedom, of the circle of his private and personal affairs now become unfamiliar, of the responsibility that every freedom entails, of the long-repressed impulses, possibilities, and dreams of his own heart that had almost become his enemies. The new atmosphere had an intoxicating effect on many; at the moment of being freed they had no other wish but to smash to pieces everything they had fought and bled for during those years. They felt they had lost or omitted something, a piece of self, a piece of development, of adaptation, of the art of living. Young men who had still been living in a child's world when the war swept them away now found the so-called world and reality to which they "returned home" completely alien and incomprehensible. And many of the older men among us believed that exactly their most im-

portant and irreplaceable years had been stolen from them
and that it was now too late to begin over again and compete
with the younger people. These were not to be envied either,
but they did have the advantage of having awakened to life in
a harsher, more sober, an unsentimental world devoid of
ideals, whereas we older men cherished periods and pictures
of a world that had represented the highest values for us and
had now turned into the amusing curiosities of day before
yesterday. Eras of time had become astonishingly short; the
young people no longer reckoned time by a life-span, a generation, or at least a lustrum, but by single years; and those born
in 1903 considered themselves divided by a chasm from those
born in 1904. Everything had become uncertain, and this uncertainty had something disturbing and often very frightening about it. But even in this perplexing world, during good
hours it sometimes seemed as though anything were possible,
and this opened wide horizons. To me, for instance, the poet
returning degraded and overwhelmed by the war, now once
more set free in private life, at times the most improbable
things seemed possible, as for instance a return of reason
and brotherhood to the world, a rediscovery of the soul, a re-
establishment of beauty, a renewed summons from the gods
in which we had believed before the collapse of our former
world. In any case, I saw no road for myself except back to
poetry, no matter whether the world still needed poetry or
not. If I was able to rouse myself from the confusions and
losses of the war years, which had almost wholly shattered
my life, and give my existence a meaning, this was possible
only through radical contemplation and reversal, through a
departure from everything that had gone before, and an attempt to submit to my angel.

It was not until the spring of 1919 that the prisoner-of-war
service for which I worked released me; freedom found me
back in a house that had been empty for a year, unheated and
uncared for. Very little remained of my earlier existence. And
so I wrote it off, packed my books, my clothes, and my desk,
locked up the deserted house, and sought a place where, alone

and in complete silence, I could begin over again. The place I found and in which, now many years later, I still live was called Montagnola and was a town in Ticino.

Three circumstances combined to render this summer an extraordinary and unique experience for me: the date 1919, the return out of the war into life, from slavery to freedom, was the most important; but there was also the atmosphere, climate, and speech of the South, and in addition, as a grace from heaven, a summer such as I have seldom seen, of a strength and warmth, a charm and splendor that lifted me up and permeated me like strong wine.

That was Klingsor's summer. During the blazing days I wandered through the villages and chestnut woods, sat on my folding chair, tried to preserve in water color something of that fluid magic; during the warm nights I sat up late beside the open doors and windows in Klingsor's little castle and attempted, with somewhat more experience and reflection than I could express with the brush, to sing in words the song of that unequaled summer. Thus emerged the story of the painter Klingsor.

Postscript to *Steppenwolf*

1941

T HERE ARE VARIOUS WAYS of understanding or misunderstanding works of literature. In most cases the author of the book is not the court competent to judge where the reader's understanding ceases and misunderstanding begins. Many an author has found readers to whom his book was more transparent than it was to himself. In addition, misunderstanding can occasionally be fruitful.

Granting all this, it seems to me that *Steppenwolf* is, among my books, the one that has been more often and more seriously misunderstood than any other. And frequently it was just those who approved, yes, the enthusiastic readers, not at all the hostile ones, who expressed themselves about the book in a way that was most disturbing to me. In part, but only in part, the reason for the large number of these cases is that this book, written by a man of fifty and dealing with the problems of that time of life, very often fell into the hands of quite young readers.

But among the readers of my book I often encountered persons of my own age who were impressed by the book but, strangely enough, were only able to see half of its subject. These readers, so it seems to me, saw themselves in the Steppenwolf, identified with him, shared his sorrows and dreams, and in doing so quite overlooked the other things the book recognizes and talks about besides Harry Haller and his difficulties. There rises over the Steppenwolf and his problematical life a second, higher, immortal world, and the "Treatise" and all those passages in the book that have to do with the spirit, with art, and with the "Immortals" set against the passionate world of the Steppenwolf a positive, cheerful, suprapersonal, and supratemporal world of faith. The book, to be sure, describes sorrows and suffering, but it is by no means the book of a man in despair but rather of a man of faith.

I cannot and naturally would not wish to prescribe to my readers how they are to understand my novel. Let each one make of it what is appropriate and helpful to him. Nevertheless it would please me very much if many of them were to realize that the story of the Steppenwolf, though it describes an illness and a crisis, does not describe one that leads to death or decline but rather the opposite—to recovery.

Favorite Reading

1945

I AM CONSTANTLY BEING ASKED, "What is your favorite reading matter?"

For a friend of world literature the question is hard to answer. I have read books by the thousands, many of them more than once, some of them over and over again, and I am opposed in principle to excluding from the circle of my sympathy or at any rate of my interest any literature, school, or author. And yet the question is justifiable and can in some measure be answered. A person may be omnivorous and proud of it, not despising anything from black bread to saddle of venison, from carrots to trout, and yet have his three or four favorite dishes. It can also happen that when someone thinks of music he means first of all Bach, Handel, and Glück but even so has no wish to forgo Schubert or Stravinsky. Thus, when I think about the matter carefully I find in every literature that I come upon realms, times, rhythms that are closer to me and dearer than others: with the Greek, for example, Homer is closer to me than the tragedians, Herodotus closer than Thucydides. Also I have to admit to myself that my relationship to all solemn, exalted writers is not an entirely natural one and my great esteem for them is not altogether unforced, whether it be a question of Dante or Hebbel or Schiller or Stefan George.

The realm of world literature I have most often had recourse to during my life and have also come to know most intimately is one that today appears to have receded so infinitely far from us as to have become a saga: Germany in the hundred years between 1750 and 1850, that Germany of which the midpoint and summit is Goethe. I keep returning to this region where I am safe from disappointment as well as

from sensationalism, I come back from excursions into the
oldest and most remote literatures, to those poets, letter
writers, and biographers who are all good humanists and yet
have the smell of the earth and of folklore. Naturally the
books that speak to me with a special directness are those in
which the landscape, the popular customs, and the language
have been intimately familiar and close to me since childhood; here I enjoy in reading that special pleasure of understanding even the slightest nuance; to return from such a
book to one I am forced to read in translation or to one that
simply does not have this organic, genuine, appropriate
speech and music is always jolting and a little painful. Of
course, it is the German of the southwest, the Alemannic and
the Swabian, in which I especially find this enjoyment. I
need only mention Mörike or Hebel, but I find it in almost all
German and Swiss authors of that blessed period from the
young Goethe to Stifter, from *Heinrich Stilling's Youth* to
Immermann and Droste-Hülshoff, and the fact that the great
majority of these splendid and delightful books exist today
only in limited numbers in public or private libraries seems
to me one of the most disturbing and ugly symptoms of our
dreadful epoch.

But blood, earth, and mother tongue are not everything,
even in literature. Over and above them there is mankind,
and there is always the astonishing and happy possibility of
discovering home in what is most distant and foreign, of loving what is apparently hidden and inaccessible and of being
able to become familiar with it. In the first half of my life,
this was proved for me by evidences of the Hindu and later
on of the Chinese spirit. As to Hinduism, I was in some
measure foreordained to it; my parents and grandparents had
been in India, had learned Indian languages, and had savored
something of the spirit of India. But that there was a marvelous Chinese literature and a specifically Chinese view of
humanity and the human spirit which not only would become
dear and precious to me but, more than that, would be a
spiritual sanctuary and a second home—of this I had no
inkling until I was over thirty years old. But then the unex-

pected occurred: I had known nothing of Chinese literature except the Shih Ching in Rückert's poetic adaptation, and then through the translations of Richard Wilhelm and others I became somewhat acquainted with, and now would not know how to live without, the Chinese-Taoist ideal of the wise and good. From two and a half thousand years' distance there came to me, who know no word of Chinese and have never been in China, the good fortune of finding in the ancient Chinese literature a substantiation of my own intuitions, a spiritual atmosphere and home that I had otherwise had only in the world that was mine through birth and speech. These Chinese masters and wise men, about whom the magisterial Chuang-tzu, about whom Lieh-Tzu and Mong-Ko have told, were the opposite of the exalted writers, they were astoundingly simple and close to the people and everyday life, they would have nothing to do with humbug and by choice lived in obscurity and contentment, and they expressed themselves in a way that repeatedly astonished and delighted me. Lao-tse's great opponent Confucius, the systematist and moralist, the lawgiver and preserver of custom, the single rather solemn personage among the wise men of ancient times, is, for example, described on one occasion in this way: "Is he not the one who knows that it will not do and yet does it?" That smacks of a composure, a humor and simplicity for which I can think of no similar example in any literature. I often remember these sayings and many others, especially when I contemplate world events and the pronouncements of those who have it in mind to rule the world during the coming years and decades and to make it perfect. They behave like Confucius the great, but behind their action there does not lie his knowledge, "that it will not do."

Nor must I forget the Japanese, though they have occupied me far less and have not supplied me with nourishment to the extent that the Chinese have. But for centuries there has been and is in Japan—a country we think of along with Germany as being warlike—something so splendid and at the same time so witty, something so inspired and also so determinedly, indeed bluntly, directed at practical life as Zen, a flower to which Buddhist India and China made their contributions but which could only attain its first full bloom in Japan. I consider Zen one of the greatest blessings a nation has ever secured for itself, a wisdom and practice ranking with that of Buddha and Lao-tse. And then at long intervals Japanese lyric poetry greatly enchanted me, especially in its emphasis on utter simplicity and brevity. One must not read any modern German lyrics when one comes straight from the Japanese, otherwise our poems seem desperately inflated and bombastic. The Japanese have made such marvelous inventions as the seventeen-syllable poem, and they have always known that an art does not profit by being made easier but rather the reverse. Once, for instance, a Japanese poet wrote a poem of two verses which said that in a forest still covered with snow a number of plum twigs burst into bloom! He gave his poem to an expert to read and the latter told him, "A single plum twig is quite enough." The poet recognized how very right this was and how far away he himself was from true simplicity; he followed his friend's advice and his poem today is still remembered.

Sometimes people laugh at the overproduction of books today in our small country. But if I were a little younger and still had my strength, I would do nothing today but edit and publish books. We must preserve the continuity of intellectual life and not postpone this labor until the countries that have been at war have perhaps recovered, nor dare we carry on the work as a brief business boom during which one need not be overly conscientious. There is hardly less danger to world literature from hastily and badly produced new editions than from the war itself and its consequences.

The Peach Tree

1945

L AST NIGHT our spring storm, the *Föhn*, swept mightily
and pitilessly over the patient land, across the empty
land, across the empty fields and gardens, through the barren vineyards and the barren forest, plucking at every branch
and trunk, howling and hissing at everything in its way,
making the fig tree rattle like dry bones, and driving whirling clouds of dead leaves high into the air. In the morning
great heaps of them lay neatly arranged, subdued and pressed
flat, behind every corner and projecting wall that offered
shelter from the wind.

And when I went into the garden I found that a catastrophe
had occurred. There on the ground lay the largest of my
peach trees, broken off close to the earth and pitched over
the steep slope of my vineyard. They do not grow to be very
old, these trees, they do not belong among the giants and
heroes, they are delicate and susceptible, overly sensitive to
injury, their resinous sap has something of ancient, too
highly bred blood lines. It was not an especially beautiful or
noble tree, the one that had fallen there, but it was, after
all, the largest of my peach trees, an old acquaintance and
friend, a resident older than I on these acres. Each year soon
after the middle of March it had opened its buds and dra-
matically displayed its rosy foam of blossoms against the
blue of a fair-weather sky and infinitely delicate against
stormy heavens, it had shuddered in the capricious squalls of
the fresh April days, burnished by the golden flame of brim-
stone butterflies; it had braced itself against the evil *Föhn*,
had stood silent and as though dreaming in the wet gray of
the rainy times, bending slightly to gaze toward its feet
where with each day of rain the grass on the steep vineyard

slope grew greener and lusher. Sometimes I had taken one
of its small blooming twigs into the house with me; occasionally when its fruit began to be too heavy I had helped
it out with a prop; also in earlier years I had been audacious
enough to try to paint it when it was in bloom. At every
time of year since I had lived here, it had had its place in
my small world and belonged to it, it had shared with me
heat and snow, storm and quietude, had added its tone to
the song, its resonance to the picture; it had gradually
grown high above the vine props and had outlived generations of lizards, snakes, butterflies, and birds. It was not
remarkable, it had not been highly regarded, but it had
been indispensable. When the fruit began to ripen I would
make the small excursion every morning from the stairway
over to it and pick up out of the wet grass the peaches that
had fallen during the night and bring them back in my
pockets, in a basket, or sometimes in my hat and set them
on the railing of the terrace.

Now at the spot that had belonged to this old acquaintance
and friend there was an empty place. The small world had
a tear in it through which the void, darkness, death, terror
looked in. The broken trunk lay there sadly, its wood looking
soft and a little spongy. The limbs had been broken in the
fall; in two weeks perhaps they would have once more worn
their rosy-red spring crowns and held them up to the blue or
the gray of the skies. Never again would I pluck a twig, never
again gather a fruit from it, never again would I attempt
to draw the capricious and somewhat fantastic structure of
its spreading branches, never again on a hot summer day
would I stroll over from the steps to rest for a moment in
its lacy shade. I called Lorenzo the gardener and instructed
him to carry the fallen tree to the barn. There, on the first
rainy day when there was no other work to be done, it
would be sawed up for firewood. Indignantly I watched him
depart. To think that you couldn't rely even on trees, they
too could slip away from you, could die, one day they could
leave you in the lurch and disappear into the great darkness!

I gazed after Lorenzo, who was having trouble pulling the heavy trunk. Farewell, my dear peach tree! At least you died a decent, natural, and proper death and for this I call you happy; you braced yourself and held out as long as you possibly could and then the great enemy wrenched your limbs from their sockets. You had to give way, you fell and were severed from your roots. You were not splintered by bombs from the air, not burnt by hellish acids, not, like millions, torn from your native earth, hastily replanted with bleeding roots, only to be seized anew and rendered homeless once more, you have not had to experience catastrophe and destruction, war and degradation around you or been forced to die in misery. You have had a fate such as becomes and is due to your kind. For this I call you blessed; you grew older better and more gracefully than we and you died with greater dignity than we who in our day must defend ourselves against the poison and the misery of a polluted world, must fight against encompassing corrosive corruption for every breath of clean air.

When I had seen the tree lying there, I had thought of a replacement, another tree to plant, as is usual with such losses. Where it had fallen we would dig a hole and let it stand open for a good while, exposed to the rain and wind and sun; into the hole we would after a while put some fertilizer, some dung from the compost heaps and all sorts of wood ash mixed with scraps, and then one day, if possible when a soft mild rain was falling, we would plant a new young small tree. Earth and air here would be completely to the liking of this newcomer, too, this child tree, it too would become a comrade and good neighbor to the vines, the flowers, the lizards, the birds, and the butterflies, in a few years it would bear fruit, every spring in the second half of March would produce its lovely blossoms and, if the fates were favorable, one day as an old and weary tree would fall victim to some storm or landslide or the heaviness of the snow.

But this time I could not make up my mind to replant. I

had set out a good many trees in my lifetime; this single one did not matter. And there was something within me that resisted renewing the cycle here at this place, giving another push to the wheel of life, nurturing a new prey for ravenous death. I do not want to do it. The place shall remain empty.

Dream Gift

1946

THIS IS AN AGE and civilization that characteristically has developed a special science, vocabulary, and literature for every separate medical, psychological, and sociological phenomenon, but no longer has an anthropology, a science of mankind. On occasion, therefore, all one's human experiences and capacities may turn into insoluble problems and astounding marvels, sometimes into fascinating, enchanting, and encouraging ones, sometimes into terrifying, threatening, and sinister ones. The human creature thus dissected, no longer whole and healthy but split up into a thousand specialties and arbitrarily selected snippets, can like a slide prepared for the microscope dissolve into a world of pictures. Many of these have human, animal, vegetable, and mineralogical resemblances in a language of form and color that is apparently unlimited, that makes use of all elements and possibilities but lacks any meaning to hold it together. The individual fragmented pictures, however, can have an unintended, magical, primeval, creative beauty; it is in fact this beauty, this enchantment of what is fragmented and freed from the whole and the real, that has attracted painters so powerfully for several decades and can lend many of their meaningless pictures such an enchanting sadness of nonexistence, such a fleeting and hallucinatory beauty that at times one thinks one finds in them something whole and genuine once more: not the unity and substantiality of the world, to be sure, but the unity and eternity of death, of decline, of mortality.

The way these painters go to work, fragmenting the whole, dissolving what is substantial, mixing the elements of form and reassembling them in new irresponsible but often marvelously attractive combinations, so do our souls operate in dreams. And it is no accident that among the new human types of our time, which did not exist before, there has been added the kind of man who no longer lives, no longer acts, is no longer responsible, does no business, makes no decisions, but only dreams. He dreams at night and often during the day as well. He has acquired the habit of writing down his dreams, and since the transcription of a dream demands many times the length of time of the dream itself, these dream authors are overbusied their whole life long, they never get to the end, they can never write down even half of what they dream; and how they manage now and then between dreams and writing to eat a meal or sew on a button is almost a miracle. These dream authors, these professional dreamers, have chosen what in wholesome people is a small part of living, a side effect of sleep, as the principal subject, the central point and pursuit of their lives. It is not our intention to disturb them in this activity or to laugh them to scorn, although occasionally we smile and shrug our shoulders. We find that however unfruitful the activity of these people is, it is nevertheless harmless and innocent, egoistic, to be sure, but in a childish fashion, a little crazy, just as every nonrepresentational painter, just as we ourselves and the whole of the present-day world are a little crazy, but not in an evil or dangerous way. A man who has happened to discover how good a glass of wine tastes may under certain circumstances become a drunkard by making a glass of wine the meaning and central point of his life; or the man who happens to discover how healthful and refreshing raw vegetables taste can and may under certain circumstances become a fanatical vegetarian and a health crank; these two are comparatively harmless species of madness and they prove nothing about the value of wine or the healthfulness of salads. The right thing, so it seems to us, would be occasionally to pay tribute both to the glass of wine and to raw vegetables, but not to let them become the axis about which our lives revolve.

That is the way it is too with dreaming and the examination of dreams. We do not believe that this, according to God's will, is a really suitable profession or principal element in human life, but we often find that too little dreaming and too little attention to our dreams are also not good. No, now and again we wish to and must lean over this charming abyss and gaze with astonishment for a while into its secrets, discovering in its broken picture sequences hints of the whole and the real, allowing ourselves to enjoy its often ineffable phantom beauties.

In a dream a few days ago I was in Ticino, in a rather strange, exaggerated, and overgrown Ticino, and I was walking with a companion through an unfamiliar suburb where the mountains looked down between walls, hedges, and new buildings. Among the structures was one called the "New Mill," many stories tall and painted bright red, and despite its lack of proportion and colossal size it had a unique charm, I had to keep looking up at it again and again. However, we were in a hurry and were walking quite rapidly; I believe we had to catch a train, we were carrying luggage, and, unsure of our way, we were pressed for time and worried. Who my companion was is unclear, but in any case he was a very close and intimate friend, someone of importance to me and my life. We came to a low wall behind which at a little distance stood some old neglected houses. I left the street, crossed the low wall in a single stride and went on in that direction, although I believed there was no road there and that we would very soon encounter gardens and private property and would be regarded as trespassers. But nothing of the sort happened, we moved forward without difficulty, constantly with this somewhat harried impatience; beside and behind us other people were walking and in the distance among other figures I saw on this street, which was no street, an old friend of mine approaching. He was completely unchanged and apparently had not grown at all older in the many years since we had seen each other. However, because of our haste and also for other reasons that were unclear, I did not want to meet him, I glanced aside and pretended not to know him, and behold, he went past us, or rather he disappeared even before reaching us, as though he had guessed my wish and fallen in with it.

And now a view appeared between the houses on our right, and it is because of this that I have not forgotten the dream and feel a desire to set down my memories of it. A view opened on a broad landscape rising gradually from where we were to great heights. "Don't you see it?" I called to my friend, without stopping. "Do look, it's incredibly beautiful!" My friend looked in the right direction but remained indifferent and did not answer. The landscape, however, spoke to all my senses and to my whole soul, it forced its way into me, I drank it up and took it with me like a great gift, a strange wish fulfillment. And it was the peculiarity of this beautiful landscape that it was at once reality and art, landscape and painted picture. It extended uphill, in the center on a promontory stood a church, villages here and there, in the background mountain ranges with a rosy glow, on the slope below the church two little wheat fields. And it was these wheat fields above everything else that made me recognize that the whole thing was not only beautiful but painted and planned; they were done partly in Neapolitan yellow, partly with a mixture of English red and a great deal of white. All cold or cool shades were absent, everything was within the range of red and yellow.

Beside us on the street a young man, a Frenchman or a French-speaking Swiss, was walking with his wife. When I called my companion's attention to the view with such eagerness and enthusiasm, the stranger smiled with a friendly but sly expression and said, "Yes, you're quite right, nothing cool, only warm colors; that's what you'd expect Cézanne to say." I nodded to him cheerfully and it was on the tip of my tongue to recite to him the colors in the picture as though to a colleague—ocher, Neapolitan yellow, English red, white, very bright madder, and so forth—but then it seemed to me that this was altogether too friendly and intimate and I restrained myself but I smiled at him and was pleased that there was someone after all who saw exactly the same thing

I did and experienced and thought about it in the same way.

From that dream, which moved on to entirely new scenes, I have retained the picture of that warm, magic landscape and I carry it with me as a gift of the god of dreams. Its colors had been my favorite colors, when I still occasionally occupied myself as a dilettante painter; they had also for a while dominated the palette of my friend, the painter Louis. And now it is an odd and rather sad fact that if I reconstruct the ideal landscape in that dream, which shone with such exciting and marvelously cheery beauty, if I reconstruct that while awake, with its Neapolitan yellow wheat fields, the towering reddish mountain church, the play of warm yellow and reddish tones, the whole legendary and festive music of its palette, then of course the landscape remains still luminously warm and beautiful but also just a little too beautiful, a little too rosy, a little bit too harmonious, a little bit too close to being sugary, yes, to being sentimental.

And now I have trouble keeping this gift unspoiled, guarding it against critical skepticism, so that I can continue in future to cheer myself with the unsullied memory of its beauty, which for the space of a dream second made me so profoundly happy. After I awoke and attempted to picture it in every particular, it seemed to me a little too beautiful, a bit pretty-pretty, a trifle too ideal, and this secret criticism cannot be smothered now, or at least only for moments. And was there not in that very understanding smile of my French-Swiss colleague, in his comment about the landscape, which he quite unnecessarily put into the mouth of old Cézanne— was there not in this sympathetic and friendly smile of the artist or expert or initiate also something sly and ominous?

Description of a Landscape

1947

F OR A WEEK NOW I have been living on the ground floor of a villa in surroundings completely new to me, a new landscape, society, and culture, and since, to begin with, I am very much alone in this new world and the autumn days in the quiet of my large handsome study seem long, I am beginning this description, like a game of solitaire. It is a kind of work that gives my lonesome and empty days an appearance of meaning; at least it is an occupation that does less harm than the important and highly paid work of so many people.

The town where I am staying lies close to the political and linguistic border of the canton on the French-speaking side. My host and friend is in charge of and lives close to a health institute which no doubt I shall soon learn more about under the doctor's guidance. At present I know nothing about it, nothing except that it is housed in a former manor house on an extensive property adorned with beautiful gardens. The very large, architecturally handsome castlelike structure encloses many inner courtyards and, I am told, a great number of patients, guards, doctors, nurses, workmen, and other employees. I see or hear almost nothing of them from my quarters in one of the new buildings. This may well be otherwise in summertime, but now in November no one ever sits on the green garden benches, and when, a few times a day, I take my short walk through the park or go over to the big house to ask about something at the office or to get my mail, then at most I meet a single nurse or mechanic or gardener's boy on the paths, on the echoing stairways, corridors, or open courtyards, and the huge building stands in complete silence as though it were untenanted.

The extensive institute itself, our little villa with apartments for the two doctors, a few modern structures that house the kitchen, washhouse, garages, stalls, carpentry shop, and other workrooms, and the plant nursery with its large beds, conservatory, and greenhouse all lie in the midst of a very large park of splendid, feudal, but also a trifle coquettish character. This park, whose terraces, walks, and stairways descend by degrees from the manor house toward the shore of the lake, is for the time being, since I am incapable of taking longer walks, my landscape and my world; to it chiefly belongs the principal part of my attention and love. The people who planted it seem to have been influenced in that operation by two tendencies, or rather passions: a passion for artistic-romantic division of the space into even, grassy lawns and clumps of trees, and the other of planting and cultivating not only handsome and well-placed trees but also the most unusual, strange, and exotic ones. So far as I have been able to see, this in general seems to be customary on the estates in the neighborhood, and also the last owner and tenant of this manor house may have brought his fondness for exotic plants with him from South America, where he owned plantations and was a tobacco exporter. Although these two passions, the romantic and the botanical, are occasionally at odds, nevertheless the attempt to reconcile them has been almost completely successful. As one wanders through the park one is sometimes attracted by surprising glimpses and noble vistas, drawn either in the direction of the open lake or back toward the façade of the castle. But at other times one is instead compelled to a closer inspection of individual plants because of their botanical interest, their age or vitality. This begins right beside the house, where on the uppermost semicircular terrace a number of southern plants are displayed in large tubs, among them an orange tree richly hung with well-rounded gleaming little fruit; it has none of that drooping, suffering, unhappy aspect usual to such plants transferred to an un-congenial climate from a different latitude; its sturdy trunk, its spherically trimmed crown, and its little golden fruit appear altogether content and healthy. And not far from it, a little to one side and closer to the shore, one is struck by an amazingly vigorous plant, a bush rather than a tree, rooted not in a tub but in the earth and bearing quite similar small, hard, ball-shaped fruit. It is a strange, highly head-strong and militant, wild, impenetrable, many-branched thorny growth, and its fruit is not as golden as those dwarf oranges. It is an impressively large, very old holly bush, and later, as one walks on, there are similar ones here and there.

Next to a few trees related to the yew and the cypress and of impressive and somewhat bizarre silhouette stands the baobab tree, lonesome and perhaps a little melancholy but powerful and healthy, immersed in its faultless symmetry as though in a dream and bearing on its upper branches, like a sign that its isolation is not to be held against it, a few heavy, massive fruits. In addition to these rarities, inten-tionally placed at intervals in the greensward as though emphatically recommended for observation and admiration, there are also, somewhat aware of their own special interest and a bit robbed of their innocence, a number of trees that are not at all rare but have been transformed through the gardener's art and bear themselves delicately and dream-ily; first of all, the weeping willow and the weeping birch tree, whose trunk and all its branches turn down at a certain height and bend back toward the roots. The result of this unnatural reversal of growth is a thick hanging roof, a living fir-tree hut or cave into which a man could disappear and live as though he were the nymph of this miraculous tree.

Among the most beautiful trees in our charming park are a few splendid old cedars, the handsomest of which touches with its upper branches the crown of a thick-boled oak tree, the oldest tree on the place, far older than park and house. There are also some flourishing sequoias, growing more vigorously in girth than in height; it may be that the frequently strong cold winds compel them to do this. For me the most splendid tree in the whole park is not one of the distinguished foreigners but a dignified, ancient silver poplar of vast size, divided not far above the ground into two mighty boles, each one of which might by itself be the prize exhibit of a park. It still retains its foliage, which can deepen in color from silver-gray through a varied scale of brownish, yellowish, indeed rosy tones into a heavy dark gray, according as light and wind play with it, whose colors, however, always have a metallic harshness and roughness. When a strong wind sways these gigantic crowns and the heavens, as sometimes happens in these early November days, still have a damp deep summer blue, or are curtained with dark clouds, it is a royal spectacle. This venerable tree would be worthy of a poet like Rilke or a painter like Corot.

The model and stylistic pattern of the park is English, not French. The attempt has been to reproduce an apparently natural primitive landscape in miniature, and in places this illusion has been almost successful. But the cautious way in which the architecture has been taken into account and the careful handling of the terrain and its slope toward the lake show most clearly that not nature and the wildwood have been at work but everywhere cultivation, thought, and garden art. And I am well pleased that all this is still evident in the park. Conceivably it would be prettier if it were left a little more to itself, if it were a bit neglected and wild; then grass would be growing in the walks and ferns in the cracks of the stone stairways and retaining walls, the greensward would contain moss, the ornamental structures would have collapsed, everything would speak of the force of nature, of indiscriminate growth and indiscriminate decay; it would permit wilderness and the thought of death access to this distinguished and beautiful world, windfalls would be lying about, and corpses, and stumps of dead trees covered with lichen. But there is nothing of the sort anywhere here. The strong, precise, and inflexible human mind and cultural will that once laid out and planted this park still control it today, maintain and cultivate it and allow not a hand's breadth for wilderness, untidiness, and death. No grass grows on the walks or moss in the lawns, neither is the crown of the oak tree permitted to encroach too far upon the neighboring cedars, nor are the espaliered trees, the dwarf trees, and the weeping trees allowed to forget their training or escape the rule by which they are formed, trimmed, and bent. And where a tree has fallen, either through disease, age, storm, or the weight of snow, and is missing, there is no disorderly place of death, no chaos of underbrush, but a small, slender, stylish young tree with two or three branches and a few leaves has been newly planted in the middle of a neat round clearing; supported by a clean strong stick that holds and protects it, it fits obediently into the order of things.

So here a creation of aristocratic culture has been preserved into a completely altered age, and the wish of the founder, that last lord of the manor who bequeathed his property to a beneficent institution, is respected and still prevails. The lofty oak and the cedar obey him as well as the meager young sapling on its stick; he is obeyed by the silhouette of each clump of trees, and his memory is honored and perpetuated by a dignified, classical monument on the last of the garden terraces, which divides the final broad lawn from the bulrushes and the water. And the single visible wound that in a brutal time was inflicted upon this beautiful microcosm will soon disappear and be healed. During the last war one of the more elevated lawns had to be plowed up and planted to grain. But right now the vacant place is waiting for the harrow and rake to eliminate this intrusive crudeness so that grass seed can be sown there once more.

Now that I have said this and that about my beautiful park, I see that I have omitted more than I have described. I owe praises to the maples and chestnuts, and have made no mention of the luxuriant, thick-stemmed wisteria of the inner courtyard, and even before all of these I should have spoken of the wonderful elm trees, the fairest of which stands quite close to my apartment, between the villa and the main building, younger but taller than the venerable oak tree beyond. This elm springs from the earth with a strong thick trunk but after a short vigorous beginning it separates into a whole nation of branches striving heavenward like a column of water spurting and dividing, slender, merry, eager for the light, until its happy upward thrust comes to an end in a high, beautifully vaulted crown.

But even if there is no room in this orderly and cultivated domain for the primitive and the wild, nevertheless the two worlds meet all along the borders of the property. The grounds that are laid out and planted have their gently descending walks ending in the sand and swamp of the flat rushy shore, and in more recent times they acquired as neighbor unclaimed nature in much more perceptible fashion left to itself. A few decades ago the creation of interconnecting canals between the lakes of the region lowered the surface of this lake by several meters and thereby a broad strip of what had once been the lake's edge was laid bare. On this strip, since no one knew what to do with it, nature was left to itself, and here now thrives in partially marshy ground mile after mile of rough and somewhat stunted forest, a jungle sprung from seeds borne there by the wind and consisting of alders, birches, willows, poplars, and many other trees, which are slowly transforming this once sandy lake bottom into a forest floor. Here and there is scrub oak too, but it does not feel altogether comfortable in this soil. And I can imagine that in summer many marsh weeds flourish and also the silvery cotton grass, and those tall feathery orchids that I know so well from the water meadows along Lake Constance. Many animals as well find refuge in this wild undergrowth, there nest ducks and other water birds, the snipe, the curlew, the heron and cormorant. I have seen swans fly by, and day before yesterday out of this woodland came two deer, making their way deliberately in little playful leaps across one of the broad lawns of our park.

What I have now, if not described, at least summarily enumerated, the elegantly tended park together with the primitive young woods on the moist new-made land, seems to be a whole landscape, but it is only the very closest environment of our house. If I stroll along the paths in these surroundings for a quarter of an hour, it is in fact a unity, a delimited small world which somewhat like a formal park in a great city suffices us for a while, gives us pleasure and can take the place of nature as a whole. In reality, however, all this—park, gardens, orchards, and encircling forest—is only the foreground and approach leading to something much grander and more uniform. If one goes downward along this pretty way from the house under the tall elms, poplars, and cedars, past the Wellingtonians with their multitudinous cones, the Wellingtonians whose thick, cinnamon-colored trunks rise so warm and well hidden behind the tent of their hanging elastic limbs, past the baobab tree and the wig tree, past the weeping willows and the holly, down to the shore, then for the first time one stands face to face with the true eternal landscape, whose characteristic is not prettiness or scientific interest but grandeur, a wide-open, simple, boundless great landscape. Behind the brownish miniature forest of reeds along the shore, waving and dancing in the wind, the lake extends for many miles, colored like the sky in fair weather and dark blue-green like glacier ice when it is stormy, and on the far side (in case it is not hidden in gray and opalescent mist as it is on many days) the low, extended range of the Jura draws its quiet but energetic lines against the heavens, which above this apparently almost flat expanse are infinitely huge. Since my years on Lake Constance I have not lived in such a landscape—and that will soon be fifty-three years ago. Expanse of lake and sky, smell of water and marsh, waving reeds, striding along the wet sand of the shore, above me in the limitless sky clouds and a few birds—how greatly I once loved all that! Since then I have without any real plan or intention always lived in landscapes somewhat closer to the high mountains, whose character is solidity, clarity of outline, which does not consist like the present landscape mostly of sky, air, mist, wind, motion. This is not the time

for me to brood or expound, otherwise this return from a
static to a dynamic world would permit of many a pretty
fantasy. Here it is again then, and it speaks to me in unforgotten accents, boundless, oceanic, moist, reflective, hiding and revealing, forever changing and altering world in
which water and sky rule over all else. Often I stand for a
long time on the shore, hat in hand and wind in my hair,
swept by the sounds and scents of my youth, challenged and
examined by a world that sharply reminds me of what is
past, that opposes and scrutinizes me like a father whose
son has returned from long wanderings, but with no feeling that my lengthy absence was disloyal. The enduring
always seems to look down upon the transient with a superiority that alternates between derision and tolerance, and
so I, an old man, find myself examined and appraised by
the spirit of this cool damp expanse, tolerated and a little
mocked without feeling myself humiliated. Every new encounter with the earth and nature is of a similar kind, at least
for our sort, for us artists: our heart comes to the elemental
and apparently eternal, warm and full of love, beats to the
measure of the waves, breathes with the wind, flies with the
clouds and birds, feels love and thankfulness for the beauty
of the lights, colors, and tones, knows that it belongs to
them, is related to them, and yet never receives in return
from the eternal earth, the eternal heavens any further response than just that indifferent, half-mocking glance of
the great for the small, of the old for the child, of the enduring for the transitory. Until we, be it in defiance or submission, in pride or despair, oppose speech to muteness,
the temporal and mortal to the eternal, and the feeling of
smallness and transitoriness becomes the both proud and
desperate consciousness of man, man that most recreant but
most capable of love, youngest but most alert, most lost but
most capable of suffering son of the earth. And behold, our
impotence is broken, we are neither small nor defiant any
longer, we no longer yearn to be one with nature but oppose
to her greatness our own, to her permanence our change-
ability, to her muteness our speech, to her apparent eternity

our knowledge of death, to her indifference our love and our hearts capable of suffering.

I have now, so it might appear, sketched out some intimation of this magnificent and magical landscape, marvelously picturesque in its autumn tones. But I am not yet through with it. In addition to the flat heavy farmland, the many gardens and parks, the shore and the lake, the wooded hills reaching almost around the whole horizon and the extensive chain of the Jura foothills, there is something more, something else commands attention: the mountains, the Alps. On most days at this time of year, to be sure, they are not to be seen, or only occasionally for a half hour or so beyond the chain of foothills something white or blue or rosy appears, a triangle or polygon, looking like cloud and yet betraying for an instant a different material and structure, pushing the wide horizon back a substantial distance and at the same time making the impression of boundlessness meaningless, for the eye gleans there an intimation, through the blue or rose, of something firm, a boundary, a wall. And twice toward evening I saw, not any such vague and isolated mountain forms momentarily showing themselves, but mountains lighted in red, their sides in blue shadow, the so familiar line of the Bernese Oberland, with the Jungfrau in the middle. They drew a boundary in the distance above the hills where otherwise everything dissolves in light and mist and sky; a very delicate and yet definite outline, they gleamed in a soft, smiling light until with the setting of the sun they unexpectedly disappeared, and the eye, however enchanted and rewarded it had been, did not miss them, so unearthly and almost unreal had been that magnificent phenomenon.

But now came a day on which I was fated to have a completely new, different, and overwhelming view of the Alps. It was Sunday, before lunch I had taken my much too short walk, all that my remaining strength permits, had returned very weary, eaten lunch, taken off my shoes and lain down on the divan, had read letters that had been waiting for several days and then with *Grimm's Fairy Tales* (oh, how many gifts unwithered after a hundred years did those two brothers bequeath to their people!) had begun to consider an answer to one of the letters but had not got far with it when I went to sleep. Presently there was a gentle tapping at my door, my little nap had not been deep in any case, and the doctor came in to tell me that he and his little boy were going for a ride and would like me to accompany them. It didn't take me long to get ready, we got in the car and drove by the shortest route to Mount Jura, famed for its view of the Alps. We passed quickly through the flat country with its vast beet fields and many fruit trees; neatly kept vineyards with low vines planted at precise intervals covered the southern slopes of the hills, then the road rose sharply through a mixed woods with brown beech leaves, the fresh green of pines, yellow of autumn larches, and led us in a short while to an elevation of a thousand meters or a little more. Now we had reached the ridge; from here on, the road ran on almost level. We climbed a few paces up an Alpine meadow grazed bare, and the view of the Alps that we had already partially glimpsed during the ascent of the mountain road, which afforded more an intimation than a view, lay revealed and open before us, a tremendous and actually terrifying sight. The whole valley and the lake lying in the depths beneath us were invisible, sunk and shrouded in a mist that had not yet thickened to fog, and that here and there stirred in soft breath, at times revealing a bit of land, but mostly producing an impression of complete stillness and immobility. If you gazed into it for a while, you could succumb to the illusion that an invisible lake down there stretched for hundreds of miles to the foot of that colossal mountain range which rose naked and clear against the heavens, beyond the world of mists. From here one sees not a single group of mountains or several, but the whole thing, the complete Alps from the extreme east of the country to their last peaks and ridges in Savoy, the backbone of Europe laid before us like that of a gigantic fish, a rigid, clear, cold, alien, yes, bitter and threatening world of rock and ice in the cold hostile blue, with here and there steep surfaces brightly lighted for a while, their eternal snow answering the light in a cold, crystalline, sober, and almost abstract way. Monstrous, silent, icy, a strong protective barricade through the middle of our world, the chain of the Alps rose into the cool autumn sky, hard and knife-edge sharp, frozen like a hundred-mile-long lava flow. My response to this spectacle was a kind of horror, a feeling of terror and cold mixed with ecstasy; like being struck by a jet of very cold water, it gave pain and pleasure, it exalted and oppressed at once. Just as, before going to sleep after the ordinary labors of the day, one may open one's window and from the commonplace, the security of the all too familiar, may lift one's eyes to the winter night sky with its coldly flaming stars, so we looked over from our mountain ridge, which with its road and hotel, summer houses and chapel made a quite civilized, domesticated impression, across the wide sea of mist to that huge, alien, rigid super-reality beyond. A little later when I had somewhat controlled that violent first impression, unsought for, a painting came into my mind. But it was not by Hodler or Calame or any other of our Alpine painters, but a man from a time long before their discovery of the Alps, the old Sienese Simone Martini; there is a picture by him in which a lonely knight is riding into the far distance, and diagonally across the picture rises a bold and naked mountain ridge, harsh and jagged, bony and thorny as the spine of a perch.

Mysteries

1947

Now and then the poet—and presumably other people as well—feels the need to turn away for a while from the simplifications, systems, abstractions, and other half and whole lies and to observe the world as it really is; in other words, not as an admittedly complicated but nevertheless ultimately surveyable and comprehensible system of conceptions but as the jungle of beautiful and terrifying, always new, completely incomprehensible mysteries that it actually is. Every day, for example, we find in the newspaper so-called world events, flat, surveyable, reduced to two dimensions, from the tension between East and West to the investigation of Japan's war potential, from industrial statistics to the assurance of some statesmen that the immense power and threat of the latest weapons of war must lead to their being abolished or beaten into plowshares. Although we know that there is no reality in all this, it being partly lies, partly a professional conjurer's trick in an amusing, artificial, irresponsible, surrealistic language, nevertheless this picture of the world daily repeated, even though it is often so crassly contradictory, each time gives us a certain pleasure, a kind of reassurance, for momentarily the world seems flat, surveyable, devoid of mysteries, and ready to adapt itself to any explanation that meets the wishes of the subscriber. And the newspaper is in fact only one among thousands of examples; it was not the first to rob the world of substance and to banish mysteries, nor is it the only one to carry on these practices for profit. No, just as the reader when he has skimmed the newspaper enjoys for a moment the illusion that he now knows essentially what has happened in the world for the last twenty-four hours and that

substantially nothing has happened that the smart editor
had not partially foretold in the Thursday edition, just so
each of us paints and misrepresents every day and every
hour the jungle of mysteries, transforming it into a pretty
garden or a flat, neatly drawn map, the moralist with the
help of his maxims, the man of religion with the help of his
faith, the engineer with the help of his slide rule, the
painter with the help of his palette, and the poet with the
help of his examples and ideals. And each one of us lives
completely content and assured in his pseudo-world and
on his map, just so long as he does not feel, through some
breach in the dam or some frightful flash of lightning, reality, the monster, the terrifying beauty, the appalling horror,
falling upon him, inescapably embracing him and lethally
taking him prisoner. This state, this illumination or awakening, this life in naked reality never lasts long, it bears death
in it, each time a person is seized by it and thrust into its
frightful whirlpool it lasts exactly as long as that person can
endure it, and then it ends either with death or with breathless flight into unreality, back to the bearable, the orderly,
the comprehensible. In this bearable, tepid, orderly zone of
concepts, systems, dogmas, allegories, we live nine-tenths of
our lives. So the little man leads a peaceable, quiet, orderly
life, though perhaps cursing a good deal, in his little house
or apartment, with a roof over his head and a floor under
his feet; and within him a knowledge of the past, of his
antecedents, his forebears whose lives were almost like his
own; and over him an order, a state, a law, a system, an
army—until in an instant all this disappears and is torn
to bits, roof and floor become thunder and fire, order and
justice confusion and chaos, peace and contentment the
suffocating threat of death, until the whole ancestral, revered, and reliable pseudo-world has burst into flame and
fragments and there is nothing left but the monster, reality.
One can call it God, this monstrous and incomprehensible
thing, this terrifying and, because of its reality, so convincing thing, but nothing is gained in understanding, in
clarification, in bearableness by a name. The knowledge of

reality, which never lasts more than a moment, can be produced by a hail of bombs in wartime, that is, by those weapons whose frightfulness, according to the words of many statesmen, will sometime compel us to beat them into plowshares. For the individual an illness is often enough, a catastrophe occurring in his immediate neighborhood, but at times, too, a momentary drop in his life's mood, the awakening from an oppressive nightmare, a sleepless night, will bring him face to face with the inexorable and for a while make all order, all comfort, all safety, all faith, all knowledge doubtful.

Enough of this. Everyone knows about it, everyone knows what it is like even if he has only been touched once or twice by the experience and believes that he has been successful in forgetting it. The experience, however, is never forgotten, and if consciousness covers it over, philosophy or faith gives it the lie, and reason rejects it, then it will find a hiding place in the blood, in the liver, in the big toe, and unfailingly one day it will assert itself in full vigor and unforgettableness. For the rest, I do not intend to philosophize about the numinous or about this experience under any other name; that is the profession of others, for the human mind, that clever, always astonishing mind, has succeeded in making out of the essentially incomprehensible, unique, demonic, unbearable a philosophy with systems, professors, and authors. Here I am not competent and I have not even been able really to read those who specialize in the riddle of life. Because it so happens, because the hour compels me to it out of the commonplaceness of my calling, I simply wish to set down, without partisanship or order, something about the relationship of the poet to the lies about life and also about the heat lightning of mystery at play behind the walls of those lies. Let me add at once: the poet as such stands no closer to the mystery of the world than any other person, he no more than anyone else can live and work without a floor under his feet and a roof over his head and without hanging over his bed a tight mosquito net of systems, conventions, abstractions, simplifications, and superficialities. He too, exactly like the newspapers, creates out of the thundering darkness of the world an order and a map, prefers to live on the surface rather than in many dimensions, prefers music to the explosion of bombs, and usually turns to his readers in what he writes with the carefully cultivated illusion that there exists a norm, a language, a system that make it possible for him to communicate his thoughts and experiences, that the reader to some extent experiences them with him and can actually assimilate them. In general, he behaves like everyone else, he carries on his profession as well as he can and is at pains not to wonder how far perhaps the ground he is standing on will carry him, how much the reader actually can accept, feel, and share his ideas and experiences, how far his faith, his picture of the world, his morality, his way of thought are like those of the reader.

*   *   *

Recently a young man wrote me a letter in which he addressed me as "old and wise." "I have faith in you," he wrote, "for I know that you are old and wise." I was having just then one of my somewhat brighter moments and did not take the letter, which was very similar to hundreds of others I receive, at one gulp, but fished out here and there a sentence or a few words and examined them with the greatest possible attention, seeking for their true substance. "Old and wise" stood there and that could, to be sure, raise laughter in an old man grown weary and irascible, who in his long rich life had often believed he stood infinitely closer to the truth than he did now in his reduced and cheerless state. Old, yes, that I was, that was true, old and worn out, disillusioned and weary. And yet the word "old" could, of course, express something entirely different! If one talked about old sagas, old houses and cities, old trees, old societies, old cultures, nothing at all deprecatory, derisive, or contemptuous was intended by the word. And so too I could only very partially claim for myself the qualities of old age; I was inclined from the many connotations of the word to permit only the negative overtones to apply to me. Well, for the young letter writer the word "old" could, so far as I was concerned, have the worth and meaning of a picturesque, gently smiling graybeard, partially touching, partially venerable; at least it had always had that added meaning for me in the times when I myself was not yet old. Well then, good, we could allow the word, understand it, and approve it as a form of salutation.

Now what about the word "wise"? Yes, what was it really intended to mean? If meant as a nothing, an imprecise generality, a common epithet, a phrase, well, one could let it pass. And if it was not that, if it was really intended to mean something, how was I to get at that meaning? I called to mind an old method I had often used, that of free association. I rested for a bit, walked up and down the room a few times, said the word "wise" to myself again, and waited for the first thing that would occur to me. Just look, what occurred to me was another word, the word Socrates. That, after all, was something, it was not just a word, it was a name, and behind the name stood not an abstraction but a figure, a man. Now what had the flimsy concept wisdom to do with the lusty, very real name Socrates? That was easy to determine. Wisdom was the quality first and unhesitatingly attributed to Socrates when his name came up, by teachers in elementary school and high school, by authorities lecturing to overflow audiences, by the authors of articles and monographs. The wise Socrates. The wisdom of Socrates —or, as the celebrated lecturers would say: the wisdom of a Socrates. More was not to be said about this wisdom. Hardly had one heard the word, however, when a reality, a truth, appeared, that is, the real Socrates, who despite all the drapery of legend was a right powerful, right convincing figure. And this figure, this old Athenian with the kind, ugly face, had expressed himself quite unmistakably about his own wisdom, he had confessed firmly and explicitly that he knew nothing, absolutely nothing, and that he had no claim whatever to the attribute of wisdom.

Here I had strayed again from the straight path and got

into the neighborhood of realities and mysteries. That's the way it was: once you let yourself be tempted into taking thoughts and words really seriously, then you were immediately in the void, in uncertainty, in darkness. If the world of scholars, of orators and lecturers, of rostrums and essays was right, then Socrates was a completely ignorant man, a man who in the first place knew nothing and believed in no knowledge or the ability to gain knowledge, and in the second place out of just this non-knowledge and disbelief in knowledge had made his strength, his instrument for questioning reality.

There stood I, an old wise man, in front of the old unwise Socrates and had to defend myself or be shamed. There was more than enough cause for shame; for despite all evasions and hairsplitting I knew quite well that the young man who addressed me as wise did not do this simply out of his own stupidity and youthful lack of intuition but that I had given him cause, had tempted him to do this, had half authorized him to do so through many of my poetic utterances in which something like experience and reflection, the instruction and wisdom of age, was detectable, and if I later, as I believe, put quotation marks around most of my poetic formulations of "words of wisdom," cast doubt upon them, indeed rejected and recanted them, nevertheless all in all I have during my whole life's activity affirmed more than I have denied, agreed or at least kept silent more often than I have taken issue, have often enough paid reverence to the traditions of the intellect, of faith, of language, of custom. Undeniably there was sometimes heat lightning in my writings, a rift in the clouds and draperies of the traditional altarpiece, a rift behind which lurked threatening apocalyptic hauntings; here and there it was indicated that man's surest possession was his poverty, his most proper bread his hunger; but all in all I had, just like everyone else, elected to turn to the beautiful worlds of form and tradition, had preferred the gardens of sonatas, fugues, and symphonies to all the fiery heavens of the apocalypse and had chosen the magical play and reassurance of language over any experience in which language ceased and became nothing because for a terrifyingly beautiful instant, perhaps ecstatic, perhaps deadly, the ineffable, the unthinkable that can be experienced only as mystery and hurt, the inner side of the world, looks at us. If the young letter writer saw in me not an ignorant Socrates but a wise man in the sense meant by the professors and article writers, then I had in large measure given him the right to do so.

Nevertheless it was still impossible to determine what part of the young man's conception of wisdom was cliché and what was experience. Perhaps his wise old man was simply a stage figure, or rather a dummy, but perhaps on the other hand that well-known series of associations with the word "wise" that I have just run through had occurred to him. Perhaps at the word "wise" his first thought had also been unconsciously of Socrates, only then with discomfort and embarrassment to have to recognize that Socrates in particular would have nothing to do with wisdom, refused to know anything about wisdom.

My examination of the words "old and wise" had thus brought me small profit. Now, in order to have done with the letter in some fashion, I pursued the opposite course and tried to gain some illumination not from any of the individual words but from the substance, from the whole concern that had impelled the young man to write his letter. This concern was a question, apparently a very simple one and apparently also simple to answer: "Has life any meaning, and wouldn't it be better to put a bullet through one's head?" At first glance this question does not seem to admit of very many answers. I could reply, "No, dear boy, life has no meaning, and in fact it would be better, etc." Or I could say, "Life, my friend, certainly has a meaning, and an exit by way of a bullet is not to be thought of." Or again: "Life, to be sure, has no meaning, but that's no reason to shoot yourself." Or once more: "Life indeed has its good meaning, but it is so difficult to live up to it or even to recognize it that one might better pick up a gun after all."

Perhaps these at first sight would be the possible answers

to the boy's question. But hardly had I begun to test the possibilities when it became obvious that there are not four or eight but a hundred or a thousand answers. And still one might swear that for this letter and this letter writer there is ultimately only a single answer, only a single door into freedom, only a single release from the hell of his distress.

To find this single answer there is no help for me in wisdom or old age. The question in this letter places me completely in the dark, for those bits of wisdom which I possess and also those bits of wisdom possessed by far older and wiser spiritual advisers are, to be sure, splendidly appropriate for books and sermons, for lectures and essays, but not for this single, real case, not for this honest patient who, though he vastly overrates the value of age and wisdom, is nevertheless in bitter earnest and who has struck from my hand all my weapons, my subterfuges and evasions with the simple words: 'I have confidence in you."

Now how is an answer to be found to this both childlike and serious question?

Something has sprung at me from this letter, something has caught me that I feel and ponder more with my nerves than with my reason, more with my stomach or sympathetic system than with experience and wisdom: a breath of reality, a blaze from the yawning rift in the clouds, an appeal from beyond, from the far side of conventions and reassurances, and there is no solution to this other than to evade and be silent or obey and accept the appeal. Perhaps I still have the choice, perhaps I can still say, I am not yet able to help the poor boy, I know as little as he, perhaps I can put his letter at the bottom of a pile of other letters and half-consciously see to its remaining there and gradually drifting out of my mind. But even as I think this I know at once that I will only be able to forget it when it has really been answered and, moreover, answered properly. That I know this, that I am convinced of it, comes not from experience and wisdom, it comes from the strength of the appeal, from the encounter with reality. And so the strength out of which I will be able to draw my answer will come not from me, not from experience or cleverness or practice or humanity, but out of reality itself, out of the scintilla of reality that this letter has brought me. So the strength to answer lies in the letter itself, it will answer itself, the youth himself will provide the answer. If he strikes a spark out of me, the stone, the old wise man, it is his hammer, his stroke, his distress, his strength alone that wakens the spark.

I cannot conceal the fact that I have already received letters with this same question very many times, have read and answered them or left them unanswered. Only the degree of need is not always the same; it is not only strong pure souls that at some hour put such questions, there are also the rich youths with their half-sorrows and half-submissiveness. More than one has already written me that I am the man in whose hands he is placing the decision: a yes from me and he will recover, a no and he will die—and strong though that sounded, I could nevertheless detect an appeal to my vanity, to my own weakness, and I came to the conclusion: this letter writer will not be healed by my yes or die by my no, but will go on cultivating his perplexity and perhaps direct his question to a number of other so-called sages, find a little comfort, a little entertainment in their answers, and put together a collection of them in a file.

And now if I, seized by necessity, illuminated by the flickering lightning of real life, allow myself to be compelled by its hardly bearable rarefied air to abrupt action, if I permit that letter once more to speak or to cry out to me, then I need not oppose it with any doubts or misgivings, subject it to any further examination or diagnosis, but only follow its cry; not to proffer my advice and my knowledge but to do the one thing that can help, that is, give the answer the youth must have and needs only to hear from another's lips to know it is his own answer, his own necessity, that he has here conjured up.

It is not easy for a letter, a query, addressed to an unknown person actually to reach the addressee, for the writer of the letter can, despite his real and distressing need, only express himself in conventional signs. He asks, "Has life a meaning?" And that sounds vague and silly, like schoolboy melancholy. But he does not really mean "life," he is not interested in philosophy, dogmatics, or natural law; what he means is simply and solely *his* life, and the last thing he wants to hear from my assumed wisdom is a lecture or a prescription on the art of living meaningfully; no, what he wants is that his true distress be seen and for a moment shared by a real human being and thereby, for this time, overcome. And if I provide him with this help then it is not I who have helped, but it is the reality of his distress that for an hour has divested me, the wise old man, of my age and wisdom, and poured over me a shining icy wave of reality.

Enough of this letter. What often preoccupies a writer after reading letters from his readers is questions such as these: While writing my books what have I, aside from the simple pleasure of writing itself, really thought, desired, meant, striven for? And then questions such as these: How much of what you intended and strove for in your work will the reader accept or reject? Yes, how much of it will be so much as noticed by the reader and absorbed into his consciousness? And the question: Has what the writer means and desires in his creations, has his wish, his ethics, his self-criticism, his morality anything whatever to do with the final effect his books produce? According to my experience, it has very little to do with it. Not even that question which generally is most important to a writer, the question about the aesthetic value of his work, about its content of formal beauty, plays really any great role. A book may be aesthetically and poetically worthless and nevertheless have a tremendous influence. Apparently these influences are often rational and calculable, were foreseeable and probable. In truth, however, what happens here in this world is also completely irrational and not subject to law.

To come back to that subject so alluring to youth, suicide: again and again I have received letters from readers with the statement that they had just been on the point of taking their own lives when this book fell into their hands, released and enlightened them, and now they were on the upgrade. About the same book, however, which had had that healing effect, the father of a suicide wrote me a harsh accusation: my thrice accursed book had been one of those that his poor son in his last days had had lying on his bedside table and it alone was to be held responsible for what had happened. I could, of course, reply to this enraged father that he was making the responsibility for his son's action much too easy for himself, if he attributed it solely to a book, but it took a good while for me to "forget" that father's letter, and to what degree I have succeeded is evident here.

At the time when Germany had practically reached the high point of its nationalistic fever curve, a woman in Berlin wrote me about another one of my books: such a shameful volume as mine must be burned, and she would see to it, and every German mother would know how to protect her sons from this book. This woman, supposing she really had sons, no doubt protected them from knowledge of my shameful volume, but from devastating half the world, from wading in the blood of unarmed victims and all the rest, she had not protected them. Curiously enough, at almost the same time another German woman wrote me about the same book: if she had sons, she would give them this book to read so that they might learn to see life and love with the eyes of this book. But in writing that book I had not intended either to corrupt young people or to instruct them in how to live, I had not given an instant's thought to either of these matters.

A quite different question, about which presumably no reader ever thinks at all, can become a concern and torment to the writer: Why must I, apparently in contradiction to all my native feelings, place my creations, the dear children of my joy and care, the fabric woven from the finest substance of my life, before the eyes of strangers and look on while they come upon the market, are overvalued and undervalued, praised and spat upon, honored or abused? Why cannot I withhold them, at most showing them to a friend but preventing their publication or not allowing it until after

my death? Is it desire for fame, is it vanity, a wish to attack
or an unconscious desire to be attacked that has brought me
again and again to send my dear children into the world
and expose them to misunderstanding, chance, vulgarity?

That is one question from which the artist never completely escapes. For the world pays us, to be sure, for our
creations, sometimes even more than they are worth, but
it pays us not with life, with soul, with happiness, with
substance, but simply with what it has to give—money,
honors, inclusion in lists of the famous. Yes, the world can
give the most unlikely responses to an artist's work. This,
for instance: an artist works for a people who are his natural
field of observation and knowledge and his natural market
as well; the people, however, allow the work created for
them to wither on the vine, they deny the artist recognition
as well as bread. Then suddenly a foreign people discover
him and give the disappointed author what he has more or
less earned: recognition and bread. Now the people for
whom the work was intended and to whom it had been
offered loudly hail the author and congratulate themselves
that one of theirs has received such distinguished recognition. And that is still far from being the strangest thing
that can happen between an artist and his nation.

There is little profit in bemoaning the unalterable and
lamenting a lost innocence, but people do it nevertheless, at
least the author does it at times. And so there is one idea that
has a great attraction for me. I wish I could through magic
make all my writings once more my private property and
rejoice in them as an unknown gentleman named Rumpel-
stiltskin. Something or other is wrong in the relationship between the artist and the world; the world itself feels this
at times, and how would it be possible for the artist not to
feel it much more keenly? Something of the disillusionment
with which the artist, even when his work has achieved
every success, regrets having surrendered things secret, beloved, and innocent rang out to me, even in my early years,
from many of the poems I loved, and most of all from a
little fairy tale by Grimm, one of the toad fairy tales. I

have never been able to reread it without a tremor and a silent anguish of soul. Since one dare not retell such a magical composition, I set down the fairy tale here at the conclusion of my essay, literally word for word.

*   *   *

An orphan child was sitting beside the city wall and spinning; then she saw a toad come out from an opening under the wall. Swiftly she spread out at her side her blue silk scarf, such as toads greatly love and which are the only things they will go upon. Forthwith the toad caught sight of it, turned about to the wall, and returned, carrying a little gold crown which it laid upon the scarf, and then went away again. The girl picked up the crown; it glittered and was made of delicately spun gold. Before long the toad came a second time: but when it did not see the crown on the scarf, it crept to the wall and from sorrow beat its little head against the wall as long as it still had strength, until finally it lay dead. Had the little girl let the crown lie where it was, the toad might well have brought even more of its treasures out of the cave.

The Omitted Word

1948

A REMARKABLE REQUEST gave my wife and me each an hour's work yesterday. A letter came from America written by an old gentleman, a pious German Jew from one of those ancient families of the Rhine and Main region. Up to the threshold of this unfriendly day those old Jewish families of the Rhineland have represented the finest and best-preserved cultural communities in Germany, one of which has its obituary and merited memorial in Wilhelm Speyer's very beautiful novel *Das Glück der Andernach*.

This old gentleman in New York, an emigrant, cultivated and pious, one of the nameless ones in that host of worthies which Germany cast out in favor of boisterous wicked men, wrote me on a question of conscience that had caused him concern, and the request he considered it his duty to address to me consisted in this: that I should leave out in any future editions of one of my books a single word. He had recently read "A Guest at the Spa" and cited a passage from it in which I quote the saying "Love thy neighbor as thyself." The patient at the spa called this saying "the wisest words ever spoken," and added, "A saying moreover that astonishingly had already appeared in the Old Testament." For the reader and letter writer in America, for the pious Jew and biblical scholar, the word "astonishingly" is not acceptable, he finds it insulting to Judaism and belittling to the Torah, and he beseeches me in solemn language to strike it out.

First of all, since my eyes were not up to it, my wife had to run through "A Guest at the Spa" in order to make sure of the context and wording of the sentence. Then I carefully reread the questionable page in that book of mine written twenty-five years ago. Of course the letter writer was right, of course it was an error, and for a Jewish reader almost

blasphemous that an author he had hitherto taken seriously
found it "astonishing" that so noble and exalted a saying
was "already" to be found in the Old Testament, that is,
long before Jesus and long before the Christian doctrine
was written down. He was right, there was no doubt about it:
my expression "astonishingly," just like the word "already"
(my correspondent, however, had taken no exception to
that), was factually wrong and hasty and stupid, it reflected
some of the combined embarrassment and arrogance with
which at the time of my childhood and schooldays popular
Protestant theology spoke to us small Protestant children
about the Bible and about Judaism, and which meant something like this: Judaism and the Old Testament were unquestionably sacred and could not be too highly respected;
however, the final thing was lacking in them, the crown:
the Old Testament was predominantly a book of severity
and the law whereas it was only the New Testament that
had brought us the true and complete conception of love
and grace, etc. When I had written that line in "Guest"
twenty-five years ago I had not been, at least at that particular moment, an informed and enlightened person; when
I quoted the magnificent saying about loving one's neighbor
it had seemed in fact "astonishing" to me that such a saying,
which one could properly call the quintessence of Christian
doctrine, or at least of Christian morality, was to be found
in the Old Testament. Right he was, that honest and concerned man in America.

But what about all this? Was the "Guest" and were all
my books written for the purpose of spreading knowledge
and objective truths among the people? Certainly they
strove above everything else to serve the truth, but in the
sense of candor, which carefully refrained from every authoritarian admixture in the expression of its ideas, a
candor whose law exposes the author to extensive sacrifice
of his person and compels him often to self-revelation, a
sacrifice that no reader has ever fully understood. Had I
ever wanted to communicate to my readers anything but
the events of my own experience and thinking, plus at
times a part of the personal road by which I had arrived

at these conclusions? Had I ever played the part of a dictator, the man of unquestionable knowledge, the priest and teacher who proclaimed his truths with the authority of his office, passing over omissions and doubts? Had not my role and task been this: to communicate to my readers not only my thoughts and convictions but also my doubts, and not to play before them the part of one speaking with authority, an initiate, but only to show myself as a seeking and erring brother?

I could not explain this to the man in America. Since in reading my books, almost all of which he knew, he had not noticed it, I would not succeed in a letter, no matter how long, in converting him to a different way of reading and understanding. He demanded of me that I strike a single word from one book and, by demanding this, that I should in the interests of the truth become guilty of a lie, I should act as though at that time, twenty-five years ago, when I wrote "Guest," I was not capable of any error or carelessness, any ignorance in respect to the Bible and theology, as though I had not at that time as today remnants of my origin and education clinging tenaciously to me. Was not that perhaps demanding a little too much?

So apparently it was a simple matter. Something was demanded of me that went against my character and taste, my literary habits, not to say simply my "principles," and to this there could really be only one answer, a refusal. But things always look simpler than they are—moral questions even more than others. If I had only been twenty years younger! Then I would not have burdened my wife with looking up the passage in the book, would not have created so many scruples for myself, would have found time to write my reader a letter of many pages explaining the matter, would have warmed to my task while writing the letter and flattered myself into the conviction that now I had really convinced and calmed my correspondent. The word "astonishingly" would have remained in my book and from then on would have documented in noble candor my unawareness and ignorance in the year 1923.

But now in fact I was older and somewhat more thoughtful, no doubt had become also somewhat less sure, and the man who wanted to have the word stricken was also not young, not a reader to be pacified and shaken in his convictions by a good letter, but an elderly gentleman whose letter was not lacking in either modesty or dignity. He was, moreover, a man of piety, a lover of the Bible, far better acquainted with the Old Testament than I was, and a rather thoughtlessly written word by me had caused him pain and aroused his concern. And something more: he was a Jew. He was a member of that nation which had given the world the Bible and the Savior and thereby had earned the hatred and grim enmity of almost all other peoples, a man of the age-old holy nation that in our godless time had endured unthinkable sufferings and had preserved itself in spite of them better than any younger nation in similar affliction: for not only had the Jews been an unequaled example (and this is true for today as well, the persecution still goes on) of solidarity, brotherly helpfulness, willingness to sacrifice, of which the world has not yet by any means become aware, they have in addition provided countless instances of heroism in endurance, steadfastness in the face of death, a dignity in misery and destruction, at the sight of which we non-Jews can only feel shame.

And so now was I to answer this friendly and dignified aged Jew by refusing him the satisfaction for which he had nobly begged, oppose to his pious wisdom my right as an author of books, as a representative of a psychological specialty, my ardor as a confessor, and, while I disillusioned and rejected him, teach him a lesson as well?

I could not bring myself to do it. It would have required a degree of certainty, of confidence in myself and the meaning and worth of my work that I could not muster up today. I wrote my reader in New York a short letter, that I had fulfilled his wish, and I wrote my publisher instructions that if there were a reprinting of "Guest," on page 154 the word "astonishingly" was to be omitted.

Happiness

1949

Man, the way God planned him and the way the poetry and wisdom of the people have understood him for many thousands of years, was created with a capacity for enjoying things even if they are not useful to him, with a sense for beauty. Mind and senses have always played an equal part in the joy man feels in beauty. As long as men are capable, in the midst of the distresses and dangers of their lives, of rejoicing in such things as these: the play of colors in nature or in a painting, an appeal in the voices of storm and sea, or in man-made music, as long as beneath its surface interests and necessities the world can be seen or felt as a whole, consisting as it does of interrelationships, from the curve of a young cat's neck to the variations of a sonata, from the touching eyes of a dog to the tragedy of a poet, an interconnection of a thousandfold riches of relationship, correspondences, analogies, and reflections, out of whose eternally flowing language their hearers derive joy and wisdom, entertainment and emotion—just so long will man again and again triumph over his ambiguities and be able to ascribe meaning to his existence. For "meaning" is precisely that unity of the multitudinous, or at least that ability of the spirit to perceive the chaotic confusion of the world as unity and harmony. For the true man, healthy, whole, unimpaired, the world justifies itself, God justifies Himself unceasingly through such marvels as these: with the coming of the cool of evening and the ending of the worker's day, there is also the reddening of the evening sky, and the magic, flowing transitions from rose into violet; or there is such a thing as the transformations of a human face when in a thousand nuances like the evening sky it is touched by the miracle of a smile. And there are such things as the spaces and windows of a cathedral, and the order of the stamens in a blossom. There are such things as a violin constructed from little boards, and the musical scale. So incomprehensible and delicate a thing, born from nature and mind, rational and at the same time suprarational and childish, as speech. Its beauties and surprises, its puzzles, its apparent immortality that nevertheless does not remove or protect it from the accidents, sicknesses, dangers to which all things mortal are exposed, these make it for us, its servants and pupils, one of the most mysterious and sacred phenomena on earth.

And it is not simply that every nation or every cultural community has created a speech corresponding to its origins and at the same time serving its as yet unarticulated goals, it is not simply that one nation can learn the language of another, admire it, smile at it, yet never completely and wholly understand it! No, for every single human being, insofar as he is not still living in a speechless primeval world or in a society mechanized through and through and thereby rendered speechless once more, speech is a personal possession. For everyone capable of language, that is, for every healthy and undismembered person, words and syllables, letters and forms, the possibilities of syntax have a particular value and meaning for him alone, every genuine language can be perceived and experienced by anyone gifted for it and with it, in a completely personal and unique fashion, even though he is unaware of it. Just as there have been musicians who loved certain instruments or certain keys or on the other hand found them questionable or distasteful, so most people, to the extent that they have any feeling for speech at all, have a special fondness for certain words and sounds, certain vowels or sequences of letters, while they avoid others, and if someone especially loves a particular poet or dislikes him, then that poet's taste and ear for language are responsible, characteristics that are congenial to the reader or the reverse. For example, I could name a whole mass of verses and poems that I have loved through the

decades and still love, not on account of their meaning, not
for their wisdom, not for the experience they contain, their
virtue or greatness, but simply on account of a particular
rhyme, on account of a particular variation in rhythm from
the accepted scheme, on account of a particular choice of
favored vowels that the poet may have hit upon as unconsciously as the reader unconsciously uses them. From the
structure and rhythm of a prose sentence by Goethe or
Brentano, or by Lessing or E. T. A. Hoffmann, one can often
draw many more conclusions about what is characteristic
in the poet, about his physical and psychological makeup,
than the sentence itself expresses. There are sentences that
might have been written by any poet at all and others that
were possible only for a single familiar word-musician.

For people like us words are the same as colors on a
painter's palette. They are numberless, and new ones keep
emerging, but the good, genuine words are less numerous
and in seventy years I have not seen a single new one emerge.
Nor are there as many colors as you choose, once you rule
out their gradations and mixtures. For everyone who talks
there are favorites and strangers among words, words preferred and words eschewed, there are everyday words that
one uses a thousand times without any fear of wearing them
out and other grand words which, no matter how much you
may love them, you utter and write only with forethought
and circumspection on the rare occasion befitting grandeur.

For me the word for happiness (*Glück*) belongs among
these.

It is one of the words I have always loved and like to
hear spoken. However much men might reason and argue
about its meaning, it still meant something beautiful, something good and desirable. And I felt that the sound of the
word corresponded to this.

To me this word, despite its brevity, had something
weighty and complete about it, something that reminded me
of gold; appropriate to gold too, in addition to its wholeness
and weightiness, it had its own luster; like lightning in
the cloud it dwelt in that short syllable which began so

meltingly and smilingly with the *Gl*, rested so laughingly and briefly in the *ü* and ended abruptly and decisively with the *ck*. It was a word for laughter and for tears, a word full of primitive magic and sensuality; if you wanted to appreciate it properly you had only to place this golden word next to a late, flat, tired nickel or copper word, such, for instance, as *actuality* or *utilization,* then everything became clear. There is no doubt about it, it never came out of a dictionary or a schoolroom, it was not thought up, derived, or put together, it was a unity, it was round, perfect, it came from heaven or out of the earth like sunlight or the face of a flower. How good, how happy, how comforting that there were such words! To live and think without them would be decline and desolation, it would be life without bread and wine, without laughter and music.

From this side, the natural and sensuous side, my attitude to the word *Glück* has never evolved or changed; today the word is just as short and golden, heavy and glowing as ever, I love it the way I loved it as a boy. But what this magical symbol means, what is intended by this word, so short and so heavy, about this my opinions and thoughts have changed many times, and only very late came to a clear and definite conclusion. Until far past the middle of my life, I obediently accepted the unproved belief that in people's mouths the word *Glück* meant something positive and unquestionably valuable, to be sure, but at bottom banal. Good birth, good education, a good career, a good marriage, prosperity in home and family, respect from others, a full purse, well-filled chests, all these things were thought of when one used the word *Glück* and I thought like everyone else. There were, so it seemed, happy people and the others, just as there were clever people and the others. We talked about happiness too in world history, we thought we knew about happy peoples, happy epochs. All the while we were living in the midst of an unusually "happy" epoch, we were lapped round with the happiness of a long peace, extensive freedom to travel, remarkable comfort and well-being as though by a warm bath. And yet we never took note of it, this happiness was all too much a matter of course, and we young people in that obviously friendly, agreeable, and peaceful epoch, if we had a high opinion of ourselves were blasé and skeptical in mood, flirted with death, with degeneracy, with that interesting chlorosis, whereas we talked about Florence of the quattrocento, the Athens of Pericles, and other vanished ages as happy. Our enthusiasm for these golden periods gradually faded, we read history, read Schopenhauer, became distrustful of superlatives and of fine words, we learned to live intellectually in a subdued and more relativistic climate—and yet the sound of the word *Glück* whenever we unexpectedly heard it with its old full golden tone remained an admonition and reminder of things of the highest value. Perhaps we thought at times that there might be simple childlike people who called these tangible possessions of life happiness, but we took the word to mean rather something like wisdom, transcendence, patience, steadfastness of soul, all of which was pretty enough and gave us pleasure, without deserving so fundamental, full, deep, and basic a name as *Glück*.

Meanwhile my personal life had long since developed to the point where I knew that it was not only not a so-called happy one but that there was no sense in trying to find so-called happiness in it. In an emotional hour I might perhaps have described this attitude as *amor fati* and yet essentially and with the exception of brief, overexcited developmental stages, I was never much inclined to pathos, and even Schopenhauer's nonpathetic, undemanding love had ceased to be my unqualified ideal since I had come to know the quiet, unostentatious, sparing, and always a little mocking kind of wisdom that had served as the soil from which sprang the reports of the lives of the Chinese masters and the parables of Chuang-tzu.

Now I don't want to fall to chattering. I have something fairly precise in mind to say. First of all, in order to keep to the point, I shall try to formulate or paraphrase what the word *Glück* contains for me today in content and significance. Today by *Glück* I understand something completely objective, to wit, the totality itself, timeless existence, the eternal harmony of the world, that which others at times have called the music of the spheres or the smile of God. This epitome, this unceasing music, this deep resounding golden gleaming eternity is pure and absolute present, it knows no time, no history, no before or after. Eternally the countenance of the world shines and laughs, all human beings, generations, nations, empires rise, flourish, and sink back again into the shadows and into nothingness. Eternally life plays its music, dances its roundelay, and whatever joy, comfort, capacity for laughter falls by chance to the lot of us transitory, weak, endangered mortals is a ray from that source, is an eye full of brightness, an ear full of music.

Now whether there ever really were those legendary "happy" men and whether even those favorites of Fortune so praised and envied, those darlings of the sun and lords of creation, only at times, only in festive and greatly favored hours or moments were illuminated by the great light, they can have experienced no other happiness, have shared in no other bliss. To exist in the perfect present, to join in the chorus of the spheres, to dance in the roundelay of the world, to join in the eternal laughter of God, that is our share in *Glück*. Many have experienced it just once, many only a few times. But he who has experienced it has not only been happy for an instant, he has also had given him some of the splendor and music, some of the light of timeless joy, and everything by way of love that has been brought into this world by lovers, everything by way of comfort and cheer that has been created for this world by artists and often after centuries glows as brightly as on its first day—all this comes from that source.

This is the comprehensive, the worldwide and holy significance that the word *Glück* has attained for me in the course of my life, and perhaps it is necessary for me to say explicitly to the schoolboys among my readers that here I am not speaking as a philologist but am telling a bit of my soul's history and that it is far from my intention to urge them to give this powerful meaning to the word *Glück* in their own everyday conversations and writings. For me, however, around this lovely short glowing golden word there has gathered everything I have felt at its sound since my childhood days. Then the feeling was certainly stronger, the response of all the senses to the sensual qualities and appeal of the word were sharper and louder, but if the word had not been so profound, so basic and so world-embracing, my conception of the eternal present, of the "golden clue" (in *Goldmund*) and the laughter of the Immortals (in *Steppenwolf*) would not have crystallized around this word.

When people who have grown old try to recall when, how often, and how strongly they have felt happiness, then they look first of all to their childhood, and properly so, for in order to experience happiness the first requisite is independence from time and therewith from fear and hope as well, and this ability in most people is lost with the years. I too, when I try to recall the moments when I shared in the splendor of the eternal present, in the smile of God, return each time to my childhood and find there the largest number and the most precious effects of this kind. Certainly more dazzling and colorful, more festively costumed and more brightly lit were the joyful periods of the years of my young manhood; my mind had a greater share in them than in those of my childhood. But when one looks closer and ever closer, there was more fun and merriment than true happiness, one was jolly, witty, humorous, making many good jokes. I remember one moment in a circle of my friends in the high bloom of my youth: in the course of a conversation an inoffensive fellow asked what in the world Homeric laughter really was, and I answered him by a rhythmic laughter that scanned in precise hexameters. There was loud applause and the clinking of glasses—but such moments as these do not stand up under later examination. That was all fun, it was merry, it tasted good, but it was not happiness. Happiness, so it seemed, when one pursued these investigations long enough, had been experienced only in childhood, in moments or hours that it was very difficult to find again, for even there, even in the region of childhood, it turned out that the glory upon re-examination was not always genuine, the gold not always wholly unalloyed. When I examined the matter very closely, only a few experiences were left, and they too were not pictures that one could paint and not stories that one could tell, they adroitly evaded questioning. If such a memory returned, it seemed at first as though it had to do with a week or days or at least a whole day, perhaps a Christmas, a birthday, or the first day of vacation. But to reconstruct a childhood day in memory required a thousand pictures, and for no single day, not even for half a one, would my memory bring together the requisite number.

Now whether they lasted for days, for hours, or even for only minutes, my experiences of happiness have been many, and even in my later days, even in old age, I have come close to it for moments. But among the encounters with happiness in the early days of my life, however often I summon them up, question and test them, one in particular has held its ground. It was during my schoolboy years, and its uniqueness, its genuineness, its primeval and mythical character, the state of being at one with the silently laughing world, the absolute freedom from time, from hope and fear, the complete nowness cannot have lasted long, perhaps minutes.

One morning I awoke, a lively boy of ten or thereabouts, with a most unusual, lovely, and profound feeling of joy and well-being that flamed through me like an interior sun, as though just now at this very instant of awakening from my good boyhood sleep something new and wonderful had happened, as though my whole boy's world, both large and small, had entered into a new and higher state, into a new life and climate, as though all that was beautiful in life now for the first time on this early morning had attained its full value and meaning. I knew nothing of yesterday or of tomorrow, I was embraced and gently cradled in a happy today. It felt fine and was relished by my senses and my soul without curiosity or calculation, it coursed through me and felt magnificent.

It was morning. Through the high window I saw suspended above the long ridge of our neighbor's roof the pure bright blue of heaven, it too appearing full of happiness as though it had something special in mind and so had donned its fairest dress. No more of the world was visible from my bed, only just this beautiful heaven and the long stretch of roof on our neighbor's house, but even this roof, this boring and desolate roof of dark reddish brown tiles, seemed to laugh, a subtle play of colors swept over a steep, shadowy slanting wall, and a single bluish glass tile among those of red clay seemed alive and happily engaged in trying to reflect some of the silent and steady radiance of early dawn. The sky, the rather rough ridge of the roof, the uniform army of brown tiles, and the airy thin blue of the single glass one seemed to have come to an understanding with one another in a beautiful and cheery way, they had obviously nothing else in mind but to laugh together in this special morning hour and to get on well with one another. Blue of heaven, brown of tile, and glass-blue belonged together, they had a meaning, they played with one another, all was well with them, and it was a fine thing and did one good to see them, to be present at their play, to feel oneself filled by the same morning radiance and well-being.

Thus I lay in bed for a lovely eternity, enjoying the dawning day together with the peaceful after-feeling of sleep, and whether I have ever tasted an identical or similar happiness on other occasions in my life, none could have been deeper or more real: all was well with the world. And whether this happiness lasted for a hundred seconds or ten minutes, it was so completely outside time that it resembled every other genuine happiness as wholly as one darting blue trout resembles another. It was transitory, it was washed away by time, but it was strong and external enough to call to me and draw me back over sixty years so that I have to make the attempt with weary eyes and aching fingers to summon it up, to smile at it, reconstruct it, and describe it. It consisted of nothing, this happiness, nothing except a harmony of the few objects around me with my own being, just a desireless sense of well-being that demanded no alteration, no heightening.

It was still quiet in the house and from outside there was no sound. If it had not been for this silence, presumably the memory of my daily chores, of getting up and going to school, would have disturbed my content. But it was clearly neither day nor night, the sweet light and the laughing blue were there, of course, but there was no sound of maids trotting over the sandstone flags of the forecourt, no slamming of doors, no scampering of bakers' boys on the stairs. This morning instant was outside time, it called upon nothing, it pointed to nothing that was to come, it was enough in itself, and since it completely contained me, for me too there was no day, no thought of getting up and going to school, or half-finished assignments or unlearned vocabulary, or a hasty breakfast in the freshly aired dining room below.

This time the eternity of happiness met its decline through a heightening of beauty, through an increase, an excess of joy. While I lay thus unmoving, and the light, silent morning world penetrated and absorbed me, out of the distance there struck through the silence something uncommon, something flashing and overly bright, golden and triumphant, full of swelling joy, full of enticing and arousing sweetness: the sound of a trumpet. And at once, now fully awake for the first time, I sat up in bed and threw back the covers, and the sound acquired another voice and then several more: it was the municipal band marching triumphantly through the streets, an altogether rare and exciting event full of resounding festiveness, which made my child's heart in my breast both laugh and sob as though all the happiness, all the magic of that blessed hour had flowed together in these rousing bittersweet tones and now poured itself forth, awakened and brought back to time and mortality. In a second I was out of bed, quivering with excitement, had rushed through the door into the next room, from whose window one could see the street. In a whirl of delight, curiosity, and desire to take part, I leaned out of

the open window, heard with excitement the proudly swelling sounds of the approaching band, saw and heard the
neighboring houses and the street awaken, come to life,
and be filled with faces, figures, and voices—and in the
same second I knew again everything that I had so completely forgotten in that state of well-being between sleep
and day. I knew that in fact today was no schoolday but a
high holiday, the king's birthday, I believe, that there would
be processions, banners, music, and merriment unconfined.

And with that knowledge I was back again, subject to
the laws of everyday life, and although this was not an
ordinary day but a holiday to which the metallic notes had
wakened me, nevertheless what had been unique and beautiful and divine in that morning magic had already vanished,
and over the lovely little miracle the waves of time, of the
world, of the commonplace had closed once more.

On Old Age
1952

O LD AGE is a stage in our lives, and like all other stages
it has a face of its own, its own atmosphere and tem-
perature, its own joys and miseries. We old white-haired
folk, like all our younger human brothers, have a part to
play that gives meaning to our lives, and even someone
mortally ill and dying, who can hardly be reached in his
own bed by a cry from this world, has his task, has something important and necessary to accomplish. Being old is
just as beautiful and holy a task as being young, learning to
die and dying are just as valuable functions as any other—
assuming that they are carried out with reverence toward
the meaning and holiness of all life. A man who hates being
very old and gray, who fears the nearness of death, is no
more worthy a representative of his stage of life than a
strong young person who hates and tries to escape his profession and his daily tasks.

To put it briefly, to fulfill the meaning of age and to perform its duty one must be reconciled with old age and
everything it brings with it. One must say yes to it. Without
this yea, without submission to what nature demands of us,
the worth and meaning of our days—whether we are old
or young—are lost and we betray life.

Everyone knows that old age brings with it infirmities and
that at its end stands death. Year after year one must make
sacrifices and endure renunciations. One must learn to
distrust one's senses and powers. The road that a short time
ago was a short stroll becomes long and wearisome, and
one day we can no longer walk it. We have to forgo some of
the foods that all our lives we have so much enjoyed. Physical joys and pleasures become rare and must constantly be

paid for at a higher price. And then all the disabilities and illnesses, the weakening of the senses, the flagging of the organs, the many pains, so often occurring in the long anxious nights—all this is not to be denied, it is bitter reality. But it would be mean-spirited and sad simply to resign oneself to this process of decline and not to see that old age has its good side, its advantages, its sources of comfort and joy. When two old people meet each other they ought not to talk simply about their damnable gout, their stiff joints and shortness of breath when climbing stairs, they ought not to exchange information just about their sufferings and annoyances but also about their more cheerful and comforting experiences and adventures. And there are many of them.

In remembering the positive and beautiful side of the life of the aged and the fact that we ancients have sources of strength, of patience, of joy that play no role in the life of the young, I am not competent to discuss the comforts of religion and the Church. This is the business of the priest. I can, however, name some of the gifts that old age bestows on us. To me the dearest of these gifts is the treasury of pictures which after a long life one carries in one's memory and to which one turns, as activity decreases, with a quite different interest than ever before. Human figures and faces that for sixty or seventy years have no longer existed on earth go on living within us, they belong to us, provide us with company, look out at us from living eyes. We see houses, gardens, cities that have since disappeared or are wholly changed as they once were, and distant mountain ranges and seacoasts that we once visited on journeys decades ago we find fresh and colorful in our picture book. Noticing, observing, contemplating become more and more a habit and exercise, and imperceptibly the mood and attitude of the beholder permeate our whole behavior. We, like the majority of men, have stormed through our years and decades of living, driven by wishes, dreams, desires, passions, impatient, tense, expectant, highly excited by fulfillment or by disappointment—and when today we cautiously leaf through the big picture book of our own lives, we are surprised at how beautiful and good it can be to have escaped that chase and pursuit and to have arrived at the *vita contemplativa*. Here in the garden of old age bloom many flowers to whose cultivation we once barely gave a thought. Here blooms the flower of patience, a noble blossom. We become more relaxed, more considerate, and the fewer our demands for participation and action become, the greater grows our ability to contemplate and listen to the life of nature and of our fellow men, to let that life stream past us without criticism and with ever-renewed astonishment at its variety, sometimes with solicitude and quiet pity, sometimes with laughter, with sheer joy, with humor.

Recently I was in my garden tending a fire, which I was feeding with leaves and dried twigs. Along came an old woman, probably close to eighty, past the whitethorn hedge; she stopped and looked at me. I greeted her and she laughed and said, "You're doing quite right with your little fire. At our age we'd do well to make friends with hell by slow degrees." That struck the tone of our conversation, in which we complained to each other of all kinds of pains and deprivations but always in a spirit of merriment. And at the end of our conversation we admitted to each other that despite everything we couldn't really be so frightfully old and could hardly count as real ancients so long as the oldest woman in the village was still alive, at one hundred.

When the very young people, in the superiority of their strength and lack of sensitivity, laugh behind our backs and find our gait awkward and straggling white hairs and scrawny necks comic, then we remember how we once, in possession of the same strength and lack of sensitivity, also laughed, and we do not seem to ourselves inferior or defeated, but rather we rejoice that we have outgrown that stage of life and have become a shade more shrewd and more patient.

Interpreting Kafka
1956

AMONG THE LETTERS my readers write me there is a particular category that keeps increasing in number and that I regard as a symptom of the increasing intellectualization of the relationship between reader and writer. The letters of this sort, usually from young readers, show a passionate concern about interpretation and explanation; their authors put endless questions. They want to know why the author chose this particular simile here, that particular word in another place, what he "intended" by his book and what he "meant," how he came upon the notion of choosing just this subject. They want to know from me which of my books seems to me the best, which is dearest to me, which brings out most clearly my views and opinions, why I expressed myself about certain problems and phenomena in a different way when I was thirty than at seventy, what relationship there is between Demian and Freudian and Jungian psychology, and so on and so on.

Some of these questions come from students in the higher schools and seem to have been prompted by the influence of their teachers; the majority, however, appear to have sprung from genuine private need, and all of them together show a change in the relationship between book and reader that can be observed spreading through public criticism as well. The cheering thing about it is the participation of the readers; they are no longer looking for passive enjoyment, they no longer simply want to swallow a book or a work of art whole, they want to master it and through analysis make it their own.

The matter, however, has its reverse side: the hair-splitting and cleverness about art and poetry has become a sport and an end in itself, and through the desire for mastery by critical analysis the elementary ability to accept, to see, and to listen, has suffered greatly. If one is content to extract from a poem or narrative its content in ideas, partisanship, information, or edification, then one is content with very little, and the secret of the art, the thing that is true and original, is lost.

Recently a young man, a schoolboy or college student, wrote me a letter with the request that I answer a series of questions about Franz Kafka. He wanted to know whether I considered Kafka's *The Castle*, *The Trial*, and *The Law* religious symbols, whether I shared Buber's opinion about Kafka's attitude toward his Jewishness—whether I believed there was a kinship between Kafka and Paul Klee—and much else besides. My answer was as follows:

Dear Herr B.

. . . Unhappily I must disappoint you completely. Your questions and the whole way in which you regard poetry comes as no surprise to me, to be sure; you have thousands of colleagues who think as you do, but your questions, which are without exception unanswerable, all flow from the same source of error.

Kafka's stories are not treatises about religious, metaphysical, or moral problems but works of the imagination. Whoever is capable of really reading a poet, that is, without questioning, without expecting intellectual or moral rewards, but in simple readiness to accept what the poet gives, to him these works in their own language give every answer that the reader can possibly wish. Kafka has nothing to say to us either as a theologian or as a philosopher but simply as a poet. That his magnificent stories have today become the fashion, that they are read by people who are neither able nor willing to assimilate poetry, for this he is not to blame.

To me, who have been a reader of Kafka since the appearance of his earliest works, none of your questions has any meaning. Kafka supplies no answer to them. He gives us the dreams and visions of his lonesome, difficult life, parables of his experiences, his distresses and moments of happiness; these dreams and visions alone are what we have to look for in him and receive from him, not the "interpretations" that ingenious exegetes can give to these creations. This business of "interpretation" is an intellectual game, a pretty enough game, suitable for people who are smart but who are strangers to art, who can read and write books about Negro sculpture or the twelve-tone scale but never find their way to the inside of a work of art because they stand at the gate fiddling at it with a hundred keys and never notice that the gate, in fact, is open.

This is how I feel about your questions. I thought I owed you an answer because your interest is serious.

Anti-Semitism
1922, 1958[*]

I

A PAMPHLET by Wilhelm Michel, entitled *Treason against the German People*, offers me an occasion to say a word against one of the ugliest and most inane forms of the new German nationalism, against the idiotic, pathological Jew-baiting of the bards of the swastika and their numerous adherents, in particular among students. The older brand of anti-Semitism was philistine and stupid, as such anti movements tend to be, but it did little harm. Today there is a kind of Jew-baiting among the misguided German youth that does a great deal of harm, because it prevents these young people from seeing the world as it is, and because it disastrously encourages the inclination to blame everything that goes wrong on some convenient devil. Whether you personally like the Jews or not, they are human beings, often infinitely more intelligent, more energetic, and better human beings than their fanatical enemies. Where you think they do harm, you may combat them, as we sometimes combat evils that are recognized to be necessary but that forever goad us to new efforts. But to regard a class of men as *the* evil of the world and take them as a scapegoat for the thousand dire sins and complacencies of your own German people, that is a grave perversion, and the harm it does far outweighs any harm that may ever have been done by Jews.

* Part I of this essay was written in 1922 and Part II was added in 1958.

II

Primitive man hates what he fears and at certain levels of his psyche civilized, educated man remains a primitive. The hatred of peoples and races for other peoples and races does not spring from superiority or strength, but from insecurity and weakness. Hatred of the Jews is a masked feeling of inferiority: toward the very old and very intelligent Jewish people the less intelligent sections of another race feel competitive envy and a shaming inferiority, and the more blatantly this base feeling parades as superiority, the more surely fear and weakness are behind it. When a truly superior, masterful man knows he is superior to someone, he will pity him, perhaps occasionally despise him, but never hate him.

We old people still remember the day when the Germans spoke with horror of the persecution of Jews in Russia and elsewhere. Whether or not they liked the Jews and esteemed them at their proper worth, they regarded the pogroms as barbarous and inhuman. Yet their minds and hearts had seldom advanced to the point of perceiving and condemning the anti-Semitism in their own people and state, which for the time being took the form not of massacres but only of juridical discriminations and a vocabulary of jibes and insults.

This seemingly trifling sin of omission had dire consequences. The same German people that was once outraged at the pogroms in other countries so outdid those atrocities a few decades later that in many countries the Germans as such have come to be regarded as far more dangerous and contemptible than the Jews or the Huns ever were.

True, this judgment is not that of the most advanced and intelligent people; like the Nazis' hatred of the Jews, it is born of fear. But such a judgment exists, it is a fact, and what such hatreds can lead to with a little incitement and organization from above, the German concentration and extermination camps have shown the world.

It is one of the tasks of the German youth to counter this hatred of the Germans with a reasonable and worthy attitude. This requires first of all an insight into the causes of the disgrace that National Socialism and above all its extermination of Jews brought upon Germany, and perpetual vigilance in avoiding the bad thinking and bad character of that generation and its leaders.

Anyone who in Germany today still or again mouths Hitlerian and anti-Semitic phrases, who closes his eyes to the terrifyingly logical concatenation of German history between 1933 and 1945, is an enemy of his country. If any of you young men are not convinced by what everybody knows, and if a seducer starts telling you the fairy tales about Jewish crimes with which Hitler and Himmler flooded their people, just remember that what the Germans did to the Jews is not a fairy tale. The history of the Third Reich and the Jews leaves no room for empty phrases.

Joseph Knecht
to Carlo Ferromonte[*]
1961

FRIEND, there is something proper and basically comforting in the way that everything, even what is apparently wholly dead and gone, is capable of recurrence and rebirth. Recently you informed me that for some time a number of your colleagues have become immersed in Buddhistic studies, especially in the literature of Zen, both in its Chinese and Japanese forms. You, it would seem, are inclined to consider this a simple fad and idle pastime; you yourself have really made up your mind not to become involved in it. Since you have broached the matter to me I am glad to give you my few thoughts about it, for the "fad" has appeared here in Waldzell too, so that I have been led to refresh my meager knowledge of the subject by reading. Above all, I have read repeatedly in recent days in that "Inscription from the Emerald Cliff," the Chinese Pi-yen Lu.

My love of the Chinese character has been known to you for a long time. Primarily it has nothing to do with Buddhism or with Zen, it was and is directed toward the splendid ancient China of the classics, which as yet knew nothing of Buddha. The old Book of Songs, the I Ching, the writings by and about Confucius and Lao-tse down to Chuang-tzu belong like Homer, Plato, and Aristotle among my teachers; they have helped to form me and to form my conception of good, wise, whole human beings. The word and concept Tao was and is dearer to me than Nirvana, and

* Both Knecht and Ferromonte are figures in Hesse's last novel, *The Glass Bead Game* (1943).

I feel the same way about Chinese painting; the traditional finished style inclining toward calligraphy seems preferable to me to the more vigorous, less controlled art of many Zen painters, closer to genius though the latter may appear. Strange and a little disturbing to me too on occasion as an old traveler and a believer in the saying *ex oriente lux* was the conception that China should have received its greatest spiritual treasure from the west, from the occidental land of India. These, however, are simply quirks of taste, not to be taken any more seriously than those fleeting wishes for a pause in history which one allows oneself occasionally in a dreamy sort of way, for instance, the wish that no Michelangelo had come along after Ghirlandaio, Piero della Francesca, and Lippi, that after Beethoven there had been no Wagner, or that Western religion had remained at the stage of primitive Christianity.

But then no more did China come to a stop with the old emperors, or with Confucius or Lao Tan, a few hundred years after its first golden period it was obviously once more in need of a light. And the light came, whether we happen to like it or not, not from the morning but by way of the Patriarch "from afar in the west"; the Buddhist teaching arrived from India and began by completely bewitching and dominating its disciples through Indian dogmatism, Indian speculation, and Indian scholasticism. The whole huge literature of the Buddhist schools was translated and commentaries on it were written, tremendous libraries grew up in the monasteries, the light from the west outshone all the old native stars. So it was, or seemed to be for a good while, that the Chinese became ascetic and pious, the dragon had been tamed. But a day came when he had digested the alien and soporific stuff he had swallowed, and the dragon stretched and woke up, and the grim old game began between victor and vanquished, between father and son, between the pedagogical and speculative West and the relaxed, fluid East. Buddhism assumed a new, a Chinese face. This roughly is the way I, a complete layman, see the prehistory of Zen.

However it will be more useful to you, I believe, if I men-

tion a few quite personal impressions that have remained
with special vividness in my mind after some study of the
"Inscription" of Pi-yen Lu. Whether I should recommend
that you commit yourself to reading the book I do not know.
It is crammed with enchanting bits and also unnerving ones,
but the kernels are enclosed in such thick hard shells that
for someone like you who already see your goals before you
quite precisely, life is probably too short to justify spending
days and weeks in deciphering such hieroglyphs. With me
it is a different matter, I have not yet concentrated so exactly on specific tasks and I wander about like a backward
student with a good appetite and clear conscience in the
boundless pastures of human intellectual history.

As you know, the kernel of the famous "Inscription" consists of short anecdotes (in the book they are called "illustrations"), some of them sayings, some instructive actions and
practices of well-known Zen masters of the early period.
Now the sayings for people like us—and for the Chinese of
the eleventh century as well—are almost all incomprehensible, their meaning can only be more or less unlocked with
the help of extensive commentaries. I give you two examples
at random:

> At the close of the summer training period Tsui-Yen
> instructed his listeners in the following words:
> All summer long as a favor to you brothers I have
> talked and talked. Look at me and see whether Tsui-
> Yen still has his eyebrows.
> Pao-fu said: Those persons who practice the profes-
> sion of thievery have emptiness in their hearts.
> Tshang-tjing said: They have thrived!
> Yün-men said: Lock the door!

Or this:

> A monk asked Hsiang-lin: What does it mean that
> the Patriarch came from afar in the West?
> Hsiang-lin replied: Weary from long sitting.

You see, this is a kind of witch's multiplication table. One feels behind it allusions, meanings, yes, incantations, these seem to be magic formulas but are not, instead they are directions for reaching precise goals, only you have to have the key to them, and in order to find that, not even the paraphrases and explanations of the "Inscription" are enough for us, for that we need a teacher who is both a Sinologist and an expert in Buddhist doctrine.

And yet there are a few of these traditional sayings of the masters that are simple and immediately impressive. One of them, it happens to be the first in the book, struck me like a revelation; I don't believe I shall ever forget it. An emperor meets the original Patriarch, Bodhidharma. With the pomposity and lack of understanding of the uninitiated worldling he asks, "What is the highest significance of the holy truth?" The Patriarch replies, "Limitless space—nothing holy." The sober greatness of this reply, Carlo, overcame me like a breath from the universe, I experienced an ecstasy and at the same time a terror as in those rare moments of immediate awareness of experience which I call "awakening" and about which we once talked in a very solemn hour. To achieve this awakening, which is not the result of cogitation but the experience of unity with the whole perceived as reality in soul and body, consciousness of this unity, is the goal toward which all disciples of Zen strive.

Now there are as many roads to this goal as there are human beings, and there are as many different kinds of guides as there are Zen masters. One can say of the students as well as of the masters that among them all types and kinds of Chinese humanity are to be found. For the most part, however, the student types are not as clearly defined in the anecdotes as the characters of the masters, but the great prize, so it seems to me, just as in our fairy tales, is more likely to fall to the simple and unpretentious than to the brilliant and versatile. Among the masters there are severe ones as well as gentle, there are lords of language and those who are taciturn, there are modest ones as well as those conscious of their own dignity, there are also angry, contentious, yes, violent masters. I have not so far discovered any other saying that has the grandeur of that "limitless space—nothing holy"; on the other hand, however, I have found a number of awakenings without words, awakenings through a blow on the ear, through being struck by a stick, through the switch of a yak's tail, through the lighting and immediate extinguishing of a candle. And then there was one master, one of the silent ones, who never answered the questions of his disciples orally but with his index finger, which he could raise in such a meaningful gesture that receptive and mature students experienced the ineffable at sight of that finger. There are stories, though, that at first reading communicate nothing at all; they sound like gossip or quarreling in the language of some completely forgotten foreign breed of man or animal—and on later inspection suddenly doors and windows open to all the heavens.

Since I talked to you at an earlier time about my kind of "awakening" long before either of us had heard of Zen, I must mention something that strikes me about the enlightened ones of Chinese Buddhism and gives me something to brood over. I know the experience myself of being struck by the lightning of perception, it has happened to me several times. Also it is something not unknown to us in the West, all mystics and very many of their followers, well and little known, have experienced it. I remind you, for example, of the first illumination of Jakob Böhme. But with these Chinese this state of awareness seems to last all their lives, at least in the case of the masters; they seem to have turned the lightning into a sun, to have nailed down the instant. Here there is a gap in my intelligence: I cannot imagine a perpetual state of illumination, a continuing condition of ecstasy. Presumably I bring too much of the attitude of the West with me into the Eastern world. I can only imagine that a person once awakened is more susceptible to a second, third, tenth awakening than other people, that in the course of nature he repeatedly sinks back into sleep and unconsciousness but never so deep that he cannot be awakened by the next bolt of light.

To round the subject off I will tell you one more remarkable and instructive story out of the Pi-yen Lu. In the tenth century there was a master named Yün-men, about whom many astonishing things are reported. His place of residence was the "Mountain Cloud Gate" in Kwangtung province in southern China. Once there came to him a seeker on a pilgrimage, a simple little man named Yüan. He had been on this journey for a long time, his pilgrimage had taken him through half of China, and here and there he had stopped at monasteries until he finally reached Mountain Cloud Gate. He was taken in, and Yün-men gave him the position of amanuensis in his own personal service. Obviously this great authority on human nature detected precious powers hidden in the simple young pilgrim of which the latter himself was unaware; for Yün-men took endless pains with him despite his slowness in understanding. I hear you ask, "How long did it take?" I reply, "Eighteen years." Day after day he summoned him on one or more occasions: "Attendant Yüan!" Each time Yüan replied, attentive and obedient: "Yes." And each time the master challenged him: "You say 'yes.' But what do you mean by that?" Taken aback and embarrassed, the attendant would again and again attempt to explain and excuse himself, but with time he instinctively realized that something was meant by the summons and the harsh criticism of his master's answer. He often taxed his abilities to the limit to justify his "yes"; presumably he meditated half his days on what answer he should give to the master next time. The great man's question and what he meant by saying "yes" was a nut that Yüan had to chew on for days and weeks and finally for the whole eighteen years. Then came a day, apparently like all the others, and once more the amanuensis heard the master summoning him by name but this time "Yüan" had an entirely different sound. It was his name, it was he himself, he alone who was now addressed, challenged, ordered, chosen, called upon!

Like lightning from the depths of heaven, like thunder from the far places of the universe came the sound: "Yüan!" And behold, the spell was broken, the veil was rent, Yüan had become capable of hearing and seeing, he perceived the world in its true form and himself in the midst of it, and the great light dawned for him. This time he did not call back, "Yes." Softly, in a faltering voice, he murmured, "I have understood."

It is a marvelous story. But there is more to it. The attendant Yüan was not simply preordained for enlightenment, long though he had had to wait for that. Still more was in store for him, as he seems to have felt and as master Yün-men felt with even greater certainty, for he kept him there three years longer, close to himself, and had a special eye to him. Then the former attendant, ready now for master-ship, was discharged and made the return pilgrimage once more through half the empire, back to his homeland, where he assumed the management of a monastery and labored there under the name of Hsiang-lin for forty years. Many maintained that he was the greatest of Yün-men's disciples. When he was eighty or more years of age and felt that his end was near, he betook himself to Prince Sung, the prefect of the region, his devoted admirer and patron of the mon-astery. He wanted to thank the prince and take his leave, for he said he had decided to go on a pilgrimage once more. One of the prince's officials sneered at him for this, saying that the abbot must certainly be senile, for how could he, aged and feeble as he was, still be able to go on a pilgrimage? But the prince took the master's part, withheld judgment, courteously took leave of him, and personally accompanied him to the door. The old man returned to his monastery, had all his monks summoned together, seated himself, and said to the silent assembly, "Here is this aged monk—who now folds forty years into a single leaf." And thereupon he entered painlessly and peacefully into the transformation.

Addio, Carlo,
Your JK

PART TWO

I · EUROPEAN AND AMERICAN LITERATURE

Caesarius of Heisterbach
1908

THE WRITINGS of the monk Caesarius of Heisterbach are among the most important sources of ecclesiastical and cultural history of the thirteenth century. Consequently they have been frequently and at times fruitfully studied by cultural historians, philologists, and Catholic and Protestant theologians. Beyond the narrow republic of specialized scholarship, however, no one knows about this modest monk, with the possible exception of a few secret lay admirers. It is as one of these that I should like to talk about him. I am too little versed in the pertinent branches of scholarship to be able to give a fair character study and criticism. But in delightful and instructive hours of reading I have become very fond of Heisterbach, the homilist and fabulist, and I consider him among the hidden treasures of our early literature; indeed, I regard him as a poet, and it is a shame that no one knows him and even more of a shame that he was not allowed to write anything except sermons and textbooks for the Cistercian monasteries.

Caesarius was born about 1180, probably in Cologne, which at that time was one of the richest and largest cities in Germany. When he died about 1245 he was prior of the Heisterbach monastery. In his early years he went to school at Saint Andreas in Cologne and acquired a quite respectable degree of scholarship. He not only learned the stereotyped liturgical Latin but also read many of the classic authors and made the language completely his own. And yet, despite his modest and passive disposition, he walked about with open eyes in the splendid, warlike Cologne of those days, and in addition to associating with theologians, priests, and ecclesiastical students he carefully observed the busy life of the city. At all events, he talks knowledgeably about trade and industry, merchant princes and goldsmiths, soldiers, handworkers, and lawyers.

But soon the gay, worldly atmosphere of Cologne became too raucous for the simple, quiet, sincere young man. He was a pious, upright person, with no great ambition or desire for physical accomplishment; he much preferred being a quiet observer and meditator; he was also something of a visionary. He liked to sit quietly constructing and thinking through fables and stories. His view of the world sprang from a desire not to reduce the confusion of daily events to a theory but to bring them unchanged into harmony with the basic principles of his faith. And since his faith was not a philosophical construction but a simple acceptance of Church dogma with the addition of a few scholastic footnotes, it is illuminating that Caesarius precisely on account of his strong sense of reality inclined to belief in miracles. If a personal and almighty God actually existed, if there really was a devil, if saints really acted as intermediaries between heaven and earth, then nothing was more natural than a miracle.

And likewise there was nothing more natural than that the young scholar should turn toward monastic life. He entered Heisterbach under Abbot Gevard and remained there all his life, an unassuming, contented, pious monk. Heisterbach was still a quite new foundation of the Cistercian order, settled by monks from Himmerode only ten years before (1189). Caesarius himself tells about his conversion: "When King Philip first abolished our archbishopric I went with Abbot Gevard to Cologne. On the way he tried hard to persuade me to become a monk, but did not succeed. Then finally he told me that precious miracle of how once in Clairvaux at harvest time when the monks in the valley were sowing the wheat the Mother of God, her mother, Anne, and Saint Mary Magdalene appeared in splendid clarity, descended from the mountains, entered the valley, dried the sweat from the monks and wafted coolness upon them, and all the rest of the story. This vision moved me so profoundly that I promised the abbot not to choose any other monastery, if God should ever grant me the will thereto. At that time I was not free since I had vowed to make a pilgrimage to the Mother of God at Rocamadour. Three months later I had fulfilled my vow and then, without one of my friends knowing about it, I entered Heisterbach."

Aside from various trips on behalf of the order, Caesarius remained from then (about 1198) uninterruptedly in Heisterbach, which he also calls Peter's Vale (Vallis Sancti Petri). In the course of time he was awarded the post of master of novices—and perhaps also the title of prior under abbots Gevard and Heinrich—which he held until he died in the middle forties.

In Heisterbach, probably quite soon, he began his literary labors and found wide recognition. In addition to theological tracts and highly valued homilies, he wrote a life of Saint Engelbert of Cologne, also a life of Saint Elizabeth, and an as yet unprinted work about the abbots of Prüm, and a book entitled *Diversarum visionum seu miraculorum libri octo,* of which only fragments have been preserved, and finally there was his principal work, *Dialogus Miraculorum,* the only one I intend to speak about here.

That, in brief, is the content of his life. It does not look like much, but turns out to be rich and astonishingly many-sided when you read the *Dialogus.*

This imposing work sprang from his experience with the novices and was written about 1122. It is a kind of textbook for novices in whom it is intended to inculcate the order's view of the world and its theology. Unfortunately no such textbooks are written today; at any rate, among those of my schooldays there is not one that will arouse interest and fame for its author in later centuries. Caesarius, to be sure, gives conscientiously formulated definitions of conversion, of contrition, of confession, of heavenly rewards and punishments, and so on, but he does not cram them down his students' throats with cruel, indigestible dryness. Rather he offers them as though incidentally, in small wholesome portions.

His *Dialogus* has twelve sections divided into short chapters, each section dealing with one principal problem either of dogmatism or of practical theology. Thus the book should really be in our eyes a monster of boredom. But it is the opposite. It is the work of a cheerful chatterer, a lonesome storyteller, the creation of a poet, the mirror of a violently animated time and likewise of a pure, good man. The chapters do not in fact contain maxims and lectures; instead, each one is a short, very well told story, sometimes side-splittingly funny, sometimes bitterly serious, sometimes touching and subtle.

The dialogue form is only a mask. The persons in the conversation are a monk and a novice. The monk teaches, the novice learns; one lectures, the other asks questions or recapitulates. But the way in which the monk teaches puts an end to the dialogue. He teaches by examples, by stories to which he then adds two or three short theological questions and answers or sometimes none at all. The beginning will be a *distinctio,* the conclusion an edifying *pensum,* but the monk warms up in telling his stories, the novice forgets to ask questions, and only after a good while do they remember the lesson, and the monk explains as an afterthought how his stories are related to the chosen theological theme.

Nevertheless this is also an excellent textbook; for the author, however far afield he may wander, is always the same reasonable, kindly, good human being, whose character is in itself educational in its effect, and he always remains the true believer and monk. When on occasion he falls into burlesque, you yet clearly feel behind the playful storyteller the serious, unshaken man of faith, and when he tells about the miracles of the Virgin Mary his descriptions are not only vivid in every particular but invested with a delicate, poetic fervor that is absolutely gripping.

The content of the book, as the title says, is predominantly miracle stories. The author is, if possible, even more of a believer in miracles than was usual in his time and he never questions a miracle. The daily intrusion of supernatural forces of good and evil into human affairs was proven, was, in fact, a matter of course. But he paints no unreal pictures, never obscures his figures in the clouds, not even in clouds of incense, but lets people remain people and presents saints, angels, and demons as similar in appearance to human beings. And his portraiture is solid, his representations are not fanciful but are memories and observations. He tells about the life of the monks, of merchants, of secular priests, about wars and crusades, about the market place and sea voyages, about clever men and fools, love stories, stories of murder and theft. Then, too, he makes no secret of the existence of evil conditions and wicked men in the church and monastery; he even occasionally seriously assails the ecumenical Church, and if he has something bad to report about a brother, perhaps even one of the brothers from his own monastery, he does so with shame and sorrow, to be sure, and with all discretion, but he does it honorably and matter-of-factly. Thus he gives valuable pictures of the lives of all classes of that time, pictures from history and church history, and always he gives the impression of unquestionable reliability. He shares the beliefs and also the superstitions of his time; he knows not only about miracles, angels, and visions but also about necromancers, soothsayers, magicians, demons, and the devil's arts. Of course, the section of Germany where he lived was particularly fruitful in these fields and produced among other things the ill-famed *Hammer of Witches*. Caesarius has been accused of credulity and naïveté. He has even been blamed for promoting superstitions and indirectly contributing to the later horrible witches' trials. I do not intend to defend him against this charge, and yet it seems to me somewhat exaggerated, all the more so since Caesarius himself is one of the most important sources of our knowledge of the contemporary world of ideas at that time and place.

All this looks quite different if Caesarius is regarded simply as an author. Then what the theologian or historian perforce regards as of principal interest becomes of secondary importance. Seen in this way, our author, who is in any case sympathetic, honorable, and estimable, increases considerably in stature.

First of all, he writes a Latin that was not better written by anyone in his time and country. It is not classical Latin. But it is as far removed from the schematic commonplace Latin of ecclesiastical speech as it is from the awkward, violent Germanized Latin of the chroniclers. It is essentially Latin felt and thought and therefore clear and pregnant, and the sentence structures in particular are simple. There is never any syntactical strain, and rhetorical devices are used only sparingly and discreetly.

As a storyteller Caesarius must be accounted an artist, and many of his stories are equal to the successful achievements of the early romantic novella writers. Here, however, limits are imposed by his intent and educational task, limits that he seldom exceeds.

More important than the construction are the vividness, the literary honesty and credibility of the stories. Almost always at the beginning there is a short note about when and from whom the author heard the story, and sometimes even this introductory sentence has a quiet suggestive power that arouses curiosity and anticipation. Then follows the story itself, brief and clear. The high points of inner denouements, which constitute the points of crystallization in sophisticated novellas, are not to be looked for here, since the stories, though in themselves self-sufficient and complete, are followed by an explanation in dialogue form of the decisive inner events. All the more trustworthy and convincing on that account are the physical actions and events. The scene, the characters engaged, their relationships to one another, the origin, progression, and solution of the plot emerge clearly, briefly, and often absorbingly. This direct discourse, despite being in Latin, often has a lively, folksy tone: short sentences sometimes without verbs and with frequent humorous twists.

Anecdotes predominate: brief examples of a conversion or a punishment, little scenes from the life of the world or

the monastery, bons mots, pertinent answers, as well as
contemporary illustrations of passages from the Bible. Often
they are not more than ten lines long, they flow inexhaustibly from a remarkably reliable and well-trained memory
and from the realistic, clear observation of the commonplace—a little treasure chest of experiences, fancies, and
axioms. Caesarius gives you solemn assurance that he has
not invented a single one of the stories or intentionally
altered it. One may believe him without hesitation even
when, with his far-reaching discretion, he suppresses the
names of people and places. Besides, he almost always gives
his sources, and many of the persons he thanks for this
or that anecdote were alive at the time of writing and in
his immediate neighborhood. Also many of the stories deal
with situations that were psychologically incomprehensible
to the author, so that on this account he sticks all the more
closely to the facts and thereby often unintentionally attains a doubly powerful effect: as, for instance, in the
grippingly detailed accounts of the suicides of monks and
nuns, whose problems of faith and whose dreadful tempta-
tions seemed foreign and terrifying to the serenely contem-
plative writer.

Giovanni Boccaccio

COMMENTS ON GIOVANNI BOCCACCIO
AS AUTHOR OF THE *DECAMERON*

1904

BECAUSE of the biased conception that the Italian Renaissance was a reawakening of classical antiquity, Boccaccio, together with Petrarch, possesses the somewhat dubious historico-scholarly reputation of being one of the harbingers of this reawakening. He zealously read and collected the Roman authors and performed some not very impressive services in encouraging the reading of the Greek philosophers. Boccaccio himself took no little pride in his philological and historical labors, whereas he seems to have attributed scant importance to his *Decameron,* and in his later years would have preferred to disown it. Until recent times scholarship too has concerned itself with his Latin works, preferring primly to avoid the *Decameron.*

So one might think that in the end the Florentine was proved right in having preferred his numerous Latin writings to the book that in reality is his principal work and also one of the most important and valuable books of the fourteenth century. Well, fortunately the longevity and fame of outstanding writings have never been dependent on scholarly judgment and, thank God, what is good and viable has constantly sustained itself, whereas even the most determined attempts to galvanize dead greatness into life have seldom or never succeeded. Thus the collected scholarly writings and the youthful poetry of Boccaccio have long since almost completely disappeared, and for us today they belong among the bric-a-brac and curiosities of the past, while his splendid book of stories is still read by thousands and continues to have all its old richness, power, and freshness. Anyone to whom the word "Renaissance" is not a scholarly abstraction but a living picture of the culture of Italian cities in the fifteenth and sixteenth centuries could, if necessary, quite easily omit from this picture the *De genealogiis deorum gentilium* and the *De claris mulieribus* but not possibly the immortal *Decameron*.

It seems unnecessary to say much about the nature and character of this famous book. Everyone knows it at least by name and everyone knows that inside a simple narrative framework it contains a collection of a hundred stories, the content of which was at that time (around 1350) especially admired in society and among the common folk in Italy. It is also known that this delightful book for hundreds of years has enjoyed a bad reputation on account of its free and occasionally coarse tone. This evil reputation, at all events, is primarily responsible for the book's great success and its enormous distribution throughout all of Europe, for without this it would never have occurred to anyone to heap so much slander on a work whose coarsest improprieties were far exceeded by numerous contemporary literary works in every country (especially Germany and France). The suppression and persecution of the *Decameron* proceeded primarily from the clergy, and in the first instance was not concerned with the sensual coarseness and vividness of the novellas but with the daring independence with which Boccaccio loved to talk about the lives and characters of the priests and monks of his time. So, for example, it is amusing to see in what direction the many editions of the *Decameron* in the fifteenth and sixteenth centuries, revised for the worse by ecclesiastical censors, were actually changed. A novella in which perhaps a beggar or nobleman seduces a woman or is betrayed by his wife remains unaltered; if, however, a priest or monk is guilty of a similar disgraceful action, the novella is not, to be sure, suppressed, nor is the language modified, but *in majoram ecclesiae gloriam*, the priest is simply turned into a knight, the monk into a duke, the nun into a burgher's daughter, and everything is now fine and unexceptionable.

This, however, is not our subject here. Of the countless questions that must arise in the mind of every attentive reader of the *Decameron*, let us choose just one: To what extent is the author of this most famous of all story collections an original writer and creator and how much of his own life and personality has he included in the book?

The hundred novellas in the *Decameron,* simply in respect to subject matter, may contain little or almost nothing truly invented by Giovanni Boccaccio. They consist of anecdotes, fables, jokes, bons mots, remarkable life histories, and other little stories which, having originated in all countries and centuries, belonged to the literary treasury of the people and the nobility and were retold by the collector partly from oral tradition, partly from older written sources. Many of them are to be found in Oriental storybooks, in the French fabliaux, and elsewhere. However, as soon as we examine not the content but the form of presentation, the book proves to be a completely self-sufficient personal work of literature in which the collector and author welded the variegated mass of material into a new book unified in spirit and execution. The powerful instrument that made possible this melting down and reshaping of old treasures was first of all Boccaccio's language. This long work, from its introduction to the last word of the hundredth novella, speaks consistently in a lively, elegant, vigorous language whose magic enchants the reader and holds him spellbound. Whether the style swells in long sonorous speeches or the narrative proceeds simply and with apparent carelessness, or takes on a graceful roguish tone, joking as it goes, it always has the same bubbling freshness, cleanliness, and vigor, never limping, never flagging, but at every instant supplely youthful, but for all its delicacy gritty and original. In many places there is no mistaking the fact that the author was a quite conscious student of the Latin classics, especially of Cicero; for example, he loves the well-constructed long, balanced period, often with almost coquettishly interlarded clauses. But if Cicero was his master in the architecture of the sentences, Boccaccio drew the language itself, the words and images, directly from the *lingua parlata* of society, the streets and the market place. Best of all in this combination was his native delicacy of feeling, a gift that alone makes an author into a poet: the secret rhythm, the sovereign personal freedom from convention and pedantry, the animation and shading of the words, the pregnant new expressions, the beautiful, self-confident style amid all the variety.

Along with the language is the transformation of unorganized and chance collections into a new, unified work of literature. The hundred novellas are not presented as narrated by Boccaccio himself. He lets each one of the ten young people of Florence—seven young women and three young men—speak; these have fled from the dying city in the year of the great plague, 1348, and are spending some time in rural sociability, their favorite pastime being the telling of interesting and witty stories. Each day one of the company is chosen king, is responsible for the entertainment of the others, and usually dictates the general theme for the stories to be told that day. This framing and arrangement of the multifarious material is masterfully carried out and constitutes not only a delicate stylistically pure idyl in mood and language, but also an authentic and outstanding description of Florentine rural and social life in the trecento. And beyond this each novella gains greatly in color and charm because it is related by a particular person and in a particular connection. Between stories there is conversation in which the company sometimes discusses the last story told; or there are banter, joking, and song. The round of storytelling is interrupted in a lively and attractive fashion that never outweighs or disturbs it.

Thus in the detail of the overall narrative, as well as in its total composition, the *Decameron* proves to be the masterpiece of a writer of genius, though the mass of his material may have been brought to him by every wind. Now it is natural to inquire whether the poet, in addition to the conception, arrangement, and language, has left behind specific traces of his personality, his life, and his character in the *Decameron*.

In older times there was much dispute as to whether the whole account of the merry country outing of the ten young people was pure invention or whether these characters were perhaps real portraits. In fact, between Florence and San Domenico, the Villa Palmieri situated on a hill above the valley of Mugnone is pointed out to travelers as the probable scene of this idyl. But however tempting it would be to identify this scene with certainty and however seriously and credibly Boccaccio describes the flight of the young people from the plague as a fact, very little can actually be established with certainty about these matters. For the author cautiously avoids describing a recognizable place near Florence. What he has to say about the position of his villa and the landscape around it fits almost any estate near Florence and simply allows no certain conclusions to be drawn.

Moreover, it is certain that Boccaccio was not in Florence during the time of the plague. His famous and detailed description of the *Pestilenza mortifera* does not therefor lose its value as an authentic account, for the plague, which came across from the Orient, raged no less horribly in Naples in the year 1348 when the author was probably living there. Now if we think we can recognize Boccaccio himself in one of those three Florentine youths who accompany the seven young ladies into the country, then the assumption that an actual occurrence is being dealt with loses much of its probability. And it is natural to be inclined to see in young Dioneo, who is king on the Seventh Day, characteristics of the author himself. Not only is this Dioneo drawn with much more affection and care and provided with many more individual characteristics than any of the other persons in the group, but he also plays the role of funmaker, entertainer, cheerer, which Boccaccio himself as author of the *Decameron* had undertaken and to which he expressly admits in the Foreword. Furthermore, it seems, vague though the indications are, that Dioneo was meant to be the lover of Fiammetta, the queen on the Fifth Day, and if this is so many doubts would be banished. For we know with a good deal of certainty who Fiammetta was.

That one of the charming ladies of the *Decameron* bears that name goes back to one of the profoundest experiences of the poet's youth. Boccaccio had spent the greater or, at all events, the more important part of his younger years in Naples. Against his inclination and natural bent he had been destined by his father to be a merchant, and it was as a merchant, after long apprentice years in Florence, that he finally came to Naples, where he soon changed horses and took up the study of canonical law, in which, however, he made no striking progress. Through his influential country-man Niccolo Acciajuoli he was introduced at the luxurious Neapolitan court, fell in love with Maria, a natural daughter of King Robert, whom he saw for the first time at Easter Sunday service in San Lorenzo (1334?). She was known officially as the Countess Aquino and was married to a prominent courtier. The young poet's not unrequited love completely filled the first part of his stay in Naples and is the subject of almost all his youthful poems. He celebrated his noble beloved, whose real name he obviously dared not mention publicly, always under the name Fiammetta, and *Fiammetta* is also the title of a novel written by him even before the *novellino*. Boccaccio left a final memorial to this love, rich in happy and bitter experiences, by giving the name of his beloved to one of the young ladies in the *Decameron*, whose beauty and amiable ways he praises in beautiful language (at the end of the Fourth Day). Even though when he wrote this his relationship with Maria had ended and the former passion had expired, nevertheless the memory of it remained the most powerful one of his life. Also this late praise may signify a final melancholy, for-giving obituary, for in all likelihood Maria-Fiammetta died during the year of the plague in Naples.

Whoever wishes to follow this thread further will find many little hints and allusions to that experience in the apparently so impersonally written work. Essential revelations about the character, inclinations, and views of the author are also to be found in his Introduction, under whose gallant and delicately playful tone unmistakable seriousness is often evident. His descriptions of the country estate near Florence are a good mirror of his way of life and his way of seeing and enjoying nature. However similar they are on occasion to the Roman pastoral writers and to some of Pliny's letters, nevertheless a subtle personal flavor is unmistakable in these enchanting pictures of nature and at times an almost modern appreciation of nature. The Third Day of the *Decameron* begins with a description of the beautiful country estate which is now popularly identified with the Villa Palmieri and its surroundings. The garden adjoining the palace is painted with particular love, enthusiasm, and great detail: the paths lined by roses and jasmine, the lawns surrounded by lemon trees and pomegranates, with grass deep green in color (*quasi nera perea*) and embroidered with bright-colored flowers, the springs, the canals, the birds in the trees and in the air. All this is presented with a love for natural beauty which the painting of that time had found no adequate means to express. Nor is the fragrance of the lemon trees forgotten, or the fine spicy sweet smell of the vineyard blossoms that deliciously fills the whole garden. Whoever has rested on a fair early-summer morning in the valley of the Mugnone, the Greve, or the Elsa can conceive of no more enchanting and fragrant description of this fruitful, rich, garden landscape, and there is nothing more delicious than to read that description in the shadows of the lemons or cypresses between the orchards and the Tuscan hillside meadows, sown with huge bright-colored anemones.

And so the introductory and encircling narrative of the ten storytellers presents itself entirely as a free and beautiful creation of Boccaccio's in which he had no hesitation in weaving unobtrusive references to emotions and memories from his own life. It is otherwise with the hundred novellas themselves; at least, the author emphasizes in his remarkable introduction to the Fourth Day that he has been at pains to keep from any alteration and is reporting all the histories exactly "as they happened," that is, as he heard them from trustworthy reporters. And yet without doubt he has given here, too, much of himself. He may have altered nothing or almost nothing in the factual content of the stories, but he surrounds them with alluring descriptions, adds long speeches, begins or ends them with general observations from his own experience and knowledge of life. In oral repetition, every story has something anecdotal about it, does not linger over descriptions, does not quote long speeches, holds to its point or resolution. This is how Boccaccio must have heard his novellas. In writing them down at leisure, however, in rounding them out, bringing them into proper proportion, and carefully stylizing them, necessarily much of his own experience was added in the agreeable elaboration of details; by no means to the disadvantage of the novellas.

When the stories tell about the business, journeys, and adventures of Florentine merchants, the author is certainly indebted in great part to his own experience for the accuracy and vividness of his descriptions. Thus in the tenth novella of the Eighth Day there is a detailed description of the practices and duties of harbor traffic. We are told how and where the foreign merchant stores and insures his wares, how the middleman learns the nature and price of the imported goods from the ledgers in the customs house, how these goods are sold and traded, etc. Similar descriptions can be found in many other places in the book.

Less frequent and less clear are the references to Boccaccio's political views and experiences. In the numerous novellas that have their scene at court, his fanatical republicanism could only have had a disturbing effect. On the other hand, his enthusiasm for the time and character of the ancient Romans is frequently and clearly evident. And least of all does he restrain his contempt for the clergy on the other side of the mountain. It is striking in itself that he shows such fondness for stories in which priests, abbots, monks, and nuns play despicable or ridiculous roles. Yet it may well be true that with the decline of monastic life and of the clergy (this was the period of the papal exile in Avignon) and with the increasing freedom of thought and life in the cities, anecdotes of this sort were especially relished and hawked about in all quarters. Nevertheless Boccaccio is not content with that. He weaves into his novellas and repeats in his introductions with visible satisfaction indignant and detailed denunciations, especially of the monks (the most characteristic one being in the seventh novella of the Third Day).

Nevertheless it is in a story about a monk (Sixth Day, tenth novella) that we come to know the author in his most attractive aspect. This is the amusing story of Brother Zippolla and his sermon on relics, one of the pearls of the *Decameron*. Boccaccio is never lacking in sparkling jokes, sharp-witted or burlesque inspirations, but in this masterly narrative he reaches the heights of a true, penetrating, pure humor such as we search for in vain among the countless later Italian story writers. The way in which the sly beggar monk, traveling about with his fake relics, outwits his outwitter, the way in which he is able to rescue himself from a highly painful embarrassment, the way he obviously derives more satisfaction from his own cleverness than from the money gained by swindling, and finally the way he comes out of the ticklish situation as an unmasked evildoer, to be sure, but unpunished, and almost with a small diabolical halo, all this was not to be found in Boccaccio's sources or in Cicero but is a product of his very own creativity. Because of its genuine Tuscan wit and grace, this particular novella has always been the favorite of the Florentines and is still so today. When around 1570 another "purified," that is, an unrecognizably mutilated edition was proposed under ecclesiastical supervision, the Florentines of their own accord insisted that at least this one story of Brother Zippolla should remain word for word unchanged in its original form.

A single novella, although here too there may be an older model, is said by a number of witnesses to represent an experience of the writer. It is the seventh novella of the Eighth Day. A student is tricked and shamefully derided by a widow and for this he takes a savage revenge.

Now we know from Boccaccio's own mouth that at the age of somewhat over forty he once fell in love with a widow. For a time she behaved encouragingly, although she had long had another lover. She spurred Boccaccio on to a fiery exchange of letters, and behind his back with her young friend made no little fun over him and his letters. That was the author's last, bitter love affair.

In the novella mentioned he tells about a student whom a lady kept waiting all one winter's night in the snow in a windy courtyard while she and her young lover laughed and made fun of her freezing admirer to their hearts' content behind the locked doors of the house. The student, however, decided to have a proper revenge. He waited for summer and then found an opportunity to lure the widow alone onto a tower far outside the city, ostensibly to perform certain magic ceremonies with her. Then he left her locked on the top platform of the tower without clothes or a place to lie down, without food or drink and without any protection against the sun, languishing and roasting for a whole blazing day, an experience that very nearly cost her her life from exposure and mosquito bites.

It might seem as though the particularly unfeeling brutality of this ignoble revenge indicated that the story was an old one and not an invention of Boccaccio's. And if he had written nothing after the *Decameron* one would certainly support this interpretation. But unfortunately we have every reason to assume that he is morally responsible for this repulsive scene and intended through it to express his impotent thirst for revenge against the beautiful and wanton widow.

For it was Boccaccio's tragicomic fate that he who spent his youth on a passionate love, who in the *Decameron* calls himself explicitly an ardent honorer, friend, and servant of women and whose earlier poems have hardly any subject but the love of women—that this same author in his later days was to become a pitiless, spiteful woman-hater. In this novella we find an isolated early expression of his contempt.

The sobering experience with the widow seems to have given him the decisive push. And soon thereafter he, the author of so many love poems and novellas about love, wrote his dreadful *Corbaccio,* one of the meanest and most contemptible books ever written against women. It seethes with the most unqualified and filthiest abuse. Its vulgar and repulsively scathing tone, however, gives us the right to laugh at the author's later disapproval of his masterwork and to take the younger Boccaccio's part against the old one.

After this change for the worse, all that was needed to make the author repent of and disown his *Decameron* was supplied in the year 1361, about five years after the completion of *Corbaccio,* by the Carthusian monk Ciani. Though Boccaccio had regretted his early esteem for women and had recanted his hymns in their honor, nevertheless he had continued to be a bitter mocker of priests and monks. But then in 1361 there appeared at his house this monk Giovachino Ciani, who succeeded—presumably beyond his own expectation—in tricking the sly, inventive, experienced rogue and enemy of monks into conversion by means of a very transparent, crude, and violent bit of practical trickery. Boccaccio was terrified and thought his end was at hand, he crept to the cross and there laid down forever his last and heaviest sin.

All that, fortunately, is now more than five centuries in the past. The *Corbaccio* has disappeared, the monk Ciani is forgotten, the picture of the aging Boccaccio has grown pale and has faded into the distance. The *Decameron,* however, and its author, *Vir juvenis Boccatius Certaldensis,* are as young and blithe and lively today as they ever were, and the delicious book provides no less pleasure now to countless young and old than it once did to the Florentines of the trecento.

Casanova

1925

WHEN I WAS A YOUNG MAN all I knew about Casanova was dark rumors. In the official histories of literature, this great writer of memoirs did not appear. His reputation was that of an incredible seducer and libertine, and about his memoirs one knew that they were truly satanic works of obscenity and frivolity. There were one or two German translations of them, old editions in many volumes long out of print, which had to be looked for in secondhand bookstores if you were interested, and anyone who owned them kept them under lock and key. I was more than thirty before I even saw a copy of these memoirs. Until then I had only known about them because they played the role of devil's bait in Grabbe's comedy. After that, however, several new editions of Casanova appeared, including two new ones in the German language, and the opinion of the world and of scholars about this work and its author changed drastically. It was no longer a disgrace, a secret vice, to own these memoirs and read them; on the contrary, it was a disgrace not to know them. And in the judgment of the critics the formerly reviled and shunned Casanova was more and more transformed into a genius.

Now however highly I prize Casanova's splendid vitality and his literary accomplishments, I would not go so far as to call him a genius. In this virtuoso of the feelings, this great practitioner of the arts of love and seduction, the heroic quality is lacking, most of all he is completely devoid of that stoic atmosphere of isolation and tragic loneliness without which we cannot picture genius. Casanova is not very differentiated or original, not even an especially unusual personality. True, he is a fabulously gifted person (and all real gifts begin with and spring from the sensuous, from a good endowment of mind and senses), he is a fellow who can do everything, and so with his versatility, his admirable education, his flexible art of living, he becomes the classical representative of the elegant type of his age. The elegant, worldly, cheerful, frivolous, and virtuoso side of the culture of the eighteenth century, of the brilliant decades before the Revolution, these we find incarnate with truly amazing perfection in Casanova. World traveler, elegant idler and playboy, agent and entrepreneur, gambler and occasional confidence man, at the same time a man of both powerful and discriminating sensuality, a master of seduction, full of tenderness, full of chivalry toward women, fond of change and yet full of devotion, this brilliant man exhibits for us of today an astounding versatility. However, all these characteristics are directed outward and this necessarily makes for a certain one-sidedness. The human ideal of an eminent reflective man of today would be neither the "genius" nor the worldling, neither the man turned completely inward nor the man turned completely outward but rather one who alternates smoothly and high-mindedly between attachment to the world and contemplation, between extroversion and introversion. However, the whole life of Casanova, who truly was not without inspiration, plays itself out entirely in the social world, and it takes very heavy blows of fate to make him for a few instants into an introvert, whereupon he at once becomes melancholy and sentimental.

What is odd and astonishing to us above everything else is the inner connection between virtuosity and naïveté in this wily artist of living. He possessed his virtuosity not only thanks to his powerful physical endowments and capacities but more than anything else to his being spared the endless crippling and stultifying school years that we consider indispensable to the taming of the young. Like all the men of his time, he enters life very young, becomes self-sufficient, has to help himself, is formed and disciplined by society and necessity and not least by women, learns to be adaptable, learns to play and to assume masks, learns guile, learns tact, and since all his gifts and impulses are directed outward and can only find satisfaction in active life he becomes a virtuoso in the art of gallantry. Through all this, however, he remains completely naïve, and even the aged Casanova, when he undertakes not without lasciviousness to recount the many love affairs of his life, is an innocent lamb in comparison with some of the problematical souls of today. He seduces dozens of girls and women but is never seized by the horror of love, its metaphysic, never grows dizzy at sight of its abysses. Only at a quite advanced old age when he is sitting in enforced loneliness in Dux in Bohemia, without fame, without women, without money, without adventures, does life begin to seem not quite so unexceptionable, becomes in his eyes just a little problematical.

And that is how he captivates us with these two enchantments, with his virtuosity in living, never to be obtained by us who have been ruined by school and the specialized professions of today, and with his remarkable innocence, his so amiable and attractive naïveté. At times it stands him in good stead, this naïveté of his, for he loads his robust conscience not only with stolen maidenheads and broken marriages, there are also juicy swindles, impostures, exploitations of many kinds with which he makes his life more amusing and finances his travels, pleasures, and love affairs. And he confronts all these blemishes to his respectability, all these burdens upon his conscience, with neither sophistication nor cynicism but with a childlike smile. He grants that now and again he played some rather broad pranks and cheated people to a fare-thee-well, but God knows how he got into it, it always happened with good intentions or at most through momentary thoughtlessness, and he is consistently successful in playfully justifying himself in his own eyes as well as those of the world.

Today there are wily scoundrels and conscienceless business operators by the thousands, as well as cultivated woman chasers in plenty; they simply do not interest us. Even the most talented man of this sort, if we compare him with Casanova, would fall short in two principal respects: the

lively, always effective example of a highly cultivated nobleman's way of life and, secondly, the high literary skill. I do
not believe that the love letters of one of today's Berlin Don
Juans or racketeers would show a higher intellectual or
stylistic level than the magazines to which these same gentlemen subscribe.

Moreover, Casanova has the advantage of his present-day
colleagues in possessing the basis of a complete external life-
style, a clearly defined culture. The elegant and charming
course of his life enchants us and awakens a yearning as
does the least bit of architecture, the smallest article of
furniture of that period—there were a unity and beauty
present then that are completely lacking in our lives. For
just this reason, too, the fear of the moralists that today's
readers may be corrupted by the reading of Casanova is
baseless. Oh no, there is no reason for such fear, alas, no.
The ship on which our hero sails forth is not so much his
personal genius or his personal immorality as the education
and culture of his time. On such soil, at such a level, a small
personal plus suffices to produce a great effect.

If we of today read Casanova with a certain melancholy,
it is chiefly because of the milieu of his life, the beautifully
elaborated culture of that outer life. This too, perhaps, is
the way it affected an educated reader decades ago. Today,
however, something more seems to have disappeared into
the past, something that Casanova possessed and that our
fathers too possessed and that even we in our youth possessed and that gave our youth much magic: reverence for
love. Be it only this Casanova kind of love, this gallant,
mothlike, somewhat overplayed and youthful perpetual state
of being in love—even this today seems to be out of style,
just like the sentimental love of Rousseau and Werther, just
like the profound and ardent love of Stendhal's heroes. Today there seems to be neither the tragic lover nor the virtuoso, there are only shallow marriage cheats or psychopaths.
That a fully competent, talented, energetic man should devote all his gifts and powers to earning money or to the
service of a political party now seems to everyone not only

understandable but right and proper—that he should devote these gifts and powers to women and to love would simply not occur to anybody today. In no truly "modern" philosophy of life, from average middle-class America to the reddest Soviet socialism, does love play any role but the insignificant one of a secondary pleasure factor in life, to be managed by a few hygienic rules.

But conceivably the modernity of today, too, will have the fate of all modernities, to endure for no more than a fleeting world-instant. Whereas the problem of love, to judge by what I know of history, after moments of diversion can always become highly relevant again.

Hans Christian Andersen

1910

WHEN WE WERE LITTLE CHILDREN and had only recently learned to read, we had, like all children, a
beautiful favorite book that was called *Andersen's Fairy
Tales*, and no matter how often we had read it, we kept returning to it again and again; it was our trusty companion
to the end of our boyhood years, our beloved childhood, with
its treasures and fairies, queens and wealthy merchants,
poor beggar children and daring fortune seekers. There next
to the incomparable Uncle Ole Luk Oie, my favorite was the
tale of the little mermaid, although it always made me sad.
How mysterious and colorful was its beginning in the palace
and gardens on the bottom of the sea. "On a calm day you
could see the sun, it was like a purple flower out of whose
calyx all light flowed." And how good and concise and illuminating was the beginning of the splendid story of the
flying trunk. "There was once a merchant who was so rich
he could plaster the whole street with gold pieces and most
of a little alley as well, but he did not do this; he had other
ways of using his money; if he handed out a schilling he got
a taler back; that's the kind of merchant he was—and then
he died."

These sentences, however, have not stuck in my memory,
I have just looked them up. I have remembered no sentences
or words but the things themselves, the whole colorful, vivid
world of old Andersen, and they were so well preserved in my
memory and were so beautiful that I was at pains in later
years not to open this book, which seemed to have been
lost, anyway. For I had, alas, discovered early and with pain
that the books from which one derives the greatest delight
in early childhood and youth are the ones that we must not

read later on, otherwise they will lose their brilliance and glamour and appear changed, sad and ridiculous.

But the story I read was good, it was not so supernatural and extravagant and artificial as I had secretly almost begun to fear, but looked out with quite honest eyes at the real world and spread over it the enchantment of fairyland, not out of vanity or silly presumption but from experience and sympathetic resignation. And the glamour was real, and as I read on and selected many of the old stories there was the same magical enchantment of earlier times, and the feared disillusionment was turned into joy and enrichment, and where perhaps it failed and did not ever possess quite all the old fullness of tone, the fault lay with me and not with old Andersen.

Now I have put the volumes in a good place where they will not grow dusty, and I shall get them down often for my pleasure. And if by any chance I should have another encounter with old Andersen, I shall not only take off my hat but acquaint myself more closely with him in grateful admiration; for he seems to me to have been a remarkable, simple, and real human being. What little one can find out about him suits admirably to this teller of tales. Growing up in poverty, he early found a patron on whom he became dependent; eager to travel, ambitious, but always in the fashion of the adventurous son in the fairy tale, Andersen finally became famous and well-to-do but never found warmth or comfort, was always starved at heart, unhappy in every love —this was the life of that strange man. And he was so very much of a child that in his disillusionment and loneliness he sat down with the little ones and thought up fairy tales for them, and although he acquired his fame principally through other works, it is really only these fairy tales that remain of him, for they are of the nature of imperishable things.

Walt Whitman

LEAVES OF GRASS

1904

WHITMAN, of course, had been known in Europe for a long time, and yet he is still too little known in Germany. To be sure, it probably won't be long before altars will be built to him, his statue will be adorned with wreaths, and his writings proclaimed as gospel. Right now there are many at work trying to make him into something that he is not, for example, a great philosopher and a prophet of more modern laws of life. Our uncultivated and thoroughly unphilosophic age no longer has any standards of measurement and rushes wildly after every true or false prophet. What haven't people made of Nietzsche, of Emerson, even of Maeterlinck! Posterity will be laughing over that for a long while. And so now "Whitman clubs" are starting to spring up here and there and so are similar expressions of an undirected enthusiasm.

The author of *Leaves of Grass* is not the most literarily gifted but he is humanly the greatest of all American poets. Actually he should be called the only or at any rate the first "American poet," without qualification. For he is the first who did not draw upon the treasuries or secondhand shops of ancient European cultures but planted all his roots in American soil. He gives voice to the first hymns from the soul of this young giant of a nation, he sings and rejoices out of a feeling of enormous powers, he will have nothing to do with anything old, anything lying behind him, but deals with an eager, proudly active present and an immeasurable, laughing future. He preaches health and strength, he is the orator of a strong young nation that much prefers to dream of its grandchildren and great-grandchildren than of its fathers. For this reason his dithyrambs so often remind us of primeval folk voices, of Moses, for instance, and of Homer as well. But he is also a man of today and so is no less fiery in preaching the *I*, the free creative man. With the proud joy of an untamed, complete human being he talks of himself and his deeds and journeys, of his home. He sings of how he comes, wellborn and raised by a model mother, from Paumanok, how he wandered through the southern savannahs and lived in tents as a soldier, how he saw Niagara and the mountains of California, the primeval forest and the buffalo herds of his native land, and he dedicates with grateful enthusiasm his songs to the American people, his people, whom he conceives of as an enormously powerful unit.

Whoever reads this book at the right hour will find in it something of the primeval world and something of the high mountains, of the ocean and the prairies. Much will strike him as shrill and almost grotesque, but the work will impress him, just as America impresses us, even if against our will.

August Strindberg

1909

ON JANUARY 22 [1909] August Strindberg will cele-
brate his sixtieth birthday. Now, just as earlier, despite his European fame, he is banned by the philistines in
Germany as he is with us [in Switzerland] and is incredibly
little known. It is said that this is due in part to the inadequacies of the German editions. I cannot verify this, but I
know that year in and year out masses of vastly inferior
books in much worse translations are read by us. People do
not like original writers, they prefer everything secondhand.
Among the Russians it fell to the lot of Gorky to become
famous among us while his far greater models are almost
unknown. This is the way it is almost everywhere, people
like what is new only if it is served up predigested and altered, diminished and adorned. This is the curse under which
Strindberg has suffered, Strindberg the pariah and martyr of
Swedish literature, a literature that is in general so popular
with us. Writers of fame and authority have tried to inter-
vene in his behalf, most recently Knut Hamsun, but these
were words written on the wind. And yet we must not
stop trying, and so here is another attempt. Let it be said
once more that this uncanny Swede belongs among the
great minds of our age, that he has written not only terrifying and shocking books but also beautiful ones of great intellectual subtlety. Suppose he is an eccentric, a neuras-
thenic, and an adventurer; really he is first of all a persecuted
and tormented man and this is so because his mind is too
shrewd and fresh and pitiless, because we would prefer to
have sugar water.

This lonely poet and weaver of thoughts, who reveals and
dissects himself just as unhesitatingly, indeed fanatically,

as he does all his subjects, is beginning to grow old, and aside from a mad, saga-like reputation in Europe, has won and encountered nothing but persecution and rejection. He needs no defender of his honor, however well earned his evil reputation! But as for his life, especially his daring mental life, he has not only lived it with independence and recklessness and perhaps enjoyed it, he has also with equal daring and courage suffered through it. He liked to take his place in the assembly of the scoffers but never in the seats of the contented and self-righteous, who will crouch beside any little discovery or small intellectual heritage in order to draw dividends from it; instead, he discarded layer after layer, not sparing what had been thought but rethinking it, and he remained a revolutionary into old age. It is true that at times he took revenge and wrote like a whiplash, but I feel no need to defend him for this; indeed, I would not want to get along without those pieces. Of his books let me mention here in particular: *Eleven One-Act Plays, On the Open Sea, The Red Room, Historical Miniatures.*

IN MEMORIAM, STRINDBERG
1949

The few great problematic thinkers of the second half of the nineteenth century did not come my way in historical sequence. The first I came to know, quite early in my school years, was Nietzsche. It was not until more than a decade later that my meeting with Dostoevsky and Strindberg took place and much later still that I came to know Kierkegaard.

When I became acquainted with August Strindberg's books, some forty years ago, he very soon took his place for me in that small group of martyr-poets, those lonely seers who not only critically recognized and intellectually explored the ambiguous, pathological, and perilous quality of their epoch, the apparently happy time of the long European peace and of liberalism and confidence in progress, but suffered it biologically, in their own bodies, these men to whom the still-unconscious problems of the times had become personal, physical and psychological distress and illness. I felt, just as I had with Nietzsche, reading him with an unforgettable shudder: here was one of the great sensitives and sufferers, a chosen one and at the same time a marked man, a most delicate seismograph for the coming convulsions, a northern brother to Nietzsche. It did not, to be sure, escape me that this suffering and quarreling, yes, quarrelsome, polemical, possessed, and embittered fanatic of true and of endangered mankind was in addition an important artist and, in many of his smaller compositions such as the one-act plays and the miniatures, a brilliant virtuoso.

But this was not the reason that for several years I repeatedly had to return to him and agonize over him, especially over his autobiographical and confessional books, among which for a time those dealing with the Parisian period were my favorites. No, it was not as an artist that he at that time moved and fascinated me but as the author of those terrifying, sad, almost monomaniacal books in which he brought the displaying of his own person and his own biography to a point of high-minded disregard of shame, in a way that somewhat later through psychoanalysis became familiar in many others but at that time was as single and challenging as a sinister darting flame and that brought a new macabre, threatening clangor into the elegant and weary atmosphere of the satiated prewar epoch. Out of his savage books in shrill tones arose much strife, much hatred, much bitterness, much harsh misunderstanding, now and again, too, spite and malice, but far stronger than all this I felt in him the deep, consuming suffering, not at all the lonely suffering of the psychopath in love with himself but rather a vicarious suffering: one that embraced us all. This won him my love.

Selma Lagerlöf

1908

THE SWEDISH AUTHOR Selma Lagerlöf was born in 1858 and has been prominent in the literary world since the beginning of the nineties. With her first work, *Gösta Berling,* she became famous in Sweden and very soon in the rest of the world. That first work was already perfect, containing all the essentials of the Lagerlöf gift; with it the author made her appearance as a finished, mature personality and since that time she has not changed in any characteristic.

It is this very fact that the person who feels compelled to criticize even what is beautiful may consider a lack in her. In Selma Lagerlöf one does not find the drama of development; her works stand like brothers and sisters, apparently of a like age, side by side, not separated by any profound difference. Perhaps this too is the womanly aspect of her talent: an almost unmoved repose in herself, deep-rooted and firm, a being and growing without division or abrupt transition. Whoever wants to may draw the conclusion from this (apparent or real) lack of conflict, struggle, and development that Selma Lagerlöf is after all not a genius. On the other hand, however, she possesses what is perhaps the most essential characteristic of the person of genius, an inner relationship with all being, a wealth of connections to all the things and creatures of the world, combined with an uncommon, lively, strong memory without which no genius and no art are possible.

In modern Swedish literature this author stands out lonely and remarkable, like some marvelous anachronism. Only the fine, far too little known Verner von Heidenstam shows at times in his best work, *Charles XII,* similar traits. The more recent Swedish writers from Strindberg to Geijerstam have nothing whatever epic about them, they are artists who work entirely subjectively, sensitively analyzing acutely differentiated perceptions, and even the farthest-sighted and most many-sided of them stick close in material and language to their own time and problems, they engage in psychology and support theses. In short, they are modern, they have the typical modern high regard for science, and they attempt to impart a certain scientific air to their books. It is precisely this that Selma Lagerlöf is entirely free from.

How much toil, experiment, and practice preceded *Gösta Berling* we do not know and I trust will never find out. Whether it appeared as the fruit of years of training and effort or as a marvelously easy, inspired achievement, *Gösta Berling*, despite all the warm personal quality of its approach and tone, has over and above this something impersonal, timeless, mythical, something that has grown out of the eternal depths of a nation's being. Its characters, its landscape, its events have been composed, they are works of art, they have the quality of conscious observation about them, but in addition they have a reality, a life of their own that permits us to regard the author not as a maker but as one inspired. It is the spirit of the earth and of the people that wanted to express itself and chose this author as its instrument. Just the way in fairy tales a poor boy runs away and on his travels meets a wise dwarf and overnight becomes rich and powerful and a king and magician, just so Selma Lagerlöf, a Swedish schoolteacher, at some hour encountered the spirit of her native land and became at its touch a great and gifted author.

She writes a style that belongs to no time, whose nuances are very womanly, at times almost homely. She constantly strolls as though in a dream on the breakneck ridge between the genial and the sentimental, between gossip and saga. In the noblest stories she turns aside from the path to pick a few flowers, and to exhibit an almost womanly sentimental love for small things. But she no more than grazes this danger, which she herself hardly suspects. While a timorous devotee shudders with fear that now she must cast off her magic robe and stand there suddenly as a miserable small-town girl, she already has the breezes of eternity playing about her forehead and is uttering words that are as precise, sustaining, and magical as the words of folksong and of the Bible.

Just so with her inventions. The characters without exception have a vivid, lifelike quality that cannot be matched; but this same magician who created them rules them with a fantastic sense of justice, rewards and punishes them according to a commonplace didactic morality, and sometimes makes an ambitious effort to sacrifice her poetry to her somewhat narrow conception of an ethical world order. These are propensities and artistic errors that would cost our greatest poets their necks, whereas in this strange woman they seem barely more than minor flaws.

In this connection I must warn against confusing this writer's morality with her piety. Her morality is that of a schoolmarm; her piety, however, is pure gold, it is inner simplicity and childlikeness, courageous trust and unstinting devotion.

So too is Gösta Berling. He is no hero, rather he is a poor devil, but for many people he has come to mean a hero, has captivated many hearts, has kindled many dazzling lights, bewitched maidens and influenced men. He is a provincial heroic figure become a myth, half still-historical person with individual characteristics, half already poetically transformed into a symbol. Everything that a tiny nation had amassed through many generations of adventure, heroism, great convulsions and great jokes, events and the storyteller's art, had hoarded and only allowed to circulate as small coin, all this becomes in this book a many-colored, rich, magnificent creation.

*   *   *

In a short time *Gösta Berling* captivated the whole world. Naïve people read it naïvely and happily as a splendid story, more sophisticated readers enjoyed it as a work of art, old people warmed themselves at its histories, and youths read it with absorption and excitement. Now if Selma Lagerlöf had been no more than the accidental vessel of a revelation, if she had simply picked up, casual and unaware, the treasures of her native tradition, if all the beauty and effectiveness were due simply to the marvelous material, then with this one great work her art would have been exhausted, or at most a sequel would have followed.

What followed, however, was quite the opposite, a great new book full of passion and splendor, *The Miracles of Antichrist*. Here her qualities and defects can be much more easily distinguished than in *Gösta Berling*. Invention, costuming, and composition of the whole are insignificant, almost dilettantish. And yet the book is marvelous. The action takes place in Sicily in a hill town on Etna and is filled with the southern sun in a way that is rare in northern books. The village life of this town is the real substance of this work, divided up into an ample series of individual pictures painted with marvelous love and even more marvelous vividness. Adroitly and effortlessly these splendid stories, each a gem, are strung together and combined with one another on the loose thread of a hardly perceptible design.

In between times many short tales and legends appeared, among them masterly things, and then followed Selma Lagerlöf's mightiest book, the first volume of *Jerusalem*. This is surely the most beautiful and greatest production of recent Swedish literature, a book about the soul of Sweden, multitudinous and yet unified, tender and powerful, realistic and visionary. The life of the Swedish peasants is portrayed in it, and I know of no other modern book in which the soul of a people has been thus expressed. Nor do I know of any work of fiction in which the religious life and experience of a community has been presented so graphically, so factually, and so sensitively.

The second part of the great work, which takes place in Jerusalem (whither the Dalekarlian community has followed a fanatic), no longer possesses this absolute native perfection. It is, to be sure, still beautiful and impressive enough to surpass many famous novels. But the way these poor mountain dwellers, strayed here from Sweden, feel themselves alien sufferers in the blazing heat of the stony Palestinian city, promised city though it is—here the author sacrifices some of her impeccable strength and assurance. The analysis of world history, the necessity for historical reflection are mostly to blame, more than the foreign soil, for the landscape as well as the oriental street life are pictured beautifully and characteristically, at times with genius.

If the first part did not exist, it would never occur to anyone to criticize the second so severely. But the first volume happens to be such a marvelous work that one reads the second with enormously heightened anticipation and judges it accordingly. For this very reason all the beautiful and absorbing things in it should not be overlooked.

In many scenes in this second part of *Jerusalem,* beautifully and unexpectedly the author's relation to Christ is indicated, a relation that in a later work, *Christ Legends,* finally finds complete expression. This relation is a thing very precious, lovely, and restorative. Selma Lagerlöf's Christ is neither historical nor dogmatic but the popular beloved Germanic Savior whom one must love as one loves the sun, whose features retain from his suffering only the radiant aspect. She talks about him simply and inexhaustibly, the way a pious mother tells her children the stories of the Savior, and in order to be able to tell a great deal and tell it accurately she has read all that was to be found of the old legends. Now she narrates them again, the well-known ones and the obscure ones, Oriental and Italian or Latin, and from her storyteller's lips they flow fresh and ardent, calming every confusion and doubt in the hearer, awakening in his soul everything that has remained pure and true and golden from the days of his childhood.

Whenever people have talked to me with harsh criticism of Selma Lagerlöf and however often I myself have felt doubts about small particulars, here I have always been a devout believer. And where in the whole world of today is there an author who would dare talk to us about Jesus like this—not symbolically, with sociological references, not historically, with critical details, nor in a proselytizing fashion like the Salvation Army, but artlessly as though the theme had no hooks and abysses? That is what Selma Lagerlöf could do.

Of Lagerlöf's remaining books—they are all beautiful and dear to me—*Arne's Treasure* seems to me to deserve special consideration. It is a novella, entirely in the grand, strict ballad style, powerful and exciting as a treasured age-old saga. Arne of Solberga, together with wife, child, and household servants, is murdered by wandering mercenaries for his treasure of gold. The murder occurred at night and the only one to escape was an adopted daughter of the house who thereafter found refuge with a poor fishmonger. She is hardly in any condition to identify the malefactors, nor does she feel called upon or able to help to clear up and avenge the evil deed. Also it appeared that the murderers, along with the treasure they had stolen, had sunk into the fjord in their attempt to flee across the ice. But the innocent victims of the murder are not at peace; visibly and invisibly, they are at work, they cause dreams and win confederates, they arouse horror here and sympathy there, they weave about the escaped murderers an invisible net. Elsalill, the surviving orphan, meanwhile has become innocently involved in an as yet tentative love-game with one of the murderers and is forced half willingly, half under duress, constantly to find and help to find clues until the robbers are discovered, an event that brings about her own death. The fleeing criminals succeed in finding refuge on a ship, which at the moment is locked tight in the ice, yet from hour to hour they expect the breaking-up of the ice and the longed-for chance for departure. But destiny is inescapable: all the bays along the shore become ice-free and navigable, barks and ships everywhere move seawards, only that one fjord and that one ship are locked tight by a wall of pack ice and the wily criminals, who have escaped so often, in the last hour succumb to their punishment. This is enormously effective, pure and inexorable as only great tragedy

is, full of the influence of unseen saga-like powers and yet
logical and illuminating.

Much by way of gratitude and praise could be said about
the splendid *Manor House Saga,* the enchanting Niels Hol-
gersson, but to what purpose? Whoever has once immersed
himself in Lagerlöf's work and come to love it must and
will long to read more of her.

Maurice Maeterlinck

1900

*S**erres chaudes* was the characteristic title of Maeterlinck's first book, a collection of poems published in
1889, in which a great talent exhibited itself with youthful,
nervous awkwardness in the pose of a decadent—distracted,
weary, and lusting for extravagant stimuli and rare artistic
sensations. In the same year, however, there also appears his
Princesse Maleine, in which, though as yet unrefined and
and overblown, almost all the enchantment of Maeterlinck's
poetry is present. Here too appears for the first time that
pale, beautiful woman with the long, heavy, dull-blond hair
who in his later works keeps returning, each time more
beautiful, more legendary, more beguiling. In *Maleine,* horror
and the supernatural are exaggerated almost to the point
of the ludicrous, and yet through the whole play runs a
strong vein of true art, visible and effective. From then on,
this sultry poetry clarifies itself in steadily nobler and freer
fashion; in 1890 *Les Aveugles* and *L'Intruse* appear, in
1892 comes *Pelléas et Mélisande,* the first work of the poet
in which his enigmatic originality lets itself flow in a beautiful, uninhibited stream. In between times the poet busied
himself with the study of Plotinus and the mystics of the
Middle Ages, and in 1894 his "first period" ends with *La
Mort de Tintagiles.* In this *"petit drame pour marionettes"* effects of demonic power are achieved. That scene in which
the sister exhausts herself in a desperate attack on the heavy,
barred door while the faint childish voice of little Tintagiles
cries out from the other side in fear of death and is slowly
extinguished—this scene quivers with the breathless, horrid
terror of a nightmare. Then came Maeterlinck's two philo-

sophical books, with the first product of his travel period, *Aglavaine et Sélysette*, sandwiched in between.

Strangely enough, the German editions of his works read just like originals, a unique occurrence in the whole range of French literature. It was not for nothing that Maeterlinck devoted himself for half his life to Novalis. His poetical works have no *esprit* at all, no elegance, no elaboration of structure; everything in them is soul, wonder, legend.

In recent times, too, there has been much talk in Germany about Maeterlinck's philosophy. *Le Trésor des humbles* (*The Treasure of the Poor*) is the name of Maeterlinck's first philosophical book. It is a kind of poetical paraphrase of the medieval mystics and it proclaims the doctrine of unconscious wisdom and that each smallest drowsy motion of our unconscious souls is more important and more true than the noblest productions of our conscious thought and action. The book contains chapters of unworldly dreamlike beauty; the devout melancholy of the hermit and the delicate, timorous soul of the mystical seeker after truth signal to us as though from the parchment pages of a late medieval breviary or book of meditations. By comparison with this hesitant, stammering wisdom, Novalis seems like a scholastic philosopher, and yet the relationship of Maeterlinck's mysticism to Novalis's *Fragments* is unmistakable. What in the German romantic blazes straight upward in a clear flame, outdoing even Fichte in energy and consistency, this appears in the Flemish dreamer as a delicate, tone-rich refraction of light, dispersed into a moody twilight of colors. Novalis is the greater philosopher, he is clear, assured, happy, and inflexible; Maeterlinck is more tremulous, almost fearful, is more delicate, more musical, gentler and deeper in mood—he is the greater poet. The last chapter in *The Treasure of the Poor* deals with "inner beauty." The soul, says the mystic, is insatiable in its longing to be filled with beauty but we do not hearken to its pleading voice. The moment we are not alone, the moment we begin to speak, we shut up our souls even more anxiously than at other times, we are ashamed of their tenderness and beauty, and we attempt to keep them away from the eyes of others. "Why not have the courage to give a noble answer to a base question?—I do not believe that there is anything on earth that beautifies a soul more insensibly and naturally than the assurance that there is somewhere not far from it a pure and beautiful being whom it can love without reserve. Therefore let it be remembered: one is not alone, the good must keep watch."

One must bear in mind the gentle soothing chords of this remarkable, noble, and solemn chapter when one reads the poet's next to last work, *Aglavaine et Sélysette*. This drama has been completely stripped of all those accidental and external elements that still clung to the author's earlier works: even scene and background, which elsewhere he uses as important factors in the mood, have here almost no contributory coloration. Simply the effect of accident and misfortune on three souls at different levels of consciousness is the subject. Into the house of Meleander and his wife Sélysette comes Aglavaine, the young widow of Meleander's brother. Through early self-knowledge and through suffering she has attained a remarkable degree of inner dignity and beauty, and she finds in the brooding Meleander a grateful friend and pupil. Artistically and psychologically the high point of the drama is the way in which Meleander's love, in constant oscillation, turns now to his splendid, clear-eyed friend, now to the unaware, beautiful, naïve Sélysette. In the one are the whole rich depths of a noble, consciously active mind and heart; in the other the hitherto unmeasured, slumbering riches of the simple child. The development consists in Sélysette being awakened through Aglavaine from her naïve tranquillity and filled with a longing for the free, conscious beauty of the artist. The awakening of this soul, which now for the first time suspects its own depths, the first awkward flutterings of its wings in the domain of wisdom and the art of life are presented with a completely new artistry, with an incomparably delicate, sensitive, chaste poetry. Aglavaine was sleeping on the grass at the edge of a deep pond. Sélysette, wandering through the garden in a torment of jealousy, has caught sight of her, has awakened her, and now the two beautiful women for the first time look straight and without reserve into each other's eyes, masks cast aside.

Once more one feels the deep difference between the two women's souls. Aglavaine keeps questioning Sélysette with increasing urgency; she, however, only smiles and does not herself know the truth.

"*Je suis tombée en me penchant . . .*" she says again and again—and dies.

Just as in this book Maeterlinck for the first time definitely and courageously does not present fate as an alien and superior force intruding from outside but places it in the souls of his characters, so he takes the same decisive step in his last philosophical work, *La Sagesse et la destinée* (*Wisdom and Fate,* 1898). When this book appeared it was said in Germany that Maeterlinck had now gone over to the teaching of Nietzsche, a proof of how naïve our time is in philosophical matters and how innocently people use Nietzsche as a philosophical yardstick. As a matter of fact, the book has nothing in common with Nietzsche except for the phrase "yea-saying to life," but is the logical development of *Treasure,* especially of its last chapter. It would be more appropriate to think of Montaigne, provided, of course, that you take the two essayists as antipodes.

Wisdom and Fate is not so rich in poetical, enigmatic, beautiful details as *The Treasure of the Poor,* but there is in it such an unmixed, pure fragrance of goodness and healing that even more than *Aglavaine* it confirmed the general faith in Maeterlinck's development and future. The influence of Emerson is often apparent; he and Novalis had been acquainted with the same ideal, to which the industrious Flemish seeker here attains. Fate and misfortune, contrary to the author's earlier conception, are no longer robbers lying in wait behind the impenetrable wall of the future; the soul that has become conscious governs itself and things, there is no power that can rob the wise of that inner harmony which is happiness. The main point of this teaching lies in the principle that one attains mastery over "things" not through harshness and physical violence but through reverence, which is the beginning of all wisdom, goodness, and beauty. To feel reverence toward all we encounter, to honor even what is alien through consideration and love, to question everything concerning its native character and speech, this is how the wise man makes friends even with what is dark and recalcitrant and comes to realize that no good or ill fortune comes from outside, that only the way we accept all that happens to us is decisive in its effect on our lives.

The public reception of this book was another demonstration that our age is essentially completely unphilosophical. But is that necessarily a defect? I think not, and without mysticism one can come to prefer Maeterlinck's "wise men" to the philosopher.

Romain Rolland

LIFE OF TOLSTOY

1922

EVERYONE who knows anything about the life of Romain Rolland knows what an important role Tolstoy played in it. Rolland was a young student in Paris when one day, tormented by profound moral doubts, torn between a vocation for art and an ethical vocation, he addressed a letter to Tolstoy, a letter to which perhaps he hardly expected an answer, a letter that was more a confession, an attempt to clarify his own mind, more an avowal and cry of despair than a question. And then something touching happened: the world-famous old Russian sent the unknown young student in Paris an answer, a charming, kindly, detailed, concerned, and comforting answer, a letter of many pages. This experience was significant in Rolland's life, and when about ten years ago he wrote his *Life of Tolstoy*, which is only now appearing in German translation, it was not only a biography, it was not only a good literary study, it was also the acknowledgment of a deep gratitude, of lifelong sincere love and admiration. That Rolland could write such a book about Tolstoy, such a human, loving, internally alive book, was an aftereffect of that letter he had once received. For the letter had shown him that Tolstoy was not only a great artist and exciting preacher but a kindly, helpful human being full of brotherly love. It is with this that Rolland's book on Tolstoy principally deals: with Tolstoy the man, with the ceaselessly painful battle of this upright, difficult life, which contained much torment and disappointment, much discouragement and self-castigation, but to which falsehood was foreign.

However, this beautiful book is by no means simply biography; it starts out with Tolstoy's works, and the literary appreciation of those works, especially the early ones, *The Cossacks, War and Peace,* and *Anna Karenina,* is masterly. The pages in which Rolland discusses *War and Peace* are among the finest he has ever written. It is a joy to see in this book what love can accomplish! The way in which the Frenchman understands the Russian, the highly cultivated connoisseur of the arts understands the naïve, boisterous assailant of art, how the socialistically inclined West European understands the Eastern mystic, how fair he is toward him, how he is never dismayed by doctrines, how he follows Tolstoy even in the most farfetched outbursts of his often iconoclastic temperament, and everywhere discovers and reveals not the errors and occasional faults but the essential life, to read this is a rare and extraordinary pleasure.

Clear though Rolland's preference is for Tolstoy's earlier masterpieces, he is nevertheless far from the current view that sees the Russian's ethical-religious journalism as an aberration, as the regrettable activity of a genius in the wrong field. Rolland courageously opposes this superficial view still widely held by us, and in so doing also finds a way of doing justice with tenderest love to Tolstoy's late fiction. In his analysis of *Resurrection,* to be sure, Rolland seems to me to place too little emphasis on that capital artistic fault which consists in the fact that the hero Nekhlyudov carries out a mission for which his whole character is inadequate. Just at this point I should have liked a fuller investigation of Tolstoy's complex psychology and an indication of the inner schism that compelled the author to place his own most personal and profoundly felt ideas and problems in the hands of a character that he portrayed far too little like himself. The way in which Tolstoy, even in the early works, sketches himself here and there, the rather nervous way he now half shows, now half hides himself, never completely identifies himself with any one character and yet is compelled to put his most personal confessions into the mouths of all his characters—this kind of compulsion to confess and at the same time to avoid confession is not just a literary game of Tolstoy's but a key to his whole psychology in those areas where it appears abnormal and eccentric.

It is not lack of understanding but love and admiration that have kept Rolland from not only indicating but interpreting the deep division, the profound sorrow in Tolstoy's life. In a significant passage in his book Rolland talks of the fact that for Tolstoy's blazing need of love, even the commandment "Love thy neighbor as thyself" had been too little, since it contained an element of egoism. But it is just here that Tolstoy's problem lies—not that of his mind or his artistry but the painful problem of his personal life—that only seldom and with difficulty did he find true love of self, whereas love for his neighbor, even if it involved sacrifice and suffering, was far easier for him.

Here I am indicating something that I miss in Rolland's book. I am not criticizing—that would be wholly impossible for me in the face of this splendid book; I simply indicate a line, give an opinion. For the rest, all I can do is express joy and gratitude and a hope that this book will find a very large audience. Some of the problems with which Tolstoy struggled are no longer timely just now—they are, however, eternal and may for any human being at any hour burst into flames again.

JEAN CHRISTOPHE
1915

In such extensive works of fiction it can easily happen that the beginning enchants us without the whole being able to sustain the same high level. In *Jean Christophe* too, naturally enough, not every page is of equal value. Artistically, poetically, I consider the first part, the account of his childhood and early youth, the most significant. But in any case there will not be a reader who will not love the whole of this work, who will not admire in addition to the conception and intuition of its most successful parts the patience and faithful work, the understanding and sense of fairness of the subsequent chapters. In the purely artistic sense a beautiful lyric poem of four lines is more perfect and valuable than any novel, including *Wilhelm Meister*. A novel like *Jean Christophe* is not only art, it is not only the behavior of a soul, it is also the attempt of a mind to comprehend intellectually and to some extent with a sense of collective justice the temper of a time, of a culture, of a section of mankind. The musician Jean Christophe is not only a character, the past vision of a poet, he is at the same time an abstraction, a bearer of rich meanings, almost a myth. He is the spirit of music, the spirit of German originality and sluggish German tortuousness, for whom the mirror, the charm, the spur, the paradisal enchantment, the lovely, dear, depraved, clever, childish, mad, splendid Paris is essential for his fate. Romain Rolland, the Frenchman, has portrayed his German hero with a love that is apparently greater than his own love for his native Paris. For a thousand pages our affectionate sympathy is steadily on the side of the struggling musician against blind, evil, mendacious Paris. Apparently almost everywhere Paris customs, Paris art, Paris manners and lack of them are treated with inexorable harshness, while the hero Christophe is the object of unvarying love. Apparently Christophe is right and Paris wrong. In reality it is not so at all, and this is one of the great charms of the book. In reality this externally wicked and corrupt Paris is the object of a deep, holy love, stands far higher than any criticism or love could place it, exists cool and mighty and becomes fateful for everyone who touches it. Frenchmen, especially those of the war years, have still very little conception of what a song has here been sung to their holy of holies. For very many Frenchmen up to the time of the war, Rolland was a poet who had converted his minor weakness of a fondness for the German character into his strength. We too thought the same thing about him. In reality Rolland is a Frenchman through and through, the true essence of the French spirit, and for that very reason it is doubly significant and valuable that this Romain Rolland was among the few who during the war took human love seriously and who in time of peace takes the so universally acknowledged international ideals seriously. This man has not only written many very intelligent and fine books, he has also forborne to take part in the hue and cry for the sake of cheap laurels. Just as he unobtrusively donated to the International Red Cross in Geneva the Nobel Prize money he had won, so he relinquished fame, friendships, his treasure of a hard-won home, and love in order to remain true to his heart . . . The time will come when the values of such persons and such actions, which today seem purely passive, will prove themselves actively. Then it will be seen that Rolland's attitude during the war was the most Christian that can be conceived of. And people will admire in his great musical novel not simply the critical intellect and great ability but also the by no means passionless love of justice, the courageous and reverent love for mankind as a whole.

André Gide

1951

MY FIRST ACQUAINTANCE with the writings of André Gide occurred between 1900 and 1910. There was *Strait Is the Gate*, which strongly reminded me, in a more Huguenot guise, of the pious atmosphere of my childhood and which engaged me in year-long controversies with its conceptions, attracting me at the same time that it repelled. Then there was *The Immoralist*, which appealed even more strongly to me. This book was dedicated to his friend Henri Ghéon, one of those close friends whose conversion later affected Gide so painfully. And in addition there was a very slender volume on which the translator had left the French title, *Paludes*, a very remarkable, capricious, rebellious little book of youthful preciosity, which confused and baffled me, now enchanting me, now angering me, and in the following years during which I moved away from Gide and almost forgot him it had a subterraneous aftereffect on me. Meanwhile, with the coming of the war of 1914, world history had burst in upon my small literary existence, and it was necessary to deal with quite different problems from my earlier ones, terrifying, deadly problems. But shortly after the end of the war when I was beginning my life in Ticino, there appeared the book by E. R. Curtius, *The Literary Forerunner of Modern France;* his postscript was dated November 1918, and since during the war years I had become friendly with Rolland and shortly thereafter had met Hugo Ball, who was preoccupied with Péguy and Léon Bloy, and because I zealously sympathized with the attempts at friendship between the intellectuals of France and Germany, the reading of this fine book in my case fell upon fruitful soil. I set about procuring books by Péguy and Suarez; above all I found myself intensively reminded of André Gide, and not only out of curiosity and a desire to learn but with the wish to revise and rectify my attitude to this writer who had remained in my memory as being so fascinating and so two-faced. Immediately I reread *The Immoralist* and *Paludes,* this time with complete surrender. Kindled by Curtius's book, my love for that seductive writer really came to life and remained constant; Gide was an author who approached his problems, so similar to mine, in so completely different a fashion, and his noble independence, stubbornness, and constantly renewed self-control of the unwearying truth-seeker continued to please me and in a strange way seem related to me. Principally Gide's development took the course of release from the pious world of faith and religious attitudes; it was the way of one overgifted and much too strictly and morally raised, who can no longer bear the narrowness and knows that the world is waiting for him, but nevertheless is not minded to sacrifice the sensibility of conscience won through that upbringing. Of course, his struggle for freedom is not simply in the intellectual sphere; it has to do with the senses as well, which demand their rights, and from the revolt of the senses against control and tutelage there emerges and grows clear the character of *enfant terrible*, of joy in exposing and stripping bare, in trapping the pious in their piously labeled lusts and depravities—in short, that element of malice and aggressive love of revenge which without doubt is a part of Gide's character and constitutes for many of his readers his most fascinating and seductive aspect. But important though this motive was in André Gide's life, however much he may have been tempted and seduced into unmasking the righteous and baffling the philistines, there was in this noble spirit something greater, impelling him toward fruition and maturity, than the ability and enjoyment of startling and shocking his readers. He was on the dangerous path of every genius who, after breaking out of a for him unbearable tradition and morality, finds himself dreadfully alone and leaderless in the face of the world and searches on a higher level for a substitute for the lost security, seeks for models or norms that

can correct and heal the far too exposed condition of the un-
fettered individual. So we see him all his life interested in the
natural sciences and studying them, and we see him explor-
ing the world of cultures, languages, and literature with a
diligence and tenacity that evokes our astonishment and admiration. What he has won in this laborious, lifelong, chivalrous battle is a new kind of freedom, a freedom from
dogma and partisanship, but in constant subjection to the
service of truth, in constant striving for knowledge. In this he
is a true brother to the great Montaigne and to that poet who
wrote *Candide*. It has always been difficult to serve the truth
as an individual without the protection of a system of faith,
of a church, of a community. In serious and exemplary
fashion André Gide has pursued this difficult course.

CORYDON
1933

The four dialogues, beginning with a natural history of
love and ending with a kind of metaphysic of love, contain
Gide's confession to pederasty and at the same time constitute
the most significant contribution to this theme made in our
time. They not only vindicate pederasty by freeing it from
the character of perversion or crime; they divest the whole
theme of that false solemnity and moralism into which it was
forced by the middle class and the law. Over and above all
this, they become a theory of love in general.

Rainer Maria Rilke

1928

F OR THE LITTLE COMMUNITY of German poetry Rilke's
death was the setting of a star, one of the few that still
remained in the cloudy skies of this time.

Now that his collected works have appeared, the reader of
these works experiences as he leafs through them, searching
for favorites with joy and melancholy, a ghostly repetition:
he opens volume after volume and finds all the phases and
stages in which he knew and loved and kept company with
this poet through the decades, often without being able to tell
whether the phases and developments were in his own (the
reader's) life or in that of the poet. Often Rilke seemed to
change for those who read him over a long period, often he
seemed to shed his skin, at times to wear a mask. Now the
collected works show an amazingly unified picture. The faith-
fulness of the poet to his own essential being is far greater,
that essential being is far stronger, than what we once called
his versatility or even his changeableness.

We pick up volume after volume, turn the pages, hum-
ming to ourselves the opening words of beloved poems, first
from one and then from another, begin to search out special
favorites and lose ourselves again in the wide bright forest of
these poems. And in each volume we find imperishable poems
that have stood the test of time, among the very earliest,
hesitant works no less than among the latest. In the first
volume we rediscover those lovely tones that so gently and
deeply entranced us thirty years ago, those quiet simple verses
full of astonishment and tremulousness of soul, such verses
as:

> Mich rührt so sehr
> böhmischen Volkes Weise,

schleicht sie ins Herz sich leise,
macht sie es schwer . . .*

and the poems of *Advent*. In the second volume the *Book of Pictures* reminds us of the powerful impression of correctitude and formal power it once made on us, and we linger for a long time over the *Book of Hours*, which once was our favorite and that of the girls we knew. In the third volume, the last of the volumes of poetry, is unfurled the classical piety of the *New Poems*, and in the *Duino Elegies* the summit of his work is attained. Remarkable, this journey from the youthful music of Bohemian folk poetry to this point and to *Orpheus*, remarkable how this poet so consistently begins with what is simplest and as his language grows, as his mastery of form increases, penetrates deeper and deeper into his problems! And at each stage now and again the miracle occurs, his delicate, hesitant, anxiety-prone person withdraws, and through him resounds the music of the universe; like the basin of a fountain he becomes at once instrument and ear.

The two following volumes contain the prose writings, among them that favorite, unforgettable *Malte Laurids Brigge*. When one considers that this book was published almost twenty years ago and though not entirely unknown, of course, has nevertheless remained in the shadows, while in the meantime dozens of perishable, fast-blooming, fast-fading successes of our so very hectic and ill-begotten prose fiction have paraded past! Rilke's *Malte Laurids Brigge* remains as splendid as on the first day.

The translations occupy the final volume of the works, and here once more all the poet's great virtues are displayed: his mastery of form, his certain instinct in selection, and his persistence in the pursuit of complete understanding. Gems like the translation of Guérin's *Centaur* are there, André Gide's *Return of the Prodigal Son* and Paul Valéry's poems. And one

---

* Songs of the Bohemian folk
Touch me so deeply—
Slipping in silence into my heart,
Make my heart heavy . . .

remembers how his love of Paris and of the French language,
together with the suffering he felt from the degradation of
the German tongue and the slovenliness of German linguistic
usage, even induced the poet in his last years to pay active
court to that beloved language and to write French poems.

1927

When the poet Rilke died a few months ago one could tell
clearly enough from the attitude of the intellectual world—
partly from its silence but even more from what was said—
how in our time the poet as the purest type of the inspired
human being, caught between the mechanical world and the
world of intellectual industriousness, is forced as it were into
an airless room and condemned to suffocate.

We have no right to denounce the times on this account.
These times are no worse and no better than other times.
They are heaven for him who shares their goals and ideals,
and hell for him who rebels against them. Now since the poet,
if he wishes to be true to his heritage and calling, dare not
commit himself either to the success-mad world where lives
are dominated by industry and organization, or to the world
of rationalized spirituality which seems on the whole to
dominate our universities, but since it is the poet's single duty
and mission to be the servant, knight, and advocate of the
soul, he sees himself at the present world-instant condemned
to a loneliness and suffering that is not every man's affair.
We all guard ourselves against suffering, each of us would
like to receive a little kindness and warmth from the world
and would like to see himself understood and supported by
those around him. So we observe the majority of our present-
day poets (their number is small in any case) in one way or
another adapting themselves to the time and its spirit, and it
is just these poets who meet with the greatest superficial success. On the other hand, others fall silent and come to destruction in the airless space of this hell.

Still others, however—Rilke belongs among them—take

the suffering upon themselves, subject themselves to fate and do not rebel when they see that the crown that other times bestowed on poets has today become a crown of thorns. My love belongs to these poets, I honor them, I would like to be their brother. We suffer but not in order to protest or to curse. We suffocate in the for us unbreathable air of the world of machines and barbaric necessities that surround us, but we do not separate ourselves from the whole, we accept this suffering and suffocation as our part of the world fate, as our mission, as our trial. We believe in none of the ideals of this time, not that of the dictators, nor that of the bolsheviks, not that of the professors, nor that of the industrialists. But we believe that man is immortal and that his image can emerge again, healed of every distortion, freed from every hell. We believe in the soul whose rights and needs, however long and harshly suppressed, can never die. We do not seek to enlighten our time, or to improve it, or to instruct it, but by revealing to it our own suffering and our own dreams we try to open to it again and again the world of images, the world of the soul, the world of experience. These dreams are in part evil dreams of anxiety, these images are in part cruel horror pictures—we dare not embellish them, we dare not disown them. We dare not hide the fact that the soul of mankind is in danger and close to the abyss. But we dare not conceal either that we believe in its immortality.

LETTERS FROM THE YEARS 1907–1914
1933

It is no accident and it is not, although at times it might appear so, by any means a simply literary matter that the figure of the poet Rilke has become of such importance for our time. A community of faithful readers love and honor his works, but Rilke's figure and life, his letters, his *nachlass*, the memories of him, are taken very seriously and gathered and cherished with much reverence. Certainly there is in Rilke and the atmosphere surrounding him a bit of snobbery, and there is a lot of it in the kind of idolatry he enjoys in certain circles. But that is simply stuck on the outside, and what we could call the Rilke cult is by no means sustained by all those ladies of the best society to whom it was a point of honor partly to acclaim this poet, partly to patronize him and to collect with piety his beautiful, often flattering letters. The phenomenon of Rilke has hardly any connection with this. It can be described in this way: in the midst of a period of violence and the brutal worship of strength, a poet becomes a favorite, indeed becomes a prophet and model, for a spiritual elite, a poet whose essence seems to be weakness, delicacy, devotion, and humility, who, however, turned his weakness into an impulse to greatness, turned his delicacy into strength, turned his psychic vulnerability and fear of life into a heroic asceticism. And this is the reason that Rilke's letters and his personal life and his legend belong so very much to his work, because in his nature he is so very typical of what is unprotected, homeless, uprooted, threatened, yes, suicidal in the spiritual man of our time. He prevails not because he was stronger but because he was weaker than the average; it is the sick and threatened quality of his nature that so powerfully summoned up and strengthened the healing, incantative, magical forces in him. And so he has become a beloved and comforting image and model for the spiritual man and artist who does not withdraw from suffering, who does not flee from and renounce his own time and its fears, nor his own weaknesses and dangers, but through them, a sufferer, achieves his faith, his ability to live, his victory. This road led him as poet to a new form, suffered for and battled for, that often resonates through and through with strain. As a human being his fate made him humble and kindly. And it is with full right that his followers reckon the many splendid letters he wrote as an essential and valid part of his work.

This new volume of letters includes the years whose most important experience and result were *Malte Laurids Brigge* —the whole book revolves around this center. But in addition there are also everywhere gifts and treasures. Descriptions (pictures, houses, gardens) of magnificent mastery, or things like the pages to Brandes about André Gide's *Strait Is the Gate*.

The little brochure *On God* puts together two letters, one a real one written during the war and the other an imaginary, literary letter from his last years, each meant as a small confession of faith.

D. H. Lawrence

1933

THREE BOOKS I have read recently have reminded me of
Lawrence, the sensitive, fiery poet who came into such
fierce conflict with his England and his age, portrayed this
deadly conflict several times in wonderful fiction, and documented it over and over again in powerful indictments.
Through his fiction (of these my favorites are *The Rainbow*
and *St. Mawr*) this strong mind speaks to men of all cultures.
His indictments are more limited; they show the personal
English biographical aspects of Lawrence's conflict. Among
the indictments belongs the very remarkable book *Apocalypse*,
which assails the British Protestants and their favorite book
of the Bible, the Revelation of St. John. With passion and
perspicuity, with the right of one mortally attacked and in-
sulted, but nevertheless with limited emotional effectiveness,
he excoriates this book from which the pious self-righteous
draw justification for their lust for power. I too have never
loved the Revelation of St. John and can get along without it
forever very easily, but I have never felt so passionately on
the subject. Although I am very well acquainted with revolt
against pietistic origins, I do not believe that it plays the same
important role with us as with Lawrence's pseudo-Christians,
but even so his battle grips us, the battle of nature and the
soul against the mechanical and the literal. It is a highly
subjective but marvelously flaming and honorable book of
battle, the last defense of a dying man against a world in
which he was destined to suffocate.

I could not make much out of *The Plumed Serpent*, Lawrence's Mexican novel, which is one of the books of this head-
strong poet that have remained closed to me; it strikes me as
forced and contrived.

On the other hand, I have now for the first time come to know *Lady Chatterley's Lover*—in the new abridged and castrated edition. Hitherto, on account of certain erotic passages, the book has been forbidden and denigrated; there was only one edition for professors and collectors of erotica but not available to the public. Since I have not seen the unabridged version, I do not know how much has been omitted and how much lost thereby. But even thus shortened, *Lady Chatterley* is one of Lawrence's great successful magical books; it glows with natural charm and passion as well as with a warring spirit against his enemies—the machine, money, the world of bloodless, dead abstractions. Now that this amazing love story finally belongs to the public, it will unquestionably win a throng of new readers in Germany too for this poet who was as headstrong as he was lovable. The translation by Herlitschka deserves praise, except that unfortunately the long passages in dialect, presumably troublesome enough in the original, are very tiresome. The poet defends love, he defends tenderness, sensuality, nature, and blood against everything that goes under the name of orthodoxy, organization, industry, theory, abstract morality. His novel is a song in praise of love, the story of the release of an educated English woman of the upper class from prudery and cynical intellectuality. Sad and yet essentially comforting and heartening is the echo of the dead poet's voice within us. We will never forget it.

1934

Between Hamsun and Lawrence there are as many resemblances as differences. By comparison with Hamsun's naïve paganism, Lawrence's differentiated, logically based, and at times somewhat neurotically tinged paganism is intellectually superior, but in blood Hamsun's more than makes up for that, and so Hamsun's optimism almost never becomes polemical, whereas Lawrence inevitably goes armed to the teeth. Hamsun's way leads with a few digressions always more clearly and naturally to pure epic, whereas Lawrence's novellas often come close to being essays: his paganism does not have Hamsun's innocence. This by no means makes Lawrence less dear to us as poet, as creator of characters and situations, despite his polemical ambiguity. In *Gypsies* there are a few portraits and likenesses of the dead author, for example, in the story "The Captain's Doll," that make us love and admire him all over again. When this writer with the hunter's and rider's instinct does not happen to be shooting down priests or running amok (something that should by no means be held against him) he can create pictures of unforgettable delicacy and translucency.

ST. MAWR
1930

Less than a year ago Lawrence died, the most original, thoroughbred English poet of our day. This last novel of his seems to me his finest. The book reeks of love and blood; its symbol, the wild, dangerous stallion that likes to break its riders' necks, represents this poet's whole character, his fawn-like closeness to nature, his alert rebelliousness. It is strange, and yet on closer consideration perfectly logical, that in the same intellectual England that, for instance, brought forth the clever, omniscient, passionless novels of Huxley, this Lawrence could have lived.

Thomas Wolfe

LOOK HOMEWARD, ANGEL

1933

SINCLAIR LEWIS, who was shrewder about the psychology of philistines than in characterizing geniuses, is said to have remarked about this astonishingly beautiful and exuberant book that it is "a colossal creation full of a deep love of life." There is some truth in this, colossal the novel certainly is, and naturally it is also "full of a deep love of life," because like every true work of the imagination it has deep, strong, sustaining roots in the senses and therefore loves and praises life. But when you come to the subtitle, which the author himself gave to his book, it does not sound like any joyful optimism or love of life; it is "A Story of Buried Life," and of the many subterranean and nocturnal aspects of this novel the foremost feeling is that of life that is buried, of the unreality of the real, of the loneliness and lostness of every man, even in the midst of a visible community. The lust for life here often takes the form of extreme despair, and this is the aspect of this apparently robust American from the southern states that especially interests us.

The lostness and despair of this writer are deep-rooted in the sensual, in surrender to sight, sound, feeling, and smell; they force their way out of a wildly beautiful and almost Rabelaisian acceptance of the senses and intoxication with them like some sinister magic flower, and they seem to be the result of a complete absence of faith in religion, authority, or tradition. The hero of the book inherits from his forefathers a vigorous, healthy, indeed overflowing sensuality, a blossoming fantasy, an enormous hunger for life, as well as a degree of kindliness and a great talent, but no magic word, no formula to control chaos, no name for God, no refuge in prayer, meditation, reverence. He stands alone between his sensuality and his aspirations as a poet, supported only by a meager formal education, leaderless, without even any strong superstitions; the innocently blooming, luxuriantly glowing world in which his senses delight stands undefended against the criticism of his understanding, the seductions of the mind; before them it shrivels, suddenly seems meaningless, lost, mortally sad, without goal or duration, an iridescent swamp.

We await the next volume by this engaging writer not because we are so anxious to read several hundred more pages of his marvelous, overwhelming song of praise to nature, to food and drink, to sex, to intoxication, to the smell of flowers, to women—but because the coming volume will have to lead the naïve young Siegfried to a spot where the beauty and the "lostness" of the world are no longer compatible, where a painful path to sublimation will have to be hewn out. One waits for it with great eagerness because this first novel leaves its hero still a youth, and beyond question the hero is the author himself. By the final page of the present excellent book he has individualized himself to such an extent and has become so keenly aware of himself that there can remain only two paths for him: descent into the merely sensual, perhaps as a drunkard like his father, or painful sublimation, responsible search for meaning. This has been hard for him because of his heritage, his parents, his sensuality, even because of his talent.

My attempt to indicate abstractly the outline of this novel can only hint at how much beauty and genius the book contains even if one subordinates its profound problem, indeed even if one dismisses it. Like a genial drinker, this enthusiast pours into himself all the juices of earth and life, eternally in love, eternally the artist—and what an artist!

1933

The young hero of this magnificent novel, Eugene Gant, is not yet twenty years old at the end of the book, and his own real novel is still to come. This first book by Thomas Wolfe, so marvelously titled, tells of Eugene's heritage, of his family, childhood, and youth. Events in the Gant family are amazing and violent, their life is a chaos of contradictions, of success and failure, of sin and magnanimity, of imagination and niggardly business enterprise. The Gant family lives its tangled, noisy life in an exuberant short-lived atmosphere in a small mountain city of one of the southern states. The rhythm of blossoming and fading, of rank growth and miserable decline, beats sadly and excitingly through the whole long book, it sings of mortality, it swings passionately between lust and death. The members of the family are wonderfully revealed in the tension of contrasts, which is the family's hallmark; they seem as completely different from one another as is possible and yet all have the same strange fear of life. The father, old Gant, is a huge drinker and eater, he smells strongly of whiskey and good, strengthening spicy food, but the life of this sensualist, whom his wife and children both despise and love, is for all its filth lighted by flashes of imagination and longing, and in the midst of his steamy, raucous, demanding drunkard's existence, his long rhetorical speeches, his playacting, his conventional morality, he stands mysterious, alone, and lost. Throughout the whole second half of the book, several hundred pages, we wait for his death; he is broken and has collapsed, the rooster has grown weak, tearful, and impotent; consumed by cancer he creeps toward death, but he does not die, he lives and lives, shadowy, half real but still there, he can find no end to the game. And the mother, who sends her children out while still young to earn money, who as housekeeper and landlady works herself to the bone and never sleeps, secretly saves and speculates, buys and sells real estate, and while her little sons are running about as paperboys and contracting tuberculosis, amasses a quite substantial fortune. A fortune she would each time gladly hand over once the worst has happened, once someone dies, once it is clear that it is now too late for reason, too late for love and kindness. We see two sons die, the dear pretty little Glover, the haggard, clever, austere Ben, and each of these death scenes is in its strange way horrifying and unique.

It is amid the parental thunderstorms, the oratorical orgies of his drunken father (who solemnly and most morally voted for Prohibition and went on drinking), amid his many brothers and sisters and the many boarders and pensioners that young Eugene grows up; clearly the story the novelist is telling is his own. Burdened by both parents with gifts and with dangers, perpetual prey to inner loneliness, he grows up not without education but without faith, standards, or comfort, and at the age of twenty, though healthy and full of intelligence, he is no less lost and abandoned in the wild, hostile world than his sick father dying for years, and yet for years continuously drinking. Here the book leaves him, on the threshold of independent life, with the equal possibilities of becoming a genius or a scamp. Intellectually he is many thousand paces further along than his father but he is just as threatened, just as lost.

The epic of the Gant family is the most powerful piece of fiction from present-day America that I know of.

J. D. Salinger

THE CATCHER IN THE RYE

1953

MANY LETTERS from very young American readers of *Steppenwolf*, some of them blasé, some of them desperate, finally and for the first time became fully understandable to me when I read this significant novel. The story concerns the experiences during a few days in the highly problematical and perilous life of a sixteen-year-old American boy. It is by no means a pretty milieu into which one looks: much too rich and much too preoccupied parents, the father a lawyer, the mother a nervous society woman with her hundred cigarettes a day; the son, hustled off to boarding schools, has just been, as so often before, expelled and is completely adrift in the midst of the fierce needs of puberty. All the characters, grownups and children, students and teachers, as in all American academic stories, are drinkers; they drink at every hour of the day and night, they speak an artificially coarse, artificially violent language, every tenth word of which is a curse—in short, it seems a hopelessly corrupt, filthy, and comfortless world in which these poor goddamn people lead their poor crazy damn lives (this is the style of their conversation). The sixteen-year-old knows nothing of his father except that he earns a great deal of money and will presumably murder him if he returns home thrown out of this last school; for his mother he has mixed sentimental feelings; toward neither any trust. A dearly loved brother had died young. There is an older brother who once wrote talented short stories but then sold and prostituted himself to Hollywood, and in addition a little sister, still a child, to whom all his tenderness belongs. And behind the façade of hard-boiled, blasé precocity we perceive, while we follow him through horrifying nights in cheap nightclubs and call-girl hotels, a soul in slow, steady development, a completely beautiful, pure, lovable and loving soul, full of noble impulses and admirable latent gifts, and as we read, this corrupt, brutal, vicious America becomes a false front, just like the behavior and language of these schoolboys. Behind the repulsive mask, barely touched by the filth, resides noble humanity, high-hearted and talented. Perhaps this dear imperiled child will sometime write poems, perhaps too, later on, he will sometime succumb and in one way or another also sell himself to Hollywood. For the time being, despite all his awkward antics and adult poses, he is a child, a runaway, a very much endangered child brimming with unused powers of soul, full of longing for the good and the beautiful, full of dignity and kindness.

Whether one reads this novel as the individual story of a half-grown problem child or as the allegory of a whole country and people, one will be led by the author along the beautiful road from dislike to understanding, from disgust to love. In a problematic world and time, poetry can achieve nothing higher.

PART TWO

II · INTELLECTUAL HISTORY

Sigmund Freud

1925

IN GERMAN SCIENCE of the last decades there are very few figures who can be compared to Freud in scope and depth of influence. And in the literature of the psychoanalysts, gradually becoming mountainous, he is really still the only one, aside from Jung in Zurich, whose work carries conviction, even outside the profession, through its lofty human and literary qualities. The beautiful and strikingly attractive thing about Freud's writings is the preoccupation of a remarkably strong intellect with questions that all lead into the suprarational, the constantly renewed, patient, and yet daring attempt of a disciplined mind to capture life itself in the net of pure science—too coarse though that net always is. The conscientious researcher and lucid logician Freud has created for himself a magnificent instrument in a language that is not only intellectualistic but razor-sharp, with its precise definitions and occasional joy in conflict and derision. Of how many of our scholars can this be said?

GENERAL INTRODUCTION TO PSYCHOANALYSIS
1919

This long-awaited book is truly what we expected it to be, the first systematic presentation of Freud's theory of the psychology of the unconscious and the technique of analysis, presented, unlike shorter earlier essays by Freud's students and disciples, by Freud himself, with the full responsibility and the complete earnestness of the discoverer and trail breaker for his new domain. All the fine qualities of his mind are to be found once more in this book, his clarity, his gift for patient theorizing, his talent for precise formulation, his wit. The three sections deal with blunders, with dreams, and with the theory of neuroses. The two first themes Freud has already systematicaliy set forth in his *Psychopathology of Everyday Life* and his *Interpretation of Dreams,* whereas a general theory of neuroses in complete form has not until now been published by him. And so this interests us most of all, and it proves to be a sterling performance. It is a pleasure to observe the consistency and cautiousness with which Freud pursues his course and draws his conclusions, the assurance of his formulations in matters that are no longer open to question and his cautiousness and modesty where he is dealing with conjectures, groping and seeking. This book gives to every man, and above all to doctors, an authentic introduction in the origin, goals, and technique of psychoanalysis.

The battle over analysis goes on, though the theory has long since silently conquered youth, and the future belongs to it. With it, psychology has been established as a science, and a first serious glimpse has been won into the laws of psychic occurrences; still more important, for the first time serious research has begun in that domain which has hitherto been outside the boundaries of science. The uninterrupted causality of psychic occurrences, the extension of the law of causality and with it the possibility of scientific investigation in this field of psychology, seems to us today a matter of course; not long ago, however, it aroused the ire and scorn of many privy counselors, just as today facts such as the existence of childhood sexuality are denied by doctors as well as laymen. Well, this battle has been fought, the basic truths of psychoanalysis have been established. They will go on being assailed, but they will never be overthrown.

But that psychoanalysis should be considered as the foundation for a new broadened, deepened philosophy of life is another question entirely. To some, the psychology of the unconscious seems destined to play this sort of role. Here we reach the point at which a number of Freud's followers have fallen away from the master. Freud himself remains completely the doctor and physicist, he examines the mechanism of psychic events without trying to make a philosophy of life

out of them, indeed he carefully avoids any metaphysical pretensions.

It is quite different with those disciples who have gone off
in various directions and, partly in an obvious spirit of dilettantism, have attempted to enlarge psychoanalysis into a kind
of religion. In fact, some of these efforts are so superficial that
one can understand Freud's defensive action against such
followers. Others, however, most of all Jung in Zurich, have
made the first admirable attempts to extend the conception of
psychoanalysis beyond medicine and make it the foundation
of a philosophy—the formulation of which, to be sure, has
not yet appeared.

It would be improper, however, to accept certain mitigat-
ing and conciliatory interpretations of Freudian psychology
while rejecting that of the real creator of this science. This is
and remains Sigmund Freud, whom one may criticize or correct in detail, but whose great achievement (together with
that of Breuer, so oddly left in the background) now has assured and permanent acceptance.

ON PSYCHOANALYSIS, FIVE LECTURES
IN WORCESTER
1919

Freud's lectures of 1909 are still the best, shortest, and
clearest introduction to psychoanalysis, i.e., to the young
science of the psychology of the unconscious and the treatment of psychic illness by raising repressed impulses into
consciousness. Freud's cool, often witty, always clear presentation is well known; the reading of each of his books is a
pleasure. It would seem that gradually a generation is growing up, even in the German higher schools, that is mature
and open-minded enough to adopt a positive attitude toward
Freud's great achievement, after twenty years of German
science's almost unanimously avoiding any practical examination of it and contenting itself with abuse and dismissal. Anyone seeking a short introduction to Freud's thought will find
it nowhere better than in these lectures.

C. G. Jung

ON THE NATURE OF THE PSYCHE

1931

AMONG TODAY'S PSYCHOLOGISTS a unique and important position is occupied by a brilliant student of Freud's, the Zurich physician C. G. Jung, who just before the World War attracted attention as the author of the talented *Symbols of Transformation*. Then, quarreling with Freud and abandoning him, he finally became the founder of a psychology centered upon his two discoveries, the "collective unconscious" and the *Psychological Types*. It is undoubtedly his theory of types for which he is best known. However it is not easy to be fair to him from a distance, for Jung is not exclusively and in fact not even principally a scholar and writer; he is first of all a doctor and the teacher of his group, and so his latest work, *On the Nature of the Psyche*, is published with contributions by some of his students and friends. One could wish for a systematic work by Jung; the "lectures" always have something slightly disillusioning about them, with their concessions to journalistic requirements of the public and other obeisances, though ironically meant, to the zeitgeist. Nevertheless the volume still contains enough that is valuable, new, and good to deserve serious consideration. One essay makes clear Jung's present attitude toward Freud, and various lectures and essays are at pains to locate Jungian psychology in present-day science and intellectual life. From a practical and medical point of view this psychology with its avowal of the "reality of the psychical" and its fine respect for the wisdom of the suprapersonal unconscious has long had a firm position on earth and can no longer be thought away; its position in present-day science, however, is not yet completely certain, and this is the real subject of debate in these volumes of essays. The tone of voice has perhaps become a little more professorial than earlier. Jung is now sixty years old and is no longer a tolerated outsider but an officially recognized great man, and nice though this is, one is nevertheless a little mournful from time to time for the eccentricity and other-worldliness of the former "occult" Jung. Well, his fine book is to be heartily commended, and he himself on his sixtieth birthday. Next to Freud, no psychiatrist of today has advanced our insight into the nature of the psyche more than he has. He does not stop at its mechanism or treat it as natural science but as philosophy. But he is rescued from the tendency to academicism by his experience as a doctor; again and again, in these new works too, he derives from his psychiatric practice a distrust of pure theory and an original, fresh point of view.

And at times, as in his essay on *Ulysses* by James Joyce, he reaches a height and magical many-sidedness of observation that arouses our wonder.

1934

In an essay on Freud, C. G. Jung takes occasion to make fun of the concept of "sublimation" formulated by Freud. For us non-psychologists, to whom awe is nothing to be laughed at, there is in all the history of mankind nothing more interesting, indeed, nothing at all of greater importance, than just this process of sublimation. That man under certain circumstances is capable of placing his impulses in the service of supra-egoistic, spiritual, religious, cultural goals, that there is such a thing as devotion to the spirit, that saints and martyrs exist, this for us is the only comfort and positive worth in world history and the one thing that history has left us. Sublimation is not, as Jung derisively says out of rancor toward Freud, an empty word without meaning, but rather it is something existent, effective, and worthy of our greatest reverence as potentiality, as ideal, as challenge. Since primeval times it has been the subject of every myth, every saga, every legend, and every story, and the Jewish contribution to this secret history of the faculty of sublimating human instincts is a great and mighty one.

Jacob Burckhardt

THE CIVILIZATION OF THE RENAISSANCE
IN ITALY

1935

. . . We salute [this publication] not simply because through
it a particular classical book (a book that has influenced
deeply and permanently the best minds of more than two generations) is at last available to people of moderate means,
but more than that, because Burckhardt in our opinion is the
noblest conceivable representative of a spiritual attitude to
which we of today are far more deeply indebted and obligated
than most of us know or admit. If in the midst of this great
cultural twilight of ours there are minds among our teachers
and writers that see their mission and duty as bequeathing to
the coming generation an indestructible spirituality that is
impervious to topical events and that can rely simply on its
own responsibility for assuming an exemplary attitude toward
the confusions and seductions of the day—if independence,
incorruptibility, and conscience are still valid ideals for
spiritual effort, then our time has the example of minds like
Burckhardt's to thank. Certainly his splendid works would be
inconceivable without his enormous knowledge, his immense
reading, and the strong element of artistry in his whole being
and work; but the foundation of it all is nevertheless his character, the severe, almost ascetic form of his intellectual
morality. Therefore we wish for those among his works that
are accessible to non-scholars, and most of all for his *Force
and Freedom: Reflections on History* and his *Civilization of
the Renaissance in Italy,* the widest circulation. It may be that
these beautiful editions, which one can get almost as a gift,

will be for many people simply picture books; nevertheless there is certain to be here and there a young seeker who will find his way to them, who will educate himself through them, who will seek models and guidelines in them and find what is good in himself confirmed and encouraged through them.

Karl Marx

DAS KAPITAL

1932

. . . I also read in *Capital* by Marx, which has appeared in a popular pocketbook edition costing almost nothing. It is no longer a dangerous book, and now no one has any excuse at all for not reading it. However, just as before, I have read only scattered passages, and much though I admire Marx I must admit that I neither love him nor share his beliefs and views. Even his model and teacher Hegel is someone I do not much love; his dazzling garrulity does not greatly entertain me, nor does his professorial assumption of superior wisdom. Granted, Marx is more factual and his critique of capitalism is essentially incontrovertible. From Hegel he derived a disgust at the self-revealing and self-appreciative spirit of the Hegel period and unfortunately transferred some of that disgust to spirit in general. If he took the spirit and spiritual nature and needs of men half as seriously as he does the phenomenon of capitalism, we would read him with greater pleasure and he would have more reliable things to say about what lies beyond capital and labor. His insight into the mechanism of economics is unquestionably gifted with genius and often prophetic; his philosophy and view of history are narrow and do not go far beyond the level of the forgotten literature of the Enlightenment of the period between Darwin and Haeckel.

Henri Bergson

1916

I SHOULD LIKE to call attention to the German edition of the works of a philosopher who at the moment has dropped out of sight in Germany, as can happen in wartime. He is Henri Bergson, the "fashionable" French thinker.

Bergson is very far away from all "fashions," although he understands the essential intellectual currents of our time and has expressed himself about them. Anyone who has found Nietzsche profitable can also find value in Bergson. Like Nietzsche, he is a champion of life against doctrine; he fights for new ways of perception and fights against the hallowed dogmas of the Kantian school. Bergson denies to the understanding, to the intelligence operating with concepts and logic, the ability of real perception, of true apprehension of what is alive. And so, for Kant's disciples and for intellectualists of every kind, he is ipso facto dismissed as no more than a romantic and poet. He forgoes all claim to the provability and universal validity of logicoscientific work, not because he does not understand it and has not mastered it, but because his strongly artistically inclined nature urges him along the path of intuition, of empathy, and of supralogical, prophetic perception. Let the professional philosophers decide how high they wish to rate Bergson as a thinker. For the rest of us, there is no reason to neglect Bergson's splendid books. They are so full of sagacity and liveliness, so fresh and personal, at the same time so admirably written and full of apt, lightning inspirations and similes that their reading alone must count as valuable and beneficial, even though for philosophers working scientifically they may contain dangers. After all, that's the experience we had with Nietzsche; in his time we began to read him with philosophical hunger and then, as years passed, his works became for us more and more a grandiose exception, the powerful record of a daring, noble, original mind whose wholly personal attitude toward the world was in itself enlightening and worth learning, whereas the actual philosophical conclusions no longer entered much into the question. It's possible that sometimes this will happen to us with Bergson, although his temperament is certainly less forceful than that of Nietzsche. In any case, his gifted books give us the splendid portrait of a thinker for whom all paths for apprehending the living world that have hitherto been investigated are inadequate, who with instinctive urgency but with well-trained mind is in pursuit of the riddle of life. Just as he sees in the capacity of intuition the highest of our faculties, so he sees life throughout as a spiritual phenomenon and finds in natural history a history of the soul. Thorough training in the natural sciences keeps him from becoming an ideologue, so that he stands far closer to Schelling than, say, to Hegel. He is the seeker, and, following in his steps, we find the journey itself, the walking and seeking, delightful. And the more we recognize his work as not yet completed, as needing many additions, many sequels, to just that extent we must treasure him as a source of the greatest stimulation.

Count Hermann Keyserling

1920

FOR ALMOST A YEAR I have heard Keyserling's *Travel Diary of a Philosopher* discussed, usually in rapturous terms, but only now has it come into my hands. I set about reading it with great excitement, as well as with that slight feeling of apprehension with which one looks at a book that has been universally and loudly praised by one's friends. The first pages, the decision to travel, the journey to India, the first experiences in Ceylon and in southern India, strengthened my anticipation and interest but also that tiny apprehension, for there was almost too much *esprit* here, there was a disturbing, almost a virtuoso empathy with any foreign world whatever! Barely has Keyserling arrived in Kandy than he is living and breathing Ceylonese Buddhism like an old monk, he knows and understands it from the bottom up, he participates in it like an epicure. And hardly has he crossed over to the mainland and proceeded through Tuticorin than he is living just as naturally and has just as quickly empathized with Hinduism and can see at a glance why Buddhism, which had enchanted him so yesterday, nevertheless turned into a fiasco in India. And shortly thereafter he is confronting Islam with the same gracefulness, the same fairness, the same almost theatrical empathy. Also the light tone in which for the most part the book is written and which, naturally enough, is much admired by most readers, easily becomes a danger for the author. In many places this philosopher chats innocently and engagingly about external views, about impressions of nature and travel, and these descriptions are, to be sure, witty and engaging but they are superficial, for Keyserling is without poetic gifts and his style, when he attempts to describe anything except thoughts and intellectual experiences, becomes feeble and journalistic.

Well, all these objections finally fell away. Taken individually, each is justified, but this travel diary as a whole is so extraordinary a performance that the weaknesses in it amount to nothing. On the whole, this is the most significant book that has appeared in Germany in years. To make the principal point at once, Keyserling is, not the first European of course, but assuredly the first European scholar and philosopher who has really understood India. Harsh though this sounds and painful though it is to say it, remembering such men as Oldenberg and Deussen, it is nevertheless true.

The thing that many artists and most of all very many so-called occultists have long known about India, the thing they sought and practiced there, the essential thing for us about Indian spirituality, this to my amazement has never been impartially observed and studied by any one of the many professors who traveled there; indeed it was not seen at all. They did not see it because it was forbidden to them. For the aspect of India in question was occultism, it was magic, it was mysticism, it had to do with the soul, it was not sufficiently denatured and neutralized to be acknowledged or even seriously noticed by Europeans, let alone by German professors. It was recognized, studied, sought out, and imitated only by occultists, by enthusiasts, by the founders of sects, by theosophists, or by sensation-hungry globetrotters. This India has now been discovered for science by Keyserling. He is the first of all the European scholars to see and give simple expression to the simple long-known fact that the Hindu way to wisdom is not a science but a psychic technique, that it has to do with an alteration in the state of consciousness, and that one educated in the Indian fashion does not attain his insights through calculation and study but sees the truths with an inner eye, hears them with an inner ear, and perceives them directly, not through cogitation.

The recognition and acceptance of this simple truth by an influential and important European thinker will have significant consequences. Keyserling, who is without the inhibitions and blinders of the academic fraternity, is in agreement with all occultists in acknowledging and commending yoga. He deplores, as do many seekers in Europe, our complete lack of a tradition and method for training in concentration, and he sees with unerring accuracy that the only method of this kind, not available, alas, to non-Catholics, that Europe has produced in the last centuries is the inspired exercises of Ignatius Loyola.

Of all the things that Keyserling says about India this will have the greatest effect, although actually it is a matter of course. It will have enormous influence, for yoga is exactly what Europe most wildly hungers for.

Now valuable though the recognition of the absolute worth of yoga and its effective formulation in this book are, however much they may remain for the majority of readers the principal point of the book, they are neither new nor are they the profoundest part of the book. The profoundest is the feeling for Hindu piety, for the Hindu's faith and for his worlds of gods, that Indian piety for which the paradoxes of every true faith create no problem, to whom every god, every idol, every myth is holy without his taking, in our sense, any one of them seriously. Here Keyserling accomplishes the extraordinary in that he as a European critically schooled thinker attains and experiences the profound naïveté of the Hindu, which appears so closely related to skepticism and yet is its exact opposite. This astonishing and truly inspiring ability of Keyserling's is explicable only from a few confessional passages in the book in which he speaks casually of his heritage and youth. There we learn, if we follow attentively this unusual soul, that from childhood it felt itself to be Proteus, that it instinctively drew back from every temptation to premature crystallization and again and again took refuge in the ideal of infinitely polymorphous plasticity. I hesitate to attempt a rough sketch of this soul from the few, only half-intentional confessions but it is this noble, flexible, inquisitive, and protean soul that gives all of Keyserling's work its magic.

Let me say a brief word too about the ethical, the educa

tional, final conclusions of this significant book. Here too Keyserling has hit upon formulations very parallel to my own, here too I found many a revealing saying happily expressed. For the last four years, in my different world as a poet, the faith I have struggled with hardest and tried most variously to express is no other than that of God in the *I* and the ideal of self-realization. Nowhere am I in complete agreement with Keyserling in his final formulations; however in what is most essential, most alive, he has everywhere strengthened me, reassured me, often led me, supported and aided me through some arresting word.

The *Travel Diary* will undoubtedly have an enormous influence. Keyserling will perhaps, next to Bergson, have the greatest influence of any thinker in present-day Europe.

Oswald Spengler

THE DECLINE OF THE WEST

1924

A GREAT DEAL of writing is going on today and one might well say that the activity of men of letters is comparable to that of arithmeticians and financiers who spend the whole day writing down innumerable ciphers—instead of reckoning with units, they reckon in millions and billions—and all this increases the use of paper. Now as for ideas, the greater part of these do not come from poets and professional writers; the interesting and inspiring material comes from the neighboring provinces, from the border region between fine literature and science. Here Oswald Spengler, author of *The Decline of the West*, still stands at the top of the list because of his wide influence and the scope and power of his gifts. Almost all the writers in this country heap such wild and violent abuse on him that one loves him for that alone. And in fact his book is the cleverest and most intelligent to appear in the last few years. Spengler's faults are not that he is mistaken here and there or draws incautious conclusions—why shouldn't he exercise the right of all human beings?—nor can it be called an error that he is politically biased and a somewhat rabid Prussian. His mistake is simply lack of humor and flexibility, a certain professorial excess of seriousness and gravity that is perceptible even in his very cultivated, readable, and engaging style.

José Ortega y Gasset

THE REVOLT OF THE MASSES

1931

NOT ALL THE WORKS of this very estimable Spanish writer have appealed to me; occasionally from behind his bravado and cheerful aggressiveness there peeks out something like philistinism and professorial decorum. But this book I cannot commend too highly, because it is one of those books in which an age can be seen struggling toward consciousness and attempting to draw its own face. Ortega y Gasset chooses to present the spiritual structure of our time through popular, often almost banal examples, but he has pictured some of them, especially the run-of-the-mill scientist and the type he calls "the self-satisfied young gentleman" with such complete clarity and expressiveness that one cannot help but be stimulated. Ultimately the book is a warning cry of the intellectual addressed to the apathetic, of the aristocrat to the standard-bearers of collective ideals, a protest of personality against the mass, and on this most significant point I can only wholeheartedly agree with the author and rejoice that these thoughts, held by a few thousand people for a long time, have now found a gripping and, one hopes, popular presentation.

1932

Though a trifle too popular in style—for this is basically a book for the few—and occasionally a trifle rhetorical, this remarkable volume is the work of one of the few men who have real knowledge of the nature of mankind, the nature of history, and therefore the state of mankind today. I am in unreserved agreement with the presentation and analysis of the mass man as Ortega gives it; it has never before been put forth so consistently and clearly. No less do I agree, and agree actively, with his conception of the state, and therefore with his conception of the only possibility for Europe's future —Europe must become a single nation. Among a series of clearly formulated and originally selected examples from history there are many individual passages of striking, witty comment, as, for example, this about historians: "One sees of the past about as much as one guesses about the future." All in all, it is a rousing, demanding, thought-provoking work that is important to Europe. The majority of German youth, instead of wrangling over their teen-age problems that will have disappeared by tomorrow, should read such books, not in order to be witty and clever about them in conversation, but to learn from them.

Leopold Ziegler

TRADITION

1936

L EOPOLD ZIEGLER is an eminent cultural critic and philosopher as well as a vivacious writer; a new work by him
may be considered an intellectual event. His latest book, *Tradition*, is a far-reaching attempt at a complete survey of the
spiritual and psychic tradition of mankind for the purpose of
unifying this vast mass of tradition from an Occidental and
Christian point of view. Ziegler postulates a unity in the human spiritual experience of all times, a new conquest and
activation of abandoned and neglected powers of the soul,
and also postulates a "catholic," that is, a worldwide, universally valid Christianity, not a Christianity that drives out
and makes war on "heathen" traditions but one that assimi-
lates them within itself. With great understanding and suggestive powers of empathy he explains in the first section the
rite, that is, the great system of customs, cultures, magic, and
ritual of the primitive stage of mankind—the world of magic.
The second section is called *Book of the Mythos* and the third
Book of the Doxa. He champions the claim of the spirit to
appropriate the experiences, exercises, and methods of inspired ways of life from all times, all nations and cultures,
and out of them to make a new universal wisdom of life for
today and tomorrow. Whether this is possible or practical to
attain remains a question. In his drive toward universality, in
his assumption that there is a supratemporal and suprana-
tional common denominator of all human spiritual experience
and art of living, he has had many noble predecessors; his
wonderful and truly creative Utopia of a universal gnosis has

exercised long before his time a magic attraction on lofty spirits in many centuries, and even if his conclusion were "only" a fiction, it would be a noble conclusion worthy of our sincerest attention. But it is more. It is not only a collection of information about magic, about yoga, about cult, myth, and customs of all times, it is a true conjuring up, a true summoning forth and making visible of the hidden, always present world that has never completely faded from human consciousness. Therein lies the living worth and great attractiveness of his book; it is a true seer who wrote it, not simply a scholar and collector. His familiarity with the wisdom of the Orient (some twelve years ago he wrote a widely praised book on Buddha) gives him the ability to see separate things as one, everywhere to concentrate upon the living basic source, not on transitory manifestations. He will be attacked and rejected by the dogmatically entrenched Christians; his universalism breaks through barriers that have always been held sacred by the churches and religious communities of Europe. And in the end it remains more than questionable whether what he understands by Christianity can be combined with the "real" historical Christianity.

But Utopias are not dreams that are to be slavishly turned into reality; they emerge in order to prompt discussion of possibilities that are as difficult as they are desirable, and to strengthen faith in those possibilities. A distinguished and vigorous mind here conjures up within the picture of what is past the spirit of what is to come. There will be no lack of criticism from many sides, for a book of this sort must encounter opposition. But there will be no lack of readers on whom it will continuously exercise an influence—and in a thousand invisible ways it will help to build the future. A short time ago the Italian Giulio Evola published his work *Revolt Against the Modern World,* which treats almost exactly the same complex of questions but with less freedom and freshness, more pomposity, and is not without occult eccentricities. We consider Ziegler more reliable.

PART TWO

III · ORIENTAL
LITERATURE

Introduction*

1929

As we set about our task of putting together a good small collection of world literature, at once we come upon the basic rule of all intellectual history: the very oldest works age the least. What is fashionable or sensational today, by tomorrow may be stale and out of date; what is new and interesting today, by day after tomorrow may be forgotten. But whatever has endured for a few centuries and is still unforgotten, has not disappeared, will presumably suffer no devaluation during our lifetimes. We begin with the oldest and most holy witnesses of the human spirit, the books of religion and myth. In addition to the Bible known to us all, I place at the head of our library that section of ancient Hindu wisdom which is called Vedanta, the essence of the Veda, in the form of a selection from the Upanishads. A selection from the speeches of the Buddha belongs with this and also the Babylonian *Gilgamesh,* the mighty poem about the great hero who ventures to fight with death. From ancient China we select the *Analects of Confucius,* the *Tao Te Ching* of Lao-tse and the splendid *Parables* of Chuang-tzu. Now we have struck the basic chords of all human literature: the struggle for standards and laws as it finds exemplary expression in the Old Testament and Confucius; the intuitive search for release from the inadequacies of earthly existence as the Hindus and the New Testament proclaim it; the secret knowledge of the eternal harmony beyond the restless, multitudinous world of appearances; the reverence for natural and psychic forces in the form of gods and the almost simultaneous knowledge or intuition that gods are only symbols and that the power and

* Drawn from Hesse's essay "A Small Library of World Literature."

weakness, the jubilation and sorrow of life reside in the hands of men. All the speculations of abstract thought, all the play of poetry, all the suffering over the fragility of our existence, all the comfort and all the humor intermixed with it find expression in these few books. A selection from the classical lyric poets of the Chinese should be added.

Of the later works of the Orient, one is indispensable to our library, that great collection of tales the *Thousand and One Nights*, a source of endless enjoyment, most rich and vivid. Although all peoples of the world have composed marvelous fairy tales, this classical magical book suffices for our collection, supplemented only by our own German fairy tales collected by the brothers Grimm. It would be most desirable to have a good anthology of Persian lyric poetry but unfortunately no such book is available in a German version; only Hafiz and Omar Khayyám have been frequently translated.

Hinduism

1923

HOWEVER WELL KNOWN and semipopular Buddhism and the concepts of so-called Vedanta are with us, Hinduism, the principal religion of India, is almost unknown and is shunned and spurned by scholars and religionists alike. This is the religion whose many-armed and elephant-headed idols Goethe once in an hour of bad temper violently rejected, though against his own deeper intuitions. However, these gods and goddesses are now coming to our notice, they have been coming for the last ten years by way of art, for suddenly the West decided that if Japanese art was valid, this must be true for India as well. And now the Hindu world of gods, with its many-armed idols, its many-breasted goddesses, its age-old stone divinities and its saints, is coming to us continuously by many paths, by way of occultism and secret societies, by way of the collector and the lover of art and curios, by way of science.

Hitherto we have seen the most religiously inventive people on earth almost exclusively through philosophical glasses; we knew them hardly at all except through the systems and theories of the old Hindus, which tried to solve religious problems intellectually. Now for the first time we are slowly beginning to have an intimation of the greatness and wonder of this true religion of the people, Hinduism, incomparable in its plasticity.

The problem that most troubles and offends the Westerner when he becomes interested in Hinduism, the fact that to the Indian, God can be simultaneously transcendent and imminent, is actually the heart of the Hindu religion. For the Indian, who is remarkably gifted in religious feeling as well as in abstract thought, no such problem really exists; from the beginning it is assumed as certain that all human knowledge and power of thought can cope only with the lower world, the human world, that the divine, on the other hand, must be approached simply through surrender, devotion, meditation, awe. And so Hinduism, which today just as three thousand years ago is the predominant religion of India, shelters peacefully and in paradisal gaiety the most monstrous opposites, the most contradictory formulations, the most opposed dogmas, rites, myths, and cults conceivable, the delicate side by side with the coarsest, the spiritual next to the massively sensual, the charitable next to the cruel and horrible.

The truth, the eternal, is not in these forms, not even in the most delicate and noble; the truth is far above them. Thus the Brahman can practice theology, the sensualist can love the philoprogenitive Krishna, the simpleton can worship the grotesque stone mask smeared with cow dung—before God it is all the same, is only in appearance a multiplicity, a mass of contradictions.

The Speeches of Buddha

1921

T HE SPIRITUAL WAVE from India that has been at work in
Europe for a hundred years, especially in Germany, has
now become generally visible and palpable; whatever one
may think of Tagore and Keyserling, the longing of Europe
for the spiritual culture of the ancient East has become unmistakable.

To put it psychologically, Europe is beginning to detect
from many symptoms of decline that the exaggerated one-
sidedness of its intellectual cultural development (this expresses itself perhaps most clearly in scientific specialization)
requires a corrective, a refreshment from the opposite pole.
This widespread longing is not for a new ethic or a new way
of thought but for a cultivation of those spiritual functions
which our intellectualized spiritual life has not done justice
to. We have found out that man can train his intellect to accomplish marvels without thereby becoming master of his
own soul. People are turning not so much to Buddha or Lao-
tse as to yoga.

Sometimes Neumann's translations* have been derided by
German men of letters because of the literalness of the seemingly endless repetitions. Some were reminded of prayer
wheels by these soothing, endlessly flowing series of meditations. This criticism, witty though it may be, arises from a
point of view that is unfair to the subject. Buddha's speeches
in fact are not compilations of a doctrine but examples of
meditation. And meditative thinking is exactly what we can
learn from them. Whether meditation can lead to different
and more valuable results than scientific thought is an idle

* This is a review of the translation by Karl Eugen Neumann.

question. The point and goal of meditation is not knowledge in the sense of our Western intellectuality but an alteration of consciousness, a technique whose highest result is pure harmony, a simultaneous and equal cooperation of logical and intuitive thinking. About the attainability of this ideal goal we are incompetent to judge, and we are children and novices in this technique. To make a beginning in the practice of meditation, however, there is no more direct path than to study these speeches of Buddha.

There are many nervous German professors who are afraid of something like a Buddhistic deluge, a drowning of the intellectual West. The West, however, will not drown, and Europe will never be a province of Buddhism. Whoever reads Buddha's speeches and through them becomes a Buddhist may have found comfort for himself—but he has taken an emergency exit instead of the Way that Buddha can perhaps show us.

The fashionable lady who now places beside that bronze Buddha from Ceylon or Siam the three volumes of Buddha's speeches will no more find that Way than the ascetic who flees from the misery of a barren everyday life to the opium of dogmatic Buddhism. When we Westerners have once learned something about meditation it will give us quite different results from those it produces for the Hindus. It will not be opium to us but rather a deepened self-knowledge, such as was the first and most holy requirement of the pupils of the wise men of Greece.

1922

Profitless though it would be to start talking today about the "religion of the future," it is nevertheless useful and worthwhile for present-day seekers to measure themselves against the few great ideals of the past. Inevitably this comparison ends in humiliating defeat. Our time sees itself culturally, the instant it compares itself with times of a true religiosity, as childishly poor and helpless. We know a great deal and our longing is genuine; genuine too is our readiness to consider our wisdom as nothing and to make a fresh spiritual start. But just here we lack all tradition, all technique, all training. Our store of wisdom concerning the inner life, the mastery of the instincts, the means of training the soul, is a nothing.

This is the point at which we are entirely right in learning from the heroes of distant times, from Jesus and the Christian saints, from the Chinese, from Buddha. Even the smallest rule of the most modest monks' order in the Middle Ages can teach us, who are completely at a loss in this respect, more about the training and cultivation of the soul than all the pedagogy of our time.

Now in this realm Buddha's speeches are a source and mine of quite unparalleled richness and depth. As soon as we cease to regard Buddha's teaching simply intellectually and acquiesce with a certain sympathy in the age-old Eastern concept of unity, if we allow Buddha to speak to us as vision, as image, as the awakened one, the perfect one, we find in him, almost independently of the philosophic content and dogmatic kernel of his teaching, a great prototype of mankind. Whoever attentively reads a small number of the countless "speeches" of Buddha is soon aware of a harmony in them, a quietude of soul, a smiling transcendence, a totally unshakable firmness, but also invariable kindness, endless patience. As ways and means to the attainment of this holy quietude of soul, the speeches are full of advice, precepts, hints.

The intellectual content of Buddha's teaching is only half his work, the other half is his life, his life as lived, as labor accomplished and action carried out. A training, a spiritual self-training of the highest order, was accomplished and is taught here, a training about which unthinking people who talk about "quietism" and "Hindu dreaminess" and the like in connection with Buddha have no conception; they deny him the cardinal Western virtue of activity. Instead Buddha accomplished a training of himself and his pupils, exercised a discipline, set up a goal, and produced results before which even the genuine heroes of European action can only feel awe. As for the "content" of that new religion or religiosity which we feel coming or which at least we long for, we will hardly discover or learn much about it from Buddha; the "content" of his teaching has long been available to us by way of philosophical channels, if only the not quite reliable detour through Schopenhauer. Then too with a "new religion" it is not so much a matter of intellectual content as of new living symbols of the primeval. To a certain extent religions come from outside, from far over our heads. Our task is simply to be prepared, to keep our "lamps" filled.

One element in the readiness will be the ability to feel awe. If we approach Buddha with the awe that is due to a holy one, if we listen gratefully to this truly holy voice, then I really do not know what harm could come of it. The warnings against the dangerous "East," which we now hear so often, all emanate from partisan camps that have some dogma, some sect, some precept to safeguard.

Chinese Literature

1911

WHAT THE WISE MEN of ancient China have to say to us may be more than many of us suppose; and yet the essentials of it can probably find room in just a few books. Of these, several of the most important, probably the most important of all, have now been made available to us.

The most famous Chinese wise man has always been Confucius and properly so, for the reason that of all thinkers he has had the strongest influence on the life and history of his country. On the whole, we are right too when we picture him as completely "Chinese," that is, formalistic to the point of pedantry, but we are unfair to the Chinese if on the basis of this judgment we consider the Chinese spirit as generally rigid and unphilosophically superficial. Against this conception Confucius himself furnishes ample evidence. That there were in China great philosophers and ethicists, whose wisdom is no less valuable for us than that of the Greeks or Buddha or Jesus, is something still little known. After all, China's greatest wise man was never really popular in his native land; compared to Confucius, his somewhat younger contemporary, he has always remained in the shadows. I am talking of Lao-tse, whose teaching has been preserved in the *Tao Te Ching*. This teaching of the Tao, the primal essence of all being, might remain a matter of indifference to us as a philosophical system or attract at most only a few interested specialists if it did not contain such a personally compelling, great, and beautiful ethic that its last German translator, a professor of theology by the way, compares Lao-tse directly to Jesus. Now for the time being, of course, Lao-tse cannot have so powerful an effect upon us non-scholars since his work is in a difficult foreign language that can only be approached through diligence and real effort. What we have here in *Tao Te Ching* is not a curio or a literary-ethnological rarity but one of the most serious and profound books of all antiquity.

Confucius is made accessible to us through his *Analects*. Of the later Chinese thinkers one of the most original and vivid is also to be had in German, at least in a selection: *Talks and Parables* by Chuang-tzu.

Chuang-tzu came three hundred years later than Lao-tse, and Grill compares his relationship to the latter with that of Plato to Socrates. It does not lie within my competence to talk knowledgeably either about the Chinese books themselves or about the work of their translator; I simply wish to report that these remarkable books have brought me, who as a layman had known of the old Orient only the Buddhistic philosophy and the philosophies related to Buddhism, wholly new treasures. The Far East, between Buddha and Christ, possessed a philosophy that never became a popular religion, whose active, living, beautiful ethic stands decidedly closer to the Christian ethic than does the Hindu-Buddhistic.

I have sometimes lamented the fact that so few fruits of the labors of our academic Orientalists have been available to us. Now that some of them are, it is greatly to be hoped that they will be influential and will increase in numbers. Knowledge of them ought not to lead us into strange paths but rather bring us a happy confirmation of what we have long greatly prized as our best possession.

1926

The Chinese philosopher Lao-tse, formerly unknown in Europe for a period of two thousand years, has in the last fifteen years been translated into all European languages and his *Tao Te Ching* has become a fashionable book. In Germany it was Richard Wilhelm who with his translations and introductions presented the classical literature and wisdom of China in unprecedented quantity. And while China is politically weak and torn and in the eyes of the great powers hardly more than a huge rich territory for exploitation to be handled with extreme care, ancient Chinese wisdom, ancient Chinese art are making their way not only into the museums and libraries of the West but also into the hearts of the intellectual young. Next to Dostoevsky, in the last ten years certainly no mind has had so strong an effect on German students, excited by the war, as Lao-tse. That this movement is going on among a rather small minority detracts not at all from its significance: the minority fascinated by it is precisely the one that counts—the most gifted, the most aware, the class of German students most ready to bear responsibility.

Our modern Western cultural ideal is so completely opposed to the Chinese that we should congratulate ourselves on having such a strong and honorable antipole on the opposite side of the globe. It would be silly to wish that the entire world could in time be cultivated in a wholly European or wholly Chinese fashion. But we should have for this alien spirit that kind of respect without which one can learn nothing and assimilate nothing, and we should reckon the Far East among our teachers at least as much as we have done for a long time for the Near East—one has only to think of Goethe! And when we read the extremely stimulating conversations of Confucius, sparkling with wit, we should not regard them as an antiquated oddity from past times but rather should remember that not only did the doctrine of Confucius guide and support the gigantic Chinese empire through two thousand years but that today his descendants are still living in China, bearing his name and the knowledge of him with pride; by comparison the oldest and most distinguished nobility of Europe seems childishly young. Lao-tse should not, of course, replace the New Testament for us, but knowing that something similar grew up under other skies and in even earlier times should strengthen our belief that mankind, however seriously it is divided into alien and hostile races and cultures, nevertheless is a unity and has common potentialities, ideals, and goals.

Despite our recent enthusiasm for China, the opinion still widely prevails that the soul of the Chinese is after all completely alien to ours. Its virtues, especially its unwearied patience and its quiet, tough industriousness, are really more of a passive nature and its sins, especially the famous Chinese cruelty, are essentially a world removed from us and fully incomprehensible. In truth these are silly prejudices. The Chinese can be cruel just as the Westerner can, and he can be pious and self-sacrificing exactly as the European can occasionally be. If we bring forth examples of Chinese cruelty, then we should at the same time mention those stories in which China and her heroism are just as exemplary as, for example, the stories of noble heroism current in our schools and drawn from the Bible or from classical antiquity.

CHINESE LEGENDS
1914

The more necessary a thorough understanding with East Asia becomes, the more pressing the purely political need for comprehension of the East is for us, just that much more important it is to acquaint ourselves with these Eastern peoples through their own thinking and character; for this purpose there is no better means than through their art and poetry. Here their folk tales play a great role, for in them, next to the theater, is the true source of spiritual nourishment for the people. What I have read of these legends corresponds exactly with the impression that the Chinese in Singapore made on me. We find much naïveté, childishness, and playfulness side by side with a great sensitivity in aesthetic matters, emphasis on poetic incident, joy in detail in general, together with a certain indifference to narrative structure (with the exception of the literary tales), belief in spirits and other animistic conceptions predominate throughout, seldom does personal superiority triumph over these demonic, controlling forces. However, by way of compensation for the limitation and primitiveness of these views, there is a system of moral and political conduct of life, an authority of custom, a sanctity of social authority based on the family, which we can only regard with amazement and admiration.

CHINESE LYRIC POETRY
1922

. . . Up to now the essence and meaning of Chinese lyric poetry has been just as foreign to the West as the essence and meaning of Chinese painting. The wealth of nuance with a limited palette, the virtuosity of the calligraphy, the noble ambition to give expression to the highest with the minimum of physical means, the infinitely delicate interplay of references, echoes, relationships, above all the fabulous art of intimation, of invitation to surmise, of withholding and sparing, all this is foreign to the present-day European. To enjoy these arts one must exercise one's ears, eyes, and fingertips and grow accustomed to the most delicate nuances.

LÜ BU WEN: *SPRING AND FALL*
1929

Lü Bu Wen was not one of the great Chinese thinkers, and his reputation among Chinese men of letters is only moderate. He was a minister and a political intriguer almost two thousand years ago, and he did not himself write his great work *Spring and Fall* but had it written for him by scholars for whom he played Maecenas. This need not disturb us, and we are very thankful that Richard Wilhelm has translated the work into German. The whole wisdom of classical China, whose true sources were in great part lost in the book burnings, is in this compendium, and in addition a mass of portraits and anecdotes. Reading it, I have spent many pleasant hours. That at this time its wisdom has been lost to the world and is only to be found in books is just as little disturbing to me as that this wisdom stands in such complete contradiction to the very unwise and consequently all the more fanatically held philosophies of life in our time—be they middle-class American or Russian bolshevist. Time passes and wisdom endures. It changes its forms and rites but at all times it rests on the same foundation: the fitting of man into nature, into the cosmic rhythm. In unquiet times man strives again and again for emancipation from this order of things; such pseudo-manumission leads only to slavery, just as the very emancipated man of today is the unwilling slave of money and the machine. Like one returning from the garishly lighted pavements of the metropolis to the woods or from the strident, rousing music of the great concert halls to the music of the sea with a feeling of thankfulness and homecoming, so I come, again and again, from all the short-lived and exciting adventures of life and the mind, back to these ancient, inexhaustible sources of wisdom. At each return they have grown no older, they stand quietly and wait for us and they are always new and gleaming as the sun is each day, while yesterday's war, yesterday's fashionable dance, yesterday's automobile today has already become old and faded and comic.

I CHING
1925

There are books one cannot read, books of wisdom by holy men in whose company and atmosphere one can live for years without ever reading them the way one reads other books. Parts of the Bible belong among these books, and the *Tao Te Ching*. One sentence from these books is enough to do you for a long time, to busy you for a long time, to penetrate deep into you. One keeps these books within easy reach or carries them in one's pocket when walking in the woods, and never reads for a whole hour in them or even half an hour but each time selects just one saying, one line, in order to meditate on it, in order amid the trash of the day and one's other reading always to hold upright the measuring stick of the great and holy.

Now to these few books a new one has been added, which I regard as good fortune for me. Naturally it is, like the few others, a book of great age, thousands of years old, but no attempt to translate it into German has hitherto been made. It is called *I Ching, The Book of Changes*, a book of Chinese wisdom and magic. One can make use of it as an oracle book in order to gain counsel in difficult life situations. One can also love and use it "just" for its wisdom. There is in the book, which I shall never be able to understand except intuitively and for moments, a system of similes for the whole world based on eight characteristics or images, the first two of which are heaven and earth, father and mother, strength and weakness. These eight characteristics are expressed each by a simple symbol, and these enter into combination with one another, resulting then in sixty-four possibilities on which the oracle is based. You question the oracle and receive perhaps this saying: "Inner truth: swine and fish. Hail! It is advantageous to cross the great water. Persistence is advantageous." Over this you can now meditate, and commentaries are provided.

This *Book of Changes* has now been lying for half a year in my bedroom and I have never at one time read more than a single page. When one studies the combinations or signs, immerses oneself in Ch'ien, the creative principle, in Sun, the gentle, this is not reading or thinking, but it is like looking into flowing water or drifting clouds. Everything is written there that can be thought and lived.

View of the Far East

1959

THE TWO "NONWHITE" peoples from whom I have learned most and for whom I have the greatest respect are the Indians and the Chinese. Both have created a spiritual and artistic culture that is older than ours and of equal value in content and beauty.

I see the golden age of Hindu thought approximately at the same time as that of the European, that is, the centuries between Homer and Socrates. During that period the loftiest ideas about man and the world that had hitherto been conceived took shape in India as well as in Greece and were developed into imposing systems of thought and faith that have not received any essential enrichment since then—this, however, they probably did not need, for today they are still in full vigor and help hundreds of millions of people endure life. In contrast to the high philosophy of ancient India there stands a completely polymorphic mythology rich in depth and humor, a folk world of gods and demons and cosmologies of luxuriant picturesqueness that continues to flourish in poetry and sculpture and as a popular faith as well. But also out of this many-colored, gleaming world there emerged the revered figure of the Buddha, the conqueror through renunciation, and Buddhism today both in its original and in its Chinese-Japanese form of Zen is proving itself not only in its native East but throughout the whole West, including America, as a religion of high morality and great powers of attraction. For close to two hundred years Western thinking has been frequently and powerfully influenced by the Hindu spirit; the last great evidence of this is Schopenhauer.

If the Indian spirit is predominantly spiritual and pious, the intellectual search of the Chinese thinkers concerns first of all practical life, the state and the family. What is required in order to govern well and successfully for the good of all, that is the principal concern of most Chinese wise men, as it was, indeed, of Hesiod and Plato. The virtues of self-control, of courtesy, of patience, of equanimity are as highly valued there as in the Western Stoa. Side by side with this there are also metaphysical and elemental thinkers, first of all Lao-tse and his poetic disciple Chuang-tzu, and after the invasion of Buddhist teaching, China slowly evolved a highly original and extremely effective form of Buddhistic discipline, Zen, which, like the Hindu form of Buddhism today, has a marked influence in the West. That Chinese spirituality has a highly and delicately developed pictorial art as companion is known to everyone.

Today's world situation has changed everything on the surface and caused endless confusion. The Chinese, once the most peaceful people on earth and the most productive in antimilitaristic pronouncements, today have become the most feared and ruthless of nations. They have barbarically fallen upon and conquered the most religious of all nations, and they constantly threaten India and every other neighboring country. We can only take note of this fact. If, for instance, one compares political France or England of the seventeenth century with that of today, it is evident that the political aspect of a nation can undergo enormous change in the course of a very few centuries, without this necessarily meaning a change in the essence of the people's character. We can only hope that throughout this time of troubles, many of the marvelous characteristics and gifts of the Chinese people will be preserved.

DATE DUE

2 hr. reserve only
11:00